E-Development:

From Excitement to Effectiveness

Edited by Robert Schware

Prepared for the World Summit on the
Information Society
Tunis, November 2005

**Global Information and Communication
Technologies Department**

THE WORLD BANK GROUP
Washington, D.C.

This volume is a product of the staff of the International Bank for Reconstruction and Development / The World Bank. The findings, interpretations, and conclusions expressed in this paper do not necessarily reflect the views of the Executive Directors of The World Bank or the governments they represent.

The World Bank does not guarantee the accuracy of the data included in this work. The boundaries, colors, denominations, and other information shown on any map in this work do not imply any judgement on the part of The World Bank concerning the legal status of any territory or the endorsement or acceptance of such boundaries.

ISBN-10: 0-821 3-6442-1
ISBN-13: 978-0-8213-6442-0
eISBN: 0-8213-6443-X
DOI: 10.1596/978-0-8213-6442-0

Library of Congress cataloging-in-publication data has been applied for.

Table of Contents

Foreword

This volume is not a compendium, but a mosaic. It tells a story. A story of how various countries, institutions and sectors have reacted to the emergence of information and communication technologies (ICT) and probed their way toward turning them into instruments of development.

It shows how, after initial years of enthusiasm, exploration and excitement, the "e- development agenda" has progressively matured into a set of policy instruments, sectoral applications and programmatic approaches. It also provides evidence that e-strategies have acquired the respectability brought by efficiency. Finally, the volume challenges some of the conventional wisdom regarding how and where ICT can best contribute to improving the lives of people in developing nations.

This volume is specifically addressed to policy makers, "e-leaders," international cooperation agencies, the private sector, and NGOs present at this second phase of the World Summit on the Information Society (WSIS) and encourages them to focus on the growing economic impact of the ICT sector. As the volume shows, ICT has touched the lives of citizens in developing countries in an ever-increasing number of ways. Technology and infrastructure have contributed to empowerment, job creation and competitiveness. This report gives the reader a sense of being at a turning point where several forces are combining to accelerate change. We have reached a critical point where the social benefits of ICT are becoming apparent and many governments are overcoming the inertia that previously prevented them from seizing the development opportunities of ICT.

The presence of telecommunications lines, computers or even Internet connectivity, however, are insufficient in and of themselves to accelerate development. The emergence of an "e-agenda" is a sign that the necessary conditions, attitudes and policies have started to coalesce to effectively utilize the potential of ICTs. Concretely, this means that we are starting to see more and more e-development projects designed to meet the essential development needs of poor countries and help them compete successfully in the international arena.

It is clear that, to achieve lasting benefits, ICT-enabled development projects must be properly planned and their implementation accompanied by a careful process of monitoring and evaluation. It is equally clear that the role of decision makers, especially at the policy level ("e-leaders"), is crucial for ensuring that the e-agenda is solidly rooted in a given nation's development agenda and serves a vision that convinces stakeholders to invest their time, energy, hope and financial resources. While quick fixes remain appealing, successful e-development projects always involve good preparation, careful design, discipline in execution, and timeliness in delivery.

It is our hope that this volume will provide useful knowledge and practical guidance on the environment conducive to successful national e-strategies, e-government and e-commerce activities, as well as e-education, e-health and e-finance projects. We look forward to pursuing the debates it may generate with interested stakeholders at WSIS and beyond. More importantly, we are eager to continue our work in the field with those who share our passion to use ICT as a tool to fight poverty and foster development.

Katherine Sierra
Vice President
Infrastructure
The World Bank

Preface

The Reality of E-Opportunities

The first phase of the World Summit on the Information Society (WSIS) in December 2003, together with the preparations for the second phase in 2005, have highlighted the importance of ICT infrastructure and applications to development. It is now quite common, and in some ways imperative, for policy makers to focus on e-education, e-health, e-commerce, e-finance and e-government as elements of an overall development strategy.

Yet the opportunities and promises of e-development also entail some major challenges. New risks are being created by the integration of ICT into the everyday operations of businesses, organizations and governments, requiring policy makers to pay vigilant attention to such issues as business process reform, behavioral resistance and cyber–security. Given the competition for limited public resources, policy makers must also be ready to ensure taxpayer money spent on e-projects generate adequate economic and social returns.

Since the first phase of WSIS, the World Bank has seen increased interest around the world in further opening telecommunication markets, building out basic backbone infrastructure, mobilizing ICT investment for challenging rural areas and addressing the potential of new Internet-based and other ICT-related services. In turn, the World Bank is supporting member countries to design and implement e-development policies, projects and measurement frameworks. These projects vary from country to country, depending on differences in institutional, legal and technological conditions, as well as development needs. To date, over 100 countries have received at least some World Bank support for information and communication infrastructure reform. An increasing number of countries are receiving support for ICT components in traditional investment projects and to design e-government applications and integrated, large-scale e-development projects (e.g., e-Sri Lanka, e-Bharat in India, e-Ghana, Vietnam ICT Development, and the ICT Sector Development Project in Tunisia).

This report attempts to distill some of the lessons learned from e-development projects, including a number undertaken with World Bank support. It avoids e-development hype in favor of realistic, down-to-earth experience drawn from users, producers, regulators, leaders and providers of ICT from our member countries, developed and developing alike. We hope that development agencies and policymakers will find the information and analysis presented in this report useful in supporting their development efforts and the design of 'e-projects'.

Mohsen Khalil
Director
Global Information and Communication
Technologies Department
The World Bank

Acronyms

ADR	alternative dispute resolution
AFDB	African Development Bank, Côte d'Ivoire
AGIMO	Australian Government Information Management Office
ANRT	National Agency of Telecommunications Regulation, Morocco
APDIP	Asia Pacific Development Information Programme
ATI	Agence tunisienne de l' Internet
ATICA	Agence pour les technologies de l'information et de la communication (Information and Communication Technologies Agency), France
BCC	Business Corporation Contract (Vietnam)
BOOT	build own operate transfer
BSNL	Bharat Sanchar Nigam Limited, India
BSP	Bangko Sentral ng Pilipinas, Philippines
BTA	Bilateral Trade Agreement (WTO)
CERT	computer emergency response team
CIF	cost, insurance, freight
CII	critical information infrastructure
CIO	Chief Information Officer
CITPO	ICT Policy Division, Global ICT Department, World Bank
CMDE	China Modern Distance Education Project
CME	continuing medical education
DAC	Development Assistance Committee of the OECD
DCITA	Department of Communications, Information Technology and the Arts, Australia
DLC	distance-learning center
DOT Force	Digital Opportunity Task Force of the G8
EAP	East Asia and Pacific region
EBRD	European Bank for Reconstruction and Development, London
ECA	Europe and Central Asia region
e-GIF	e-Government Interoperability Framework (UK)
EIB	European Investment Bank, Luxembourg
ESD	electronic service delivery
EU	European Union
FBI	Federal Bureau of Investigation, USA
FDI	foreign direct investment
FLN	Ford Learning Network, Ford Motor Company
GATS	General Agreement on Trade in Services
GCNet	Ghana Community Network
GDP	gross domestic product
GICT	Global Information and Communication Technologies Department, a joint department of the World Bank and the International Finance Corporation
GIS	Geographic Information System
GITR	Global Information Technology Report (World Economic Forum, INSEAD, *info*Dev)
GPT	general-purpose technology

GSM	Global System for Mobile Communications
HDI	Human Development Index of the UNDP
IADB	Inter-American Development Bank, Washington, DC
ICA	International Council for Information Technology in Government Administration
ICANN	Internet Corporation for Assigned Names and Numbers
ICT	information and communication technology
ICT4D	ICT for development
IDA	Infocomm Development Authority, Singapore
IFC	International Finance Corporation, a component of the World Bank Group
IP	Internet Protocol
IPR	intellectual property rights
ISO	International Organization for Standardization
ISP	Internet Service Provider
IT	information technology
ITU	International Telecommunications Union, Geneva
KAM	Knowledge Assessment Methodology (World Bank)
KEI	Knowledge Economy Index (World Bank)
KIA	Kotoka International Airport, Ghana
LAC	Latin America and Caribbean region
LAN	local area network
LDC	least-developed country
MAHE	Manipal Academy of Higher Education, India
MDB	multilateral development bank
MDGs	Millenium Development Goals
MENA	Middle East and North Africa region
MHz	megahertz
NBER	National Bureau for Economic Research (USA)
NEI	Networked Economy Index (of the GITR)
NERA	National Economic Research Associates (South Africa)
NOIE	National Office for the Information Economy, Australia
NORAD	Norwegian Agency for Development Cooperation
NREN	national research and education network
NTCA	National Telecommunications Cooperative Association (US)
OBA	output-based aid
OBHE	Observatory on Borderless Higher Education, UK
ODA	official development assistance
ODR	online dispute resolution
OECD	Organisation for Economic Cooperation and Development
OER	open educational resources
OGCIO	Office of the Government Chief Information Officer, Hong Kong
OSS	open source software
PC	personal computer
PPP	public-private partnership
PRM	Performance Reference Model (U.S. government)
PRSP	Poverty Reduction Strategy Paper
PTT	Post, Telegraph and Telephone

REN	regional education network
RP	Reference Paper (WTO)
RTC	Record of Rights, Tenancy and Crops (India)
SAC	Shanghai Aerospace Computer System Engineering Co., Ltd., China
SII	Internal Taxation Service, Chile
SME	small and medium enterprise
SMS	short messaging service
SMT	surface-mount technology
SMU	Sikkim Manipal University of Health, Medical and Technological Sciences, India
SSA	Sub-Saharan Africa region
SSL	secure sockets layer
SUBTEL	Subsecretaria de Telecommunicaciones, Chile
UNCITRAL	United Nations Commission on International Trade Law
UNCTAD	United Nations Conference on Trade and Development
UNDP	United Nations Development Programme
UNECA	United Nations Economic and Social Commission for Africa
UNELAC	United Nations Economic and Social Commission for Latin America and the Caribbean
UNESCAP	United Nations Economic and Social Commission for Asia and the Pacific
UNESCO	United Nations Educational, Scientific and Cultural Organization
UNESCWA	United Nations Economic and Social Commission for Western Asia
UNICTTF	United Nations Information and Communications Technology Task Force
UNPAN	United Nations Online Network in Public Administration and Finance
UNU	United Nations University
UPOL	University of Phoenix Online, USA
USAID	United States Agency for International Development
USOTEC	U.S. Office of Technology and Electronic Commerce
UTL	United Telecom Limited, India
VAT	value-added tax
VC	venture capital
VoIP	Voice over Internet Protocol
VSAT	very small aperture terminal (for downlink of a satellite signal)
W3C	World Wide Web Consortium
WAN	wide area network
WEF	World Economic Forum
WGIG	Working Group on Internet Governance (www.wgig.org)
WIDER	World Institute for Development Economics Research (United Nations University)
WiFi	wireless fidelity (any type of 802.11 network, whether 802.11b, 802.11a, dual-band, etc.)
WiMax	802.16 fixed broadband wireless access systems employing point-to-multipoint architecture
WIPO	World Intellectual Property Organization
WSIS	World Summit on the Information Society
WTDR	World Telecommunications Development Report (ITU)
WTO	World Trade Organization
YOK	Yuksek Ogrenim Kurumu (Higher Education Council), Turkey

Acknowledgments

This volume was produced by a World Bank team consisting of Subramaniam Janakiram, Boutheina Guermazi, Charles Kenny, Bruno Lanvin, Gareth Locksley, Isabel Neto, Ronald Perkinson, David Satola, Randeep Sudan and Charles Watt. Several e-leaders contributed to Chapter 4, lending a concrete dimension to the chapter. These included Lidia Brito, former Minister of Research and Higher Education of Mozambique; Markus Kummer, former e-envoy of Switzerland; Mart Laar, former Prime Minister of Estonia; Errki Liikanen, former EU Commissioner for Enterprise and the Information Society; and Lucio Stanca, Minister of Innovation and Technology, Italy.

Valuable contributions and comments were received from external reviewers and World Bank colleagues Paulo Baioni, Deepak Bhatia, Subhash Bhatnagar, Carlos Botelho, Yann Burtin, Arsala Deane, Andi Dervishi, Antonio Estache, Henry Forero, James Guida, James Hanna, Robert Hawkins, Sudhakar Kaveeshwar, Michel Maechler, Kayoko Shibata Medlin, Craig Neal, Lorenzo Pupillo, Shobha Shetty, Ramesh Siva, Eduardo Talero, Robert Valantin, Robert Whyte, Cesar Yammal, Degi Young and Christine Zhen-Wei Qiang. The guidance and support of Pierre Guislain, Manager of the Policy Division of the Global ICT Department of the World Bank Group, is deeply appreciated. The team also benefited from the research and administrative support of Naomi Halewood and Marta Priftis. Special recognition to Peggy McInerny and Mark Wahl for editing work, cover art and interior layout.

Overview

E-Development:
From Excitement to Effectiveness

by Robert Schware

Information and communication technologies (ICTs) are increasingly being recognized as essential tools of development—tools that can empower poor people, enhance skills, increase productivity, and improve governance at all levels. The success of ICT-enabled development (or e-development) will thus not be measured by the diffusion of technology, but by advances in development itself: economic growth and, ultimately, achievement of the Millenium Development Goals.

This volume examines a wide range of issues related to e-development, with a focus on the requirements and realities of using ICTs to advance development goals. The report does not attempt to present a comprehensive overview of e-development. Rather, it highlights key issues that have immediate relevance to policy makers in developing nations who make decisions on investments and development goals. Two issues, e-government and e-education, are highlighted in particular because ICT applications in these areas can lead to significant development outcomes (e.g., improved transparency and ac-

countability of government, more educated populations). They can also be successfully deployed through public-private partnerships, leveraging limited government funding to achieve greater impact, while building out crucial infrastructure.

Chapter 1 examines the limited data available on the impact of e-development at the macroeconomic level and reviews the major requirements of successful implementation of ICT-based development projects. Chapter 2 reviews the components of an enabling policy environment for e-development, including the need to facilitate the market penetration of personal computers to tap the full benefits of the information age. Chapter 3 explores the design of effective strategies for e-development, noting that they must be rooted in a nation's broader development strategy and utilize rigorous monitoring and evaluation. Chapter 4 looks at the qualities of leadership needed to successfully implement e-strategies and features the observations of a number of individuals who have led e-development efforts in countries around the world.

Chapter 5 examines the opportunities and challenges of ICT-based government applications (e-government) and offers a number of suggestions on how nations can best organize their efforts to introduce such applications. Chapter 6 explores the enormous opportunities that ICT-based applications hold for expanding affordable access to university and continuing education in developing nations. Finally, Chapter 7 considers the expanding role of the international community in building an equitable digital society accessible to all.

E-development is not easy

Although ICT-enabled projects can contribute greatly to the achievement of development goals, they are risky endeavors. Poorly designed projects can waste precious resources that could be devoted to competing development needs. Lack of crucial pre-requisites, including affordable access to infrastructure, the rule of law and strong government and market institutions, can derail even well-designed projects. To date, the track record of e-development is short, complex, and difficult to measure. Difficulties include the cross-sectoral dimension of the applications, the potential time lag between project implementation and the moment when benefits are realized, and the limited investment resources available in developing countries. Given the opportunity cost of investing in ICT-based projects, rigorous and hard evidence on impact and good practices is urgently required.

A recent survey found, for example, that only forty percent of companies that adopted on-line purchasing systems actually saved money when they deployed such systems as part of a change management process. The figure for companies that introduced such systems without a change management program was only three

percent.[1] Available evidence also suggests that firms, governments, and civil society face difficulties in exploiting ICTs to their full potential in least-developed countries (LDCs); one recent study estimated that a majority of public sector IT applications in LDCs are either partial or total failures, a finding equally true for the private sector.[2]

Yet when deployed well, ICTs can accelerate development outcomes. Recent World Bank surveys of over 20,000 firms in roughly 50 low- and middle-income countries show that firms in developing countries which use ICT show faster sales and employment growth, as well as higher labor and total factor productivity, than firms which do not use ICT.[3] An analysis of advanced Internet use across the world (see Annex 1), however, suggests that the "digital divide" is very much part of the broader "development divide," a finding that should temper some of the more optimistic hopes for e-development as a tool for "leapfrogging" stages of development. Another cautionary consideration is that network externalities come into effect only after a critical mass of ICT users has been reached. Thus the development of ICT infrastructure may need to reach a certain critical threshold before the effect of network externalities show a positive impact on development and spur further ICT investment.

Lessons to date indicate that successful ICT-enabled projects must be: (a) suitable to the level of a given country's development; (b) relevant to the needs of targeted users; (c) integrated with infrastructure, applications, and skills development; (d) designed and implemented within a broader process of institutional and business process change; (e) coordinated as one part of an overall national development strategy; and (f) continuously monitored and evaluated for feedback.

No access without infrastructure

For most developing countries, lack of adequate infrastructure remains *the* major obstacle to the uptake of ICT. ICT infrastructure is, however, enormously expensive. The upfront investment needed to build out modern telecommunications networks, particularly broadband networks, far exceeds the resources of most developing nations. Several decades ago, the ICT sector was in the hands of state-owned enterprises. Following a wave of PTT privatizations and regulatory reform in developing countries that began in the 1990s, however, the private sector became the primary source of ICT investment in developing countries. Despite a noticeable decline of overall North-South investment flows in the last few years, continued rollout of physical infrastructure suggests that these flows have been replaced by a combination of South-South FDI flows, domestic private financing, and other sources.

As a result, many innovative partnerships between governments, businesses, and civil society have been formed to build networks and deploy advanced ICT applications in such sectors as government, commerce, and education. Such public-private partnerships allow developing countries to overcome the obstacles of insufficient resources, expertise, and project management skills and to leverage limited government funds to achieve far greater impact. Morocco, for example, built an effective regulatory framework and then used a GSM license auction to attract over US$1 billion investment in its mobile telephony market.[4] Chile allocated subsidies by public tender that resulted in private operators building public pay phones in 7,850 localities in underserved areas of the country.[5]

Creating the "right" enabling environment

If there is no access without infrastructure, it is equally true that there is no investment without an enabling regulatory environment. Given the competition for international investment dollars, developing countries must create conditions that make it attractive for outside investors to invest in ICT networks. Yet the complexity of these networks and the applications they facilitate, such as e-commerce, means that enabling policy frameworks must address issues far more complicated than a fair return on investment.

The basic goal of regulatory reform should be to create a stable, open environment that encourages confidence in the ICT market. A major step towards this goal is to establish clear and transparent governance structures and respect for the rule of law. Basic principles that support regulatory reform include encouraging market-based approaches and ease of market entry; promoting business confidence and clarity; enhancing transactional enforceability; ensuring interoperability (of systems, standards, networks, etc.); and protecting intellectual property and consumer rights. All developing countries will need to adapt their legal and regulatory frameworks not simply to improve access to telephony, but to better support broadband services, given that most e-applications require higher bandwidth and permanent Internet connections. Harmonization of legal frameworks across countries, moreover, is needed to ensure the cross-border interoperability of Internet-based applications. In the East Asia and Pacific region, for example, research on 23 countries showed that isolated activities of individual countries were ineffective in addressing this challenge and that harmonization of their legal frameworks was required.[6]

Globally, the trend in regulation is to minimize licensing hurdles by establishing general authorization regimes and to adopt technological neutrality. Many countries are accordingly moving away from service-specific licensing regimes to embrace converged licensing approaches, relieving investors from restrictive and burdensome licensing rules.[7]

For developing countries, certain regulatory issues (e.g., digital signatures or the security of online transactions) may not appear immediately relevant. However, these issues may be encountered much earlier than anticipated in the development process. For example, successful operation of telekiosks or Internet cafés—both cost-effective ways to provide access to the Internet and advanced ICT applications to large numbers of people—requires a legal framework that addresses the protection of intellectual property rights and consumer privacy.

Analysis of e-commerce worldwide reveals that it depends significantly on a supportive institutional environment, including national respect for "rule of law" and the availability of credible payment channels, such as credit cards.[8] In China, for example, only 13 percent of online transactions are paid for online, compared to 42 percent paid cash-on-delivery (COD) and 24 percent via remittances sent by mail.[9] Thus even when regulatory reforms establish a positive enabling environment for ICT, if the financial system is not sophisticated enough to support electronic transactions such as inter-bank electronic payments and bank credit cards, a country will find it difficult to reap the benefits of e-business. In the Middle East, for example, only 18 percent of banks (most of which are foreign) offer e-banking services. The absence of digital certification laws and the low level of credit card penetration in Arab countries are major factors that discourage banks from going online. In the case of Jordan, the total transaction volume of Visa credit cards in 2004 was estimated at US$258 million, of which online payments accounted for only US$2.5 million, not even 1 percent of the total.[10]

The crucial ingredient: Monitoring and evaluation frameworks

Although the positive impact of ICT-enabled projects on development has been documented over the past decade, the evidence has not yet been aggregated in a way that can easily convince decision makers at the policy level. To a large extent, the case for ICT for development still needs to be made.[11] Monitoring and evaluation (M&E), including the use of indicators closely linked to broader development processes, is the key to ensuring cost-effective deployment of ICT-based projects.

Unfortunately, the trend in ICT-based development projects has made such investments more difficult to track. At roughly the same time that investment in the ICT sector shifted from public to private sources, a stronger international commitment to reduce poverty (e.g., the Millenium Declaration and Goals) changed the focus of international donors from infrastructure and technology *per se* to ICT applications that could promote development. Many donors have subsequently "mainstreamed" ICTs in their development assistance programs, using ICT in different projects (e.g., health or education) as a tool of development. As a consequence, the ICT component of these projects is often difficult to quantify or even identify.

Effective M&E requires both upstream linkages (i.e., with national development objectives) and downstream accountability (i.e., measuring results with proper tools). Most importantly, e-strategies should refrain from re-inventing the wheel and integrate existing M&E indicators into the design of national e-development plans. Moreover, an M&E system must be comprehensible not only to the designers of e-strategies, but to domestic participants (e.g., the government, ministries, enterprises, and civil society) and external stakeholders (e.g., investors, donors, partners) as well.

For example, if an e-strategy includes distance education initiatives, it is important that such activities (and their outputs) be connected not only to broader e-strategy objectives (e.g., promoting e-literacy or enhancing the use of ICTs in education), but also to the objectives of the country's general development strategy (e.g., promoting general educational goals or developing general ICT usage) and more generic policy objectives (e.g., diversifying a traditional economy). Alternatively, if a country adopts a policy objective (e.g., "to become a knowledge society within twenty years" or "to stimulate the growth of the national ICT sector") various strategic goals will need to be articulated to assess progress towards this objective. Such goals could include, for example, providing primary education to 80 percent of a class age by a certain date or generating a certain percentage of national income through the ICT sector by a certain date.

E-government and the need for leadership

ICT has deeply changed the way in which government functions, for example, through office automation and the growing ubiquity of Web-based services. The advent of e-government and e-procurement, for instance, has allowed greater transparency and accountability across governmental agencies. The record of e-government projects in both developed and developing countries has, however, been mixed. A survey conducted by Richard Heeks of the University of Manchester in 2003 found that 35 percent of e-government initiatives were total failures in developing and transitional countries, 50 percent were partial failures, and only 15 percent were successes.[12]

While sophisticated e-government applications may appear to be the provenance of advanced industrial nations, many middle- and lower-income developing nations have begun to successfully adopt such applications. Often, a good e-government entry point is a department that is widely perceived to be corrupt and inefficient, such as procurement, customs or licensing, where cost savings can justify the initial investment. In 1997, the South Korean government introduced an e-procurement system that offers online information on more than 420,000 standardized products. The system replaced a procurement process that was widely regarded as corrupt, complicated, lacking accountability, and non-transparent. As of 2002, the government's investment of US$26 million had generated savings estimated at US$2.5 billion a year. The system has enhanced transparency and public trust, and allows for cross-agency comparisons of procurement, making the system more accountable.[13]

Chile introduced an online taxation system in 1998 that has considerably improved the national tax service and made it easier for citizens to access vital tax information. Three years after project launch, over 400,000 taxpayers had checked their tax assessments online, some 183,548 sworn returns and 89,355 income tax returns had been received online, and the Chilean exchequer had collected US$1.943 billion in taxes.[14]

Not all e-government initiatives will be based on networked computers. In certain developing countries, mobile telephone networks offer a more immediately usable platform for e-government applications. An application in the Philippines provides a good example of how mobile phones can be used in innovative ways. Globe Telecom's G-Cash application enables micro monentary transactions between families, friends, and local merchants. The text-based messaging service allows users, including those without bank accounts or credit cards, to send money phone-to-phone, buy goods and services, pay for business permits, and receive micro-financing and international remittances.

The development of e-government services can be a major latent market for the ICT sector in developing countries, particularly the software industry. By implementing such services, not only does government benefit, but the IT sector gets a kick start. One of the key lessons of e-government initiatives to date is the need to avoid an "agency-centric" or "silo" approach to the use of ICT. Avoiding this problem requires an overarching architecture that can guide the development of applications across various ministries, departments and government agencies. The absence of such an architecture can lead to sub-optimal results and, often, conflicting and incompatible applications. Thus a developing nation that chooses to "enter" the e-government market in a specific sector must first develop an architecture that will allow future applications to interoperate with one another.

It should be pointed out that e-government applications are major transformational exercises in change management. ICT implementation challenges hierarchies by demanding horizontal communication between government institutions. In addition, productivity increases associated with ICT applications can create redundancies, introducing an additional element of tension. Strong leadership is thus needed to successfully deploy national e-strategies. One pitfall of such strategies is to ignore or underestimate the inertia and rigidities of the public sector, meaning that e-leaders must have sufficient power and authority to implement decisions across multiple government departments. It is also vital that such leaders be able to formulate an overall vision of e-development and communicate this vision to stakeholders across multiple layers of society.

The potential of ICTs to expand tertiary education

A major application area with great potential for developing countries is e-learning. Since the early 1990s, both public and private higher education institutions in most countries have struggled to keep up with growing enrollment demand. Particularly in developing countries, governments have been forced to balance education system needs against fiscal realities. This is especially true given the priority that these nations have placed on achieving the Millennium Development Goals in primary and secondary education.

Today, the majority of global e-learning applications are found mainly in the developed world. By comparison, developing countries have made only small beginnings in the field. Yet it is in the latter countries that e-learning holds the greatest chance of bridging the access, cost and quality gaps in higher education, a global enterprise that is struggling to reach the one-quarter of 18-to-25 year-olds currently enrolled in higher education. Total estimated student enrollment in global higher education in the year 2000 was around 90 million. By 2003, more than 100 million students were enrolled in higher education worldwide.

The changing landscape of global higher education is reflected in changed student profiles in most countries. According to the U.S. Department of Education, over 5.9 million, or 39 percent, of all students enrolled in higher education programs in the USA in 2004 were over the age of 24. This number is projected to reach 6.6 million in 2007 and 6.9 million in 2012. In Canada, around 30 percent of undergraduate students are over the age of 25; in Australia, New Zealand, Denmark, Norway and Sweden, over 20 percent of first-year university students were over the age of 27 in 2000.[15]

New systems of distance learning and Web-enabled education and training programs can be used to reach remote and underserved regions and segments of the population, as well as to accommodate working adults that seek flexible learning options. The emerging trend for working adults worldwide is to access online education programs without leaving their jobs. For adults in developing nations, such programs allow them to complete advanced educational degrees without incurring the high travel and living costs, or stringent visa requirements, of studying abroad.

In China, close to one million students are estimated to be studying online today.[16] In the United States in 2003, there were 1.9 million online higher education students. This figure increased to 2.6 million students (a 24 percent increase) in 2004, meaning that 16 percent of all higher education students in the United States were studying online.[17] Very conservative estimates project that the online e-learning sub-sector will become a global, US$150 billion plus industry by 2025.[18]

Although the majority online providers of higher education programs are based in the United States, several providers have made promising starts in developing countries, including China, Mexico, Turkey, India and China. Most successful providers of ICT-based higher education programs today, which generally combine online learning with some kind of face-to-face instruction, are commercial ventures. Public-private partnerships may thus offer developing nations a cost-effective way to both expand infrastructure and access to affordable higher education.

The growing role of the international community

An increasing amount of international effort has been devoted to building information societies over the last few years. Chief among these efforts are the European Union's "e-Europe Initiative," the G-8 Digital Opportunity Task Force (DOT Force), the United Nations ICT Task Force (UNICTTF), and the process surrounding the World Summit on the Information Society (WSIS) of the International Telecommunications Union.

The international community now faces a number of challenges and expectations with respect to e-development. On one hand, it is expected to support national efforts to build information societies and bridge the digital divide. On the other hand, it has a responsibility to respond to challenges that are broader than those faced by individual nations, such as the technical, economic, and policy rules that will constitute universally accepted rules of the game. This category of activity includes norms and standards (e.g., the International Telecommunications Union), trade agreements (the World Trade Organization), but also to some extent, issues of global governance (e.g., the Working Group on Internet Governance). It also includes international financial support for regional infrastructure and other types of cross-border cooperation, as well as facilitating collaboration on issues such as cyber-security.

One crucial responsibility of the international community at present is to help develop analytical and policy tools that allow developing nations to better conceptualize the role of ICT in development, including monitoring and evaluation frameworks for ICT-enabled projects. Another crucial responsibility is to facilitate long-term investment in relevant areas of e-development by both donors and private investors. Finally, the international community must provide forums where e-development issues can be discussed openly and professionally by both developed and developing nations.

Measuring the benefits of ICT and the success or failures of specific projects is particularly urgent because current data is limited. ICT projects are difficult to track and there is insufficient rigorous data to serve as the basis for policy decisions. Certain organizations are now tracking different aspects of ICT. The ITU's *World Telecommunications Development Report* (WTDR),[19] for example, focuses on telecommunications. *The Global Information Technologies Report* (GITR) edited by the World Economic Forum also tracks ICT, but from a strong private-sector perspective.[20] In addition, a recent report produced by the WSIS Task Force on Financing Mechanisms provides helpful information on tracking ICT investments.[21]

The MDG+5 Summit of September 2005 and the second phase of the WSIS in November 2005 offer an unprecedented window of opportunity that will not be repeated in the near future. The former has the ability to make ICT a priority of the development agenda, whereas the latter can make development the main objective of ICT-

related international debates. The ambition of the international community should be to seize this moment to reconfigure the ICT-for-development debate from both sides. By accepting the expanded roles described here, international organizations, business and civil society are in a position not only to turn the information revolution into an instrument of global prosperity, but also to shape the ways in which they interact with each other in the face of other global challenges.

Notes

1 S. Yusuf. 2004. Innovative East Asia: The Future of Growth. New York: Oxford University Press.

2 See R. Heeks. 2003. "Information Technology, Government and Development." Report on the IT, Government and Development Workshop, 26 November 1998. Manchester, England. http:www.man.ac.uk/idpm/itgovsem.htm. Accessed July 2005.; and C. Kenny and C. Qiang. 2003. "ICT and Broad-Based Development." in ICT and Development. Washington, DC: Global Information & Communication Technologies Department, World Bank.

3 C. Qiang, G. Clarke, and N. Halewood. "The Role of ICT in Doing Business" in World Information and Communication Technologies for Development Report, 2005. Edited by C. Qiang. Washington, DC: World Bank, 2005.

4 See ITU, "The Role of Effective Regulation: Morocco Case Study," ITU, Geneva, 2002; and B. Wellenius, C. Rosotto and A. Lewin, "Morocco: Developing Competition in Telecommunications," CITPO Working Paper, GICT Department, World Bank, Washington, DC, 2004.

5 Bjorn Wellenius, "Closing the Gap in Access to Rural Communications: Chile, 1995–2002," infoDev Working Paper, World Bank, Washington, DC, 2001.

6 D. Satola, R. Sreenivasan, and L. Pavlasova, 2004. "Benchmarking Regional e-Commerce in Asia and the Pacific and Assessment of Related Regional Activities," in "Harmonization of Legal and Regulatory Systems for E-Commerce in Asia and the Pacific: Current Challenges and Capacity Building Needs." United Nations, New York.

7 Examples include member states of the European Union, India, South Africa, Tanzania and Zambia.

8 Firms in the Dominican Republic, for example, have found that residents are not ready to take advantage of e-commerce offerings, largely because credit card fraud in the country is the seventh highest in the world. Kirkman et al. 2002. "The Dominican Republic Readiness for the Networked World." Information Technologies Group. Center for International Development. Harvard University, Cambridge.

9 Yusuf. 2004. Innovative East Asia.

10 Arab Advisor Group. 2005. "An Analysis of e-Commerce Adoption in Jordan and the Gulf Region based on Reported Figures from Visa International." Arab Advisor Group: Amman, Jordan.

11 See, for example, K. McNamara. 2004. Information and Communication Technologies, Poverty and Development—Learning from Experience. Washington, DC: infoDev, GICT Department, World Bank.

12 See Richard Heeks. 2003. "Achieving Success/Avoiding Failure in e-Government Projects: Topic Summary. "eGovernment for Development Information Exchange, University of Manchester, Manchester, UK. Available at http://www.egov4dev.org/topic1smry.htm. Accessed July 2005.

13 World Bank. 2004. "Korea's Move to E-Procurement." PREM Notes, no. 90, July 2004. Poverty Reduction and Economic Management Network, World Bank: Washington, DC.

14 World Bank. "Chilean Tax System Online." abstract, E-Government, GSPR net (Governance and Public Sector Reform Sites): Washington, D.C. Available at http://www1.worldbank.org/ publicsector/egov/chile_taxcs.htm. Accessed July 2005.

15 OECD. Education at a Glance. Paris: OECD, 2003.

16 Estimate of contributing author Ron Perkinson, based on conversations with universities and accumulated market appraisal data regarding a range of university distance providers.

17 Sloan Consortium, Entering the Mainstream: The Quality and Extent of Online Education in the United States, 2003 and 2004, Sloan Center, Olin and Babson Colleges, Franklin W. Olin College of Engineering, Needham, Massachusetts, http://www.sloan-c.org/resources/survey.asp. Accessed July 2005.

18 Michael T. Moe, "The Book of Knowledge: Investing in the Growing Education and Training Industry," Merrill Lynch & Co., Inc., New York, 2000.

19 See ITU. 2003. World Development Report. Geneva.

20 A forthcoming World Bank publication. World Information and Communication for Development Report 2006: Trends and Policies for the Information Society, " will address these issues from the perspective of national governments and international donors.

21 WSIS. 2004. "The Report of the Task Force on Financial Mechanisms for ICT for Development: A Review of Trends and an Analysis of Gaps and Promising Practices." ITU, Geneva. Available at http://www.itu.int/ wsis/documents/doc_multi.asp?lang=en&id=1372|1376|1425|1377. Accessed July 2005.

Chapter 1

Look Before You Leap:
The Bumpy Road to E-Development

by Isabel Neto, Charles Kenny,
Subramaniam Janakiram, and Charles Watt

It has become commonplace to laud the potentially huge role that the Internet and networked computing can play in the development process. To date, however, we know little about the impact of these technologies, and it remains relatively difficult to evaluate the effectiveness of past and current practices in the field. This is in part because e-development is not an end in itself, but rather a process that uses modern ICTs to increase productivity, trade and the delivery of services. In the end, the measure of success of ICT in development will not focus on the spread of technology, but on overall progress towards economic growth and, ultimately, progress towards the Millenium Development Goals.[1]

Compounding the difficulty of evaluating the potential of an intermediate tool such as e-development is the rapid pace of change in the ICT sector and the broad applicability of the technologies involved. The general purpose and cross-sectoral nature of networked computing (which provides solutions in fields as diverse as educa-

tion, health, commerce and finance), and the fact that there is often a time lag before the positive effects of ICT use become apparent, has limited progress in estimating macroeconomic impact and the evaluation of ICT-based projects.[2] The role of governments in fostering electronic development is a relatively new area of practice and research in particular. Nonetheless, given the opportunity cost of investing in ICTs rather than in other areas of development, we need to find methods to increase the success rate of e-development as well as to monitor and measure the impact of ICT-related investments to increase our stock of best practices and lesssons learned.

This chapter first reviews what we know about the impact of e-development projects, examining evidence at both the macro and project level, and briefly examines the role of the ICT sector in national economies. It then outlines the challenges of e-development opportunities, explores the drivers and preconditions of successful ICT-based development projects and discusses the components of a holistic approach to project

Box 1.1. Core definitions used in this report

E-development is development that makes use of ICTs or ICT applications to provide information and knowledge services to enhance productivity, efficiency and quality of life. For the purpose of this report, e-development refers specifically to the use of the Internet and networked computers to contribute to development processes. The term refers to both the production of goods and services in the area of computing and networks (the "ICT sector"), as well as the use of networked computers across economic and social sectors.

Information and Communication Technologies (ICTs) consists of hardware, software, networks and media for the collection, storage, processing, transmission and presentation of information (e.g., voice, data, text, images), as well as related services. Communication technologies consist of a range of communication media and devices, including print, telephone, fax, radio, television, video, audio, computer and the Internet. ICT can be split into ICI and IT.

Information Technology (IT) refers to hardware and software used to collect, store, process and present information.

Information and Communication Infrastructure (ICI) refers to physical telecommunications systems and networks (e.g., cellular, broadcast, cable, satellite, postal) and the services that utilize them (e.g., Internet, voice, mail, radio and television).

Information and Communication Technologies Sector (ICT Sector) is the combination of manufacturing services industries that capture, process, transmit and display data and information electronically. The ICT sector is complex and is more readily understood in terms of its impact on business, government and the individual citizen.

ICT applications, or e-applications, are hardware and software solutions that utilize ICTs to meet business, public administration, social and other needs. Such applications are also sometimes referred to as *informatics*, a term that conveys ICT as a way of doing things. A new vocabulary is emerging with reference to the electronic character of applications using the prefix "e." Examples of such applications include conducting business transactions on the Internet (e-commerce), using networked computers both as a general pedagogical tool and to impart the skills needed for successful ICT-enabled projects (e-education), providing information to health managers, health professionals and the general public (e-health), and using networked computing to increase a government's transparency and inclusiveness (e-governance). While terms such as e-education, e-government, e-commerce, and e-health can refer to the applications themselves, they can also refer to the principles or strategies behind these applications.

implementation. Finally, it concludes with some pointers on the way forward.

The chapter and the report as a whole will focus on the use and impact of networked computing. This is not to downplay the importance of other types of ICTs such as mobile phones and broadcast radio, many of which are widespread in developing countries today and have a proven track record of developmental impact. But precisely because the track record of networked computing is both shorter and less well understood, there is a considerable need for research and discussion on this topic.

Part I. What (little) is known about the impact of ICT on economic growth

Looking at broad macroeconomic data, there appears to be strong a link between the level of welfare and the existence and use of ICT in developing countries. For example, the correlation between the UNDP Human Development Index (HDI),[3] a measure of general development that includes non-income factors, and the networked economy index (NEI),[4] a broad measure of e-development, is very strong across countries (see figure 1.1).

Similarly, rich countries have more Internet users, more personal computers (PCs) and more bandwidth than poor countries—a set

of conditions described as the "digital divide" (see table 1.1). This relationship should come as no surprise. While rich countries spend a somewhat larger percentage of their GDP on ICT (see table 1.2), it is clear that the major reason for smaller stocks of ICT in developing countries is that ICTs are consumption and investment goods —and rich countries have more money to invest and consume.

E-development is clearly a product of more general development, then. The more interesting question is the extent to which e-development can also be a *driver* of general development. The cross-country evidence reviewed below suggests that investment in ICT production facilities and investment in ICT equipment have both been a direct source of economic growth in many countries.

Looking at ICT production, 'transition' countries such as the Czech Republic, Slovakia or Hun-

Table 1.1 Internet usage, PC ownership and ICT infrastructure by region of the world, 2002/2003

	Internet users, 2002		PCs, 2002		International bandwidth (Gbps), 2003			
	per 1,000 inhabitants	per US$m of GDP	per 1,000 inhabitants	per US$m of GDP	per 1,000 inhabitants	per US$m of GDP	per Internet User	per Broadband subscriber
SSA	9.3	19.9	12.0	23.2	3.8	8.0	0.4	126.0
EAP	54.6	42.5	34.3	26.7	47.0	36.6	0.9	5.5
ECA	72.2	29.9	74.9	27.9	141.0	58.1	2.0	82.2
LAC	82.5	25.5	68.2	20.7	62.5	19.0	0.8	19.0
MENA	45.1	16.0	47.9	17.0	24.5	8.7	0.5	9.1
SAR	13.4	28.1	6.8	14.3	2.7	5.7	0.2	26.5
Developing world	41.5	30.8	32.3	23.0	38.4	28.4	0.9	10.5
World	103.0	19.4	102.4	18.4	363.6	68.4	3.5	22.2

Source: World Bank, "Financing Information and Communication Infrastructure Needs in the Developing World: Public and Private Roles," World Bank, Washington, DC, 2005.
Note: PC – personal computer. SSA – Subsaharan Africa; EAP – East Asia and Pacific; ECA – Europe and Central Asia; LAC – Latin America and the Caribbean; MENA – Middle East and North Africa; SAR – South Asia Region. These regions correspond to World Bank groupings. For more information, see http://www.worldbank.org/html/extdr/regions.htm.

Table 1.2. Investment in and expenditures on telecommunications and ICTs by region, 1995–2004

	Investment in telecommunications			Average ICT expenditure (% of GDP)
	Investment per capita (average 1995–2002)	*Investment as % GDP (average 1995–2002)*	*Investment in US$ millions (cumulative total 1995–2002)*	
SSA	6.1	1.0	22,600	6.3
EAP	17.3	1.4	231,800	6.1
ECA	14.7	0.7	55,000	5.8
LAC	35.9	0.9	131,600	5.6
MENA	19.6	0.6	29,500	5.2
SAR	2.6	0.6	27,000	5.2
Developing world	13.7	1.0	497,400	5.7
Developed world	138.5	0.5	985,500	8.2
World	34.2	0.6	1,482,900	6.5

Source: World Bank. 2005. "Financing Information and Communication Infrastructure."
Notes: (a) See Table 1.1 for explanation of regional acronyms. (b) ICT expenditures include external spending on information technology (tangible spending on information technology products purchased by businesses, households, governments, and education institutions from vendors or organizations outside the purchasing entity), internal spending on information technology (intangible spending on internally customized software, capital depreciation and the like), and spending on telecommunications services and other office equipment.

gary have seen economic growth driven in no small part by their ICT industries (see figure 1.2).[5] Vietnam has also experienced recently dynamic growth in the software industry, which expanded by over 40 percent in a single year, 2002 to 2003 (38 percent for domestic software services and 50 percent for export software services). In that same year, the hardware industry in Vietnam grew 27 percent. Although the US$2.1 billion ICT sector in Vietnam is relatively small, even when compared to countries like the Philippines or Indonesia, it has made considerable progress in just six years.[6] Again, in Estonia, the overall ICT sector employed roughly 4,300 people in 2002, generating US$41 million per annum in taxes on the basis of US$172 million in revenues.[7]

In leading ICT production countries such as India, the sector has not only grown in size but also complexity. India's share of the global market for outsourced customized software grew from 11.9 percent in 1991 to 18.5 percent in 1999, reflecting total market growth of 55 percent.[9] There has been significant development within this segment of the software market, as Indian companies progressively demonstrate their ability to move away from "on-site" or "body shopping" services to turnkey projects. Whereas the on-site element contributed 90 percent of India's software exports in 1988, this percentage fell to 40 percent by 2000.[10] The drift upwards in value-added software and services in India is supported by an examination of ISO 9000 and SEI-CMM quality certifications. Of the 31 companies that were certified worldwide in May 2002 at Level 5, the highest certification level, all 16 non-U.S. companies were Indian.[11]

Figure 1.1 Human development and networked economy indexes

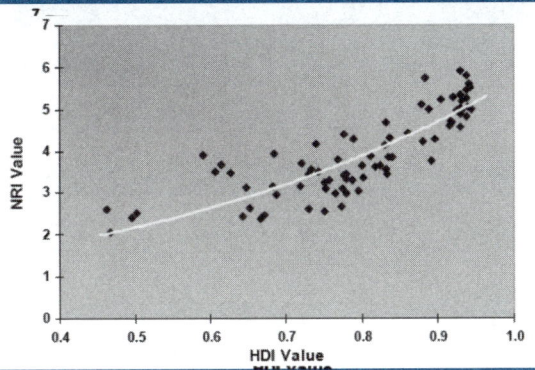

Source: B. Lanvin and C. Qiang. "Poverty 'Eradication:' Using ICT to Meet the MDGs; Direct and Indirect Roles of E-Maturity," in Dutta, S., B. Lanvin and F. Paua, eds. 2004. *Global Information Technology Report 2003–04.* Oxford University Press. Accesible at http://www.weforum.org.

On the ICT usage side, investments in ICT have the potential to significantly reorganize how goods and services are created and distributed. ICT applications can create new markets, new products and activities (such as online outsourcing of services) and new ways of organizing how society operates. Ideally, these activities can enable countries to diversify their economies, enhance their export competitiveness and produce high value-added services that boost local economies.

Recent World Bank surveys of over 20,000 firms in roughly 50 low- and middle-income countries provide evidence that firms in developing countries which use ICT show faster sales and employment growth, as well as higher labor and total factor productivity, than firms which do not use ICT [9]. The surveys also suggest that in countries where respondents considered ICT services to be of high quality, companies use email and Web services for business at higher rates.

Figure 1.2 ICT sector contribution to GDP growth, selected countries, 1995–2001

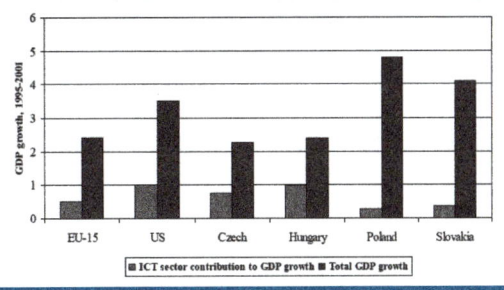

Source: Based on van Ark and Piatkowski[8]

Of note, 60 percent of the exporters and 80 percent of the foreign-owned firms that were surveyed used email and websites, as compared to 20–30 percent of micro, non-exporting domestic firms. This result echoes a recent study which shows that the export performance of Indian firms that have adopted more advanced e-business tools has been better than that of other firms in international markets. Indeed, the type of e-business technology, together with the skill intensity of the workforce, were shown to be the most significant factors influencing export performance.[10] Another recent study at the cross-country level suggests that access to the Internet affects the export performance of firms in developing countries, stimulating exports from poor to rich countries.[11]

Having said that, there is also evidence from developing countries that limits to ICT use in some sectors of the economy may well be based on practical calculations of cost and benefits. A recent study of small- and medium-scale enterprises (SMEs) in the food processing, textile and tourism sectors of Kenya, Tanzania and Uganda confirms that ICT usage differs by sector in the developing world.[12] This finding seems to result from differing cost-benefit analyses in sectors with differing production and marketing structures. The most advanced ICT use in the three countries studied was in the tourism sector of Tanzania and Kenya, where SMEs are mainly safari tour operators. Flexibility and rapid coordination are especially important in this sector, which is oriented mostly towards foreign customers. (The tourism sector is also characterized by management with the highest level of education, as well as the highest absolute stock of ICT capital.) The food and textile sectors in the three countries used ICT significantly less. This study also found that the stock of ICT capital had a negative impact on labor productivity, save for the tourism sector, where a relatively high capital intensity had a positive impact on labor productivity.

Growth accounting analyses of the impact of ICTs reflects the micro and macro data presented above. Across the world, per capita economic growth is driven by three factors: investment in equipment and infrastructure (i.e., physical capital, including stocks of ICT), investment in human capital (i.e., skills and education), and efficient use of labor and capital, which increase total factor productivity (TFP). As seen earlier in table 1.2, there has been considerable and growing investment in ICTs worldwide over the last ten years. There is every reason to believe that this investment has played a role in increasing global output and labor productivity, but the evidence is elusive on whether this ICT investment has earned economic returns above the normal rate outside the ICT production sector, and some questions as to who benefits from TFP gains within the production sector.

Some developing economies *have* seen significant labor and total factor productivity gains from ICT production, particularly the Newly Industrialized Economies (NIEs) of Asia,[13] where large

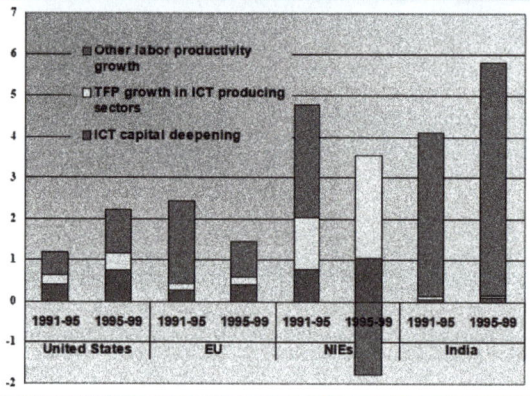

Figure 1.3. Contribution of ICT to labor productivity growth, selected countries and years (% of GDP)

Source: Qiang, Pitt and Ayers. "Contribution of ICT to Growth." *Note:* Data for the EU is the average for the following countries: Austria, Denmark, Finland, France, Germany, Italy, The Netherlands, Portugal, Spain, Sweden and the United Kingdom. NIEs stands for the Asian Newly Industrialized Economies: Hong Kong SAR, South Korea, Singapore and Taiwan Province of China.[15]

ICT producing sectors may have had a considerable economic impact through gains in total factor productivity (see figure 1.3).

For most developing countries, however, ICT use is likely to have a bigger impact than ICT production because the ICT industry is concentrated in relatively few countries, and because productivity gains in ICT production appear to accrue to users, not producers. Looking at the beneficiaries of TFP gains, East Asia has by far the largest share of IT production in the developing world. However, even countries where technology exports constitute a higher share of total exports in the region have failed to see more rapid overall productivity growth, perhaps in part because returns accrue to (largely U.S.) patent owners, rather than ICT manufacturers, in what has become an increasingly commoditized business.[14] It is also worth noting that even in poorer developing countries such as India that have led the way in ICT exports from low income countries, the sector remains very small compared to the overall economy.

On the usage side, ICT investment will have promoted labor productivity, but given the remarkably rapid growth in ICT investment worldwide over the last ten years, it is not improbable that countries and companies have invested in ICT until the return on this investment matches the return on other types of investments. This phenomenon might explain the elusive nature of total factor productivity gains due to ICT investment around the world. The above-mentioned study of SMEs in Kenya, Tanzania and Uganda, for example, suggested that investment in ICTs does not have a significant impact on enterprise returns or export performance, and can even have a negative impact on labor productivity. The negative impact of ICT investment on labor productivity can be interpreted either as an over-investment in ICT (i.e., the non-divisibility of equipment in case of small enterprises),[15] or as the result of the substantial learning required during the initial ICT adoption phase and resultant lags before full economic benefits are felt.[16] Over-investment in ICT can also be attributable to poor choices of both hardware and software, a decision made more difficult by their wide price ranges.

To conclude, a growing ICT industrial base in some developing countries has created significant investment and employment opportunities, while a growing number of applications for new ICTs have created numerous opportunities for industries across the world to invest in the use of computers. Developing countries have already garnered significant returns as a result. Where evidence is less clear is of supra-normal returns to investment and leapfrogging opportunities. E-development is crucially dependent on broader development, this is unsurprising given its cross-cutting application. Furthermore, evidence of considerable 'spillovers' of the type that justify government intervention to subsidise expanded use are limited at the macroeconomic level for ICT as a whole. This suggests the need for caution in the development of significant programs of sector-specific interventions favoring ICT investments over other types of investment.

Part II. Policies for the development of IT sectors in developing nations

Developed, middle-income and developing nations can all reap benefits from having a healthy IT supply sector, as we have seen. Software industries in particular can have a considerable impact on employment, pay and economic performance.[17] At the same time, developing countries face considerable challenges in promoting and sustaining ICT-enabled innovation and new business creation. They struggle not only to attract private investment (local and international) to expand IT services, they find it difficult to expand IT-enabled businesses in varied sectors of their own economies.

As part of their economic development strategy, some governments are making substantial efforts to develop national IT sectors that can compete globally. Countries such as India, Malaysia, Greece, Israel, Singapore and the Republic of Korea have taken a pro-active stance to encourage IT-led growth, investing seed capital in start-up companies, establishing joint ventures, and creating high technology parks and export initiatives.[18] Even skeptics of intervention appear to agree that governments in East Asia have played an important role in the development of the local IT manufacturing industry. They have pursued this goal through direct investments in human resources and technology development (e.g., Taiwan's Industrial Technology Research Institute), as well as through incentives for private investment in the industry. Current initiatives by the government of Russia reflect a similar strategy (see box 1.2).

A major latent market for the IT sector in developing countries is the development and delivery of e-government applications. By implementing these services, not only does government benefit, but the IT sector is given an important demand-boost. In Estonia, for example, legislation created a favourable environment for the industry; governmental departments then actively procured innovative solutions from local companies, including online taxation applications, an "X-road" initiative to modernize national databases, and an ID-card initiative. The Estonian government has contributed a stable 1 percent of its total budget to financing ICT expenditure.[19]

Box 1.2 Information technology: Russia's next natural resource[a]

In an effort to jump-start its economy and diminish its dependence on natural resources, Russia has made local IT development one of its top priorities.[21] The country set aside US$650 million in 2005 to invest in hi-technology initiatives, such as the e-Russia program, which encompasses both e-government and e-health services (e.g., putting medical records online).

In 2005 software exports are already growing by 40 percent to 50 percent annually, and by 2010, the government hopes that Russian programmers' contributions will make up 7 percent of global software exports, and a $40 billion market To spur further growth, the country hopes to develop regional, government-sponsored IT research and development centres, or "techno-parks," similar to those of Bangalore, India. At the same time, the government is hoping to reassure investors by cutting red tape and amending the tax code to create simplified regimes favorable to the IT industry. Former Soviet Union President Mikhail Gorbachev when addressing a gathering of Massachusetts software industry executives in April 2005 stated "Russian society is ready to make a breakthrough. The high level of education and the potential of our science enable us to take our place in the post-industrial economy."

The development of IT industry groups has also begun beyond Russia. The RUSSOFT Association, for example, is an association of the largest and most technically competent software developing companies in Russia, Byelorussia, and Ukraine. Headquartered in Saint Petersburg, the association comprises more than 70 companies and 6,000 highly qualified, professional software engineers.

While these efforts are supporting Russia's attempts to attract significant investment in the sector, analysts note that the country faces a growing list of emerging-market competitors (including Poland, Hungary and Estonia) seeking to get their own slice of the IT industry.

[a] "IT is Russia's next natural resource," quote from Leonid Reiman, Minister of Information Technology and Communications of the Russian Federation, at the Russian Economic Forum, London, United Kingdom, April 12, 2005.

Source: Pruitt, S. 12 April 2005. "Russia looks to make IT its 'next natural resource." ITworld.com, IDG New Service, London Bureau.

At the same time, not all government efforts to promote ICT sectors are successful. One example of an intervention that failed to deliver was the attempt of the Indonesian government to promote a software production center as part of its Action Plan for 2001–2005. The Bali Camp software development house began operations in 1999 with 50 programmers. It grew to supply software modules to both domestic and international markets. At one time, its clients included global IT companies such as Microsoft, Oracle, Cisco and IBM. However, the inability of Bali Camp to attract and retain good IT staff, pay competitive salaries and develop programming specialties beyond legacy system re-engineering all but forced it to close.

Similarly, Hong Kong's US$100 million venture capital fund for ICT was unable to find attractive investments. The Malaysia Multimedia Supercorridor, which started in the mid-1990s with a government-backed venture capital fund, ten years of tax freedom and a promise of US$10 billion in infrastructure investment, attracted less than US$500 million in private investment, far below the government target. Reasons cited by companies for not moving to the Supercorridor included concerns over the monitoring of Internet traffic, red tape, slow visa approval, as well as weak intellectual property protection, infrastructure and the skills base of the local labor market.[20]

Overall, macroeconomic evidence suggests that IT production, while a growing source of investment and employment opportunities, is unlikely to generate far higher economic and social returns than other investments. This, combined with a patchy record of success in specific interventions designed to attract IT industries and growing international competition in the sector suggests that sector-specific government inter-ventions should be designed with care and limited in extent. Evidence to date also suggests that the most significant policies that governments can introduce to attract IT industries are the same that attract industries in general –macroeconomic stability, limited red tape and corruption, investment security, a strong infrastructure and human capital base and so on.

Part III. Broad-based e-development is a complex venture

Turning to the use of ICT in development programs, while projects can garner significant returns, e-development solutions can also be costly, with a high failure rate among large initiatives. Lack of physical and human capital, absence of the institutions required to successfully implement ICT-enabled projects and fragmented ICT strategies are some of the difficulties faced by developing countries when deploying such projects.[21]

The use of networked computers in schools provides an instructive example of the uncertain cost-benefit ratio of ICT-based development projects. Numerous studies suggest that computers can provide students individualized interactivity, a more satisfying learning experience and marketable ICT-related skills. Yet the annual cost of providing just one computer to every 20 students is between US$78 and US$104 per student per year. In some developing countries, annual discretionary educational expenditures per secondary student are below US$20. Furthermore, the impact of computing and Internet connectivity on improved test scores is mixed, suggesting that the broader educational environment (including the quality and training of teachers, as well as the quality and integration of digital instruction

Box 1.3 Gyandoot: Electronic government and the rural poor

Gyandoot is an information and communication project designed to provide government services to the population of Dhar (Madhya Pradesh, India) via telekiosks. The project was intended to provide inhabitants of remote regions (primarily tribal peoples and the very poor) a cost-effective alternative to traveling to district headquarters to access such services as obtaining land records, information on market prices, and government entitlements (welfare schemes, public distribution of food, pensions, grants, etc); file grievances; and access email or a village newspaper.

Recent evaluations of the project show that more than 78 percent of users surveyed are satisfied with the services. However, usage is low, financial sustainability of the project is doubtful, and the poorest residents of the district are not using Gyandoot. Out of the 38 telekiosks surveyed, 10 were not operational; the average use calculated for 18 telekiosks over a period of two years was only 0.62 users per day. Usage is also deteriorating over time. Revenue generated from Gyandoot services was also grossly inadequate to reach the breakeven point. According to one survey of 221 poor people, only 9 (4 percent of the total) had used Gyandoot and only 31 percent of the target group was aware of Gyandoot, which offers only a few services that directly benefit poor people.

Among the key lessons learned from the project are that appropriate technology is a necessary but insufficient condition for the success of ICT projects. Community participation and ownership of such projects is needed, project implementation should be the responsibility of grassroots-based organizations and individuals who have appropriate incentives to work with marginalized groups, services offered by such projects must benefit targeted users (in this case, poor people), and awareness-raising campaigns must be conducted during deployment.

Sources: Indian Institute of Management (IIM). 2002. "Gyandoot—Rural Cyber Cafés on the Intranet." and; S. Cecchini and M. Raina. 2003. "Electronic Government and the Rural Poor."; and http://gyandoot.nic.in.

materials) is an important determinant of the success or failure of ICT-enabled education projects.[22]

Studies of e-procurement suggests that this generally mixed picture may extend to applications beyond education. For example, a recent survey found that only forty percent of companies that adopted on-line purchasing systems actually saved money when they deployed such systems as part of a change management process. The figure for companies that introduced such systems without a change management program was only three percent.[23] Available evidence also suggests that firms, governments and civil society face difficulties in exploiting ICTs to their full potential in least-developed countries (LDCs); one recent study estimated that a majority of public sector IT applications in LDCs are either partial or total failures,[24] a finding equally true for the private sector. Box 1.3 highlights an example of an e-government initiative which has won several awards – still, usage is low, especially for the poorer population, and the project may not be sustainable.

Even if e-strategies are carefully developed and implemented, project costs can threaten the sustainability of ICT-enabled applications. The Enlaces program in Chile, for example, is often considered one of the most success- ful e-education projects to date (see box 1.4), but implementation of the program was only possible due to significant funding from the Ministry of Education and generous grants from Telefónica CTC, among others. Secur-

Box 1.4 The Enlaces e-education program in Chile

One of the key aims of the Enlaces program in Chile was to address educational exclusion in rural and deprived urban areas by linking primary and secondary schools via basic e-mail services and gateways to the Internet. The program began as a prototype in six schools in Santiago in 1991 and was later scaled up to the national level. By 2004, the program had reached more than 93 percent of the subsidized school population. Close to 80 percent of all classroom teachers had been trained and more than 8,500 schools were part of the program, which now comprises virtually all urban schools and a growing proportion of rural schools. Evaluations by the World Bank, UNESCO, and the U.S. Agency for International Development concur that the Enlaces project is one of the most successful programs in the Chilean Educational Reform. (For more information, see http://www.enlaces.ufro.cl.)

Among the factors accounting for its success was an integrated strategy which focused not only on infrastruc- ture, but also attention to teachers and teacher training. This strategy sought to create a social network of educators and pupils facilitated by user-friendly technology and decentralized support, together with respect for the autonomy of participating schools in how they use the program's technologies. With respect to content, hundreds of software titles for all areas of the curriculum have been distributed to schools, and the Ministry of Education has invested heavily in a comprehensive educational portal.

Enlaces demonstrates what can be done when there is sufficient political will coupled with the technical expertise and financial resources needed to implement an ICT-based education project. However, the program is not sustainable in isolation and relies on government funds and donations. As of 1996, total project costs for a small primary school with 75 students averaged US$78 per student annually, or roughly 8 percent of Chile's annual recurrent expenditures per student in primary education. (Annual per student costs in large schools were much lower, US$21 per student, or 4 percent of recurrent government expenditures per student).

As of 1998, the budget provision for Enlaces was around US$120 million. Central government funding of around US$60 million has been supported by long-term loans provided by the World Bank (US$20 million). Additional support has been provided by Telefónica CTC, the largest telecommunications service provider in Chile, which donated 10 years of Internet service (1998–2008) to more than 4,000 schools (an estimated value of more than US$1 million per year). The Chilean private sector (i.e., mostly parents) and other education projects unrelated to Enlaces have contributed nearly 20 percent of the present hardware in primary schools (K-8), and more than 30 percent of that in secondary schools.

Sources: Hinostroza, E. 1993. "Teaching the Learning."; Potashnik, M. 1996. "Computer in the Schools."; Hepp, P. et al. 2004. "Technology in the Schools."; and International Institute for Communications and Develoment. 1998. "ICTs in Developing Countries."

ing permanent funding and thus ensuring sustainability of the project remains an issue.

Part IV. Success in applying ICT depends on macro drivers and preconditions

Having briefly examined the complexity of e-development projects, let us now examine what makes such projects successful. What are the general drivers of e-development at the macro-economic level? What are the challenges to successful implementation of e-development projects? Some of these difficulties are directly linked to the preconditions for e-development, while others are linked to implementation. Identifying potential hurdles can help policy makers to avoid the many pitfalls that can cause failure.

Level of economic development

It is an obvious but important point that people living on a dollar or two a day are unlikely to either afford advanced ICT equipment or have the skills to use it.[25] In addition to affordability concerns, general lack of capital and high interest rates in some countries create significant obstacles to the development of the ICT sector, not to mention the lack of functioning banking and credit systems. ICT infrastructure and a functioning banking system, for example, are crucial preconditions for e-commerce. Additionally, the ability of ICT to facilitate trade and open new markets will be limited by weak transport infrastructure.[26] Investment in ICTs alone is insufficient for business growth, then.[27]

Another consideration that may lower expectations of e-development is that network externalities come into effect only after a critical mass of ICT users has been reached. The development of ICT infrastructure may thus need to reach a certain threshold before the effect of network externalities begin to have an impact on additional ICT investment.[28] Accordingly, the impact of ICT technologies may be lower in lower-income countires, a finding supported by data indicating that less-advanced economies and regions are benefiting less from the Internet than already well-off economies and regions. Similarly, ICT use in lower-income countries may initially exacerbate internal inequalities. ICT rollout, which provide new opportunities to wealthy urban populations, but not poor rural populations, may encourage income divergence.[29] Unless specific policies targeting the poor are implemented (whether or not they directly involve ICTs), both income and gender divides within countries may grow as a result of the ICT revolution.

A simple regression analysis confirms the lesson that general development is key to e-development (see Annex 1). Roughly 80 percent of the variation in number of secure Internet servers between individual countries can be predicted on the basis of GDP per capita alone. It is thus apparent that the "digital divide" between advanced industrial and developing nations is part of a broader "development divide," a finding that should temper optimistic expectations of e-development as a tool for "leapfrogging" stages of development.

Having said that, the same analysis suggests that countries can significantly influence the development impact of ICTs through carefully designed interventions that improve the climate for investment and project success. The regression technique suggests that improving policies and institutions to encourage investment while extending access to telecommunications infrastructure can dramatically extend use of e-commerce at a given level of income per capita.

Infrastructure

A reliable and affordable telecommunications network, not to mention a reliable electricity infrastructure, has to be in place to harness the potential of ICT. Lack of infrastructure is one of the most important impediments to greater use of ICT identified by government officials, entrepreneurs and observers, particularly the lack of efficient, low-cost telecommunications services. Poor infrastructure performance strongly affects a country's growth prospects, as do high bandwidth costs. Numerous empirical studies have demonstrated that there is a close correlation between income growth, on one hand, and the quality and quantity of information infrastructure, on the other. In part this will be because poor infrastructure deters ICT use.

Accordingly, while one analysis suggests that 53 percent of the gap in PC use between the United States and Sub-Saharan African is accounted for by income differentials, fully 41 percent of the gap might be attributed to the disparity in telecommunications infrastructure.[30] The experience of e-government programs also suggests that ICT infrastructure is at the heart of successful deployment and sustainability.[31]

ICT infrastructure is costly to establish and maintain, costs that are further aggravated when a population is sparsely distributed over large areas. In such cases, service is usually limited and expensive; ICT costs, particularly Internet fees, can be prohibitively high. Given the limited resources of developing countries, e-development projects need to be designed with the understanding that access to ICTs, particularly advanced services, will continue to be of a lesser extent and lower quality in poorer countries for some time to come. Chapter Two discusses policy and regulatory approaches that should improve the reach of information infrastructure in developing countries.

Skills

Another critical precondition and/or driver of successful ICT projects is skilled human capital. The use of ICT depends on a solid pool of skilled workers. Adoption of ICT has thus been associated with considerably increased demand for skilled labor. A recent study of e-business shows that skill intensity of the workforce was one of the two most significant factors influencing the export performance of Indian firms (the other was the type of technology used).[32] The need for human capacity implies that there is a need for technical training, as well as for general education and the capacity to commercially exploit the information and knowledge that ICT makes available.[33] With respect to general education, a recent study found that a one-year increase in average schooling results in a one percentage point increase in PC penetration.[34]

The capacity of users to exploit local content on the Internet and to take part in its production depends on levels of literacy, education and mastery of the technologies concerned. For example, in Ethiopia, a country in which 60 percent of the adult population is illiterate and less than 1 percent of the relevant age group pursues tertiary education, 98 percent of Internet users in the late 1990s had a university degree.[35] This barrier may be sufficiently formidable to deter ICT diffusion, even if the long-term benefits outweigh short-term costs. Lower educational achievements, particularly in science and technology disciplines, constrain girls and women in particular from accessing ICT infrastructure and services.[36]

Institutions

While existing differences in physical ICT access and skills should be of concern to policy makers, having the right institutions in place is also essential. Although physical infrastructure correlates with much of the variation in basic

Internet use, ICT activity also depends significantly on appropriate legal and regulatory frameworks, particularly respect for the "rule of law."

Legal and regulatory reform in the telecommunications sector can play an important role in promoting competition and ICT investment, causing ICT prices to drop and extending access to more advanced ICT services. Differences in regulatory quality generally account for a large part of the gap in technology use between countries. One recent paper, for example, estimated that one-third of the Internet usage gap between the United Sates and the Middle East and North Africa region was associated with the difference in regulatory regimes.[37] (See chapter 2 for a discussion of the elements of a conducive policy environment.)

Analysis of e-commerce worldwide reveals that it depends significantly on a supportive institutional environment, including the availability of reliable payment channels, such as credit cards. This finding implies that well-functioning financial and credit institutions are key drivers of successful e-commerce applications.[38] In China, for example, only 13 percent of online transactions are paid for online, compared to 42 percent that are paid cash-on-delivery (COD) and 24 percent via remittances sent by mail.[39]

Legal and regulatory frameworks also ensure security (i.e., they facilitate digital commerce and ensure secure transactions),[40] increase trust (perhaps the most important factor in determining a willingness to purchase online) and protect privacy. In fact, an institutional environment that facilitates the building of transactional integrity is critical to the development of e-commerce.[41]

Part V. The need for a holistic approach to ICT implementation

Given poor ICT infrastructure rollout, low ICT skills, a weak institutional environment and lack of network externalities, firms and individuals in many developing countries may have little incentive to use new technologies. Even when the preconditions that affect ICT adoption are met, many challenges to the successful implementation of e-development projects remain. Available experience lends itself to several lessons: in particular, it appears that successful ICT-enabled projects:

- are well-suited to the level of a given country's development;

- are relevant to the needs of targeted users;

- integrate infrastructure, applications and skills development;

- are developed and implemented within a broader process of institutional and business process change;

- are designed with awareness of the complexity of such change;

- are coordinated as part of a larger strategy; and

- are continuously monitored and evaluated for feedback.

Developing a vision for e-development that is holistic in approach is the key to effectiveness. Such an approach keeps in mind the impact of an ICT project at the macro level, necessary cross-sectoral interactions and local specificities. Governments or public sector firms also need to develop appropriate and realistic implementation strategies, ensuring coordination across sectors and appropriate sequencing. Coordination between projects, particularly those that can share resources, infrastructure, etc., can lead to cost savings.[42]

The following subsections discuss these lessons in greater detail, using examples from e-government applications as illustrations. As the illustrations make clear, thinking through project objectives, context, funding mechanisms and content in a holistic manner gives ICT-enabled projects much better chances of success.

ICT suitable to the level of development

ICT-enabled projects should be adapted to the level of development of a given country. The business model for e-development will thus differ from country to country, based on their unique economic, social, political and technical infrastructure and ICT know-how. Figure 1.4 illustrates how, given a country's stage of development (top arrow), its policy choices and e-development focus—both at the infrastructure (middle arrow) and applications level (bottom arrow), of which e-government is an example —are likely to change.

ICT relevant to user needs

ICT applications need to be sufficiently relevant and provide value to targeted users. What information is really useful to local end-users in, say, rural areas? What, for example, would motivate a small-scale farmer in a remote area to plug into the World Wide Web? In the absence of sufficiently relevant applications in health, education, governance or employment, rural area shop owners, small business firms and individuals have little incentive to use ICT technology.

One recent failure of a "build it and they will come" model of computer networking occurred in Vietnam, where a donor-financed project provided five Centers for Poverty Reduction each two PCs, Internet and email access, electronic

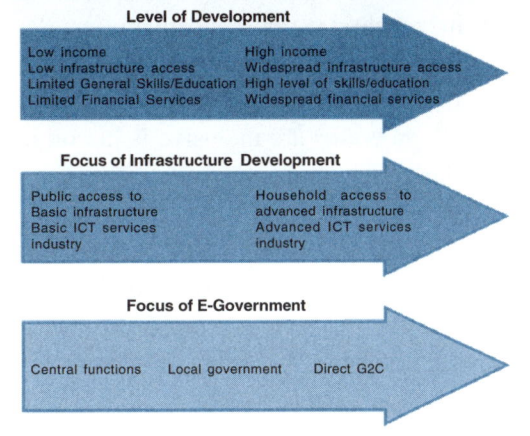

Figure 1.4. The focus of e-development activities changes with the level of development

libraries of community planning and poverty reduction literature, and computer and software training. Although the project aimed to improve collaboration between the centers, use of the Internet for collaboration or program research was minimal. When potential users were questioned as to why there was such limited use of the networked equipment, one common answer was that other centers were not seen as particularly valuable sources of information.[43]

Relevant local content implies that the material is "comprehensible" (i.e., content in local languages and adapted to local needs) and locally produced (i.e., applications and content produced by local individuals, NGOs or community groups). As a sign of how significant a problem this remains, 70 percent of pages on the World Wide Web are still in the English language, suggesting a relative dearth of material in the local languages of poor people in developing countries. Encouraging community ownership and participation in project design can help ensure that e-development projects are demand driven and will be appropriate to the needs and preferences of users. This is especially important when designing rural information and knowledge systems.[44] Addressing the need for relevant content also has a gender dimension. Involving women, as well as men, in content development and project design leads to locally appropriate content that is valuable to both genders. More broadly, ensuring that ICT programs are inclusive is important to broad-based development (box 1.5).

Integrating infrastructure, applications and skills development

When developing a specific ICT project, it is essential to take into account the disparate elements that will affect its performance. For example, it is necessary to ensure an electricity supply when deploying ICT equipment; training may be needed so that intended users can actually benefit from the services offered; and, in schools, curricula may need to be redesigned to use ICT to support problem solving, group learning and research. If only some of these elements are attended to, project failure is likely (see Box 1.6).

Integrating ICT projects into broader processes of change

Achieving major impact (whether economic, social or even democratic) with e-government applications calls for a more substantial, sometimes revolutionary, transformation of public administration processes.[45] Initiatives in India, for ex-

---

Box 1.5 Using ICT policies to rectify racial and gender imbalances

Local political and social conditions may impose requirements on the ICT sector in certain countries to enhance ownership by and employment of specific racial and/or gender groups. For example, lack of talented young black South Africans in the ICT sector (and their lack of involvement in ICT business start-ups) caused industry groups to draft an "ICT Empowerment Charter" along the lines of South Africa's Broad-Based Black Economic Empowerment Act. Originally intended to take effect March 1, 2005, the Charter is a voluntary and inclusive industry initiative which calls for all participating firms to meet mid-term (2010) and long-term (2015) targets for 33 indicators. Should large numbers of ICT firms achieve these goals, the racial and gender balance of equity holdings, management control and professional participation in this sector, traditionally dominated by white males, will have changed profoundly.

In South Korea, the government has undertaken an ICT initiative intended to promote higher education and workforce participation among females. A virtual university program, Ewha offers 152 full-credit courses to 8,799 female students across South Korea. The initiative is part of a national program to create fifteen virtual institutions—partnerships between 65 universities and 5 companies, each operating within an existing university system. Ewha is based on the belief that women will reap the greatest benefit from the push toward higher education. (Women today hold 35 percent of high-level IT positions in corporate South Korea.) These institutions have developed new educational programs using various ICTs, such as satellite broadcasting, videoconferencing, video on demand and the Internet, and offer a range of educational courses, from single Internet courses to retraining opportunities, as well as complex projects that make innovative use of new technologies.

Sources: ICT Empowerment Charter Working Group, South Africa. www.ictcharter.org.za; ILO. 2001. *World Employment Report 2001.* Geneva, Switzerland.

Box 1.6 How *not* to deploy computer labs in high schools

Starting around 1997, the Dominican Republic began the installation of computer labs in hundreds of high schools throughout the country. Each was equipped with 20 networked computers, productivity software, and a VSAT (very small aperture terminal) Internet connection. The goals of the project were not simply to provide connectivity and hardware, but also to facilitate learning in different subject areas in every high school, regardless of its location.

While the effort succeeded in creating labs in virtually every high school in the nation, results have been mixed. In some schools, computers remained in their boxes more than four years after project launch, mostly due to inadequate or absent electrical capacity. In connected schools, while students are reported to show an increased interest in their studies, computers in the labs are generally not being used for educational purposes: unstructured access periods are dominated by chat, games, and Internet surfing. ICT integration into the curriculum is also mixed across subjects and lower than initially hoped.

Computer labs provide a resource not only for students but also for community members. However, most labs are closed after school and on weekends, as well as during the summer holidays. Other problems include limited community participation (and little or no preparation for the host school), overlap with other connectivity programs, and assorted technical difficulties. Operating costs are significant and ongoing financing of the labs remains an unsolved challenge.

Source: http://cyber.law.harvard.edu/bold/devel03/modules/episodeIII.html#case. For more information, see Kirkman et al. 2002. "Dominican Republic Readiness."

ample, have included the computerization of district offices and the provision of PCs to rural development agencies (District Information System of National Informatics Centre, DISNIC, and Computerized Rural Information Systems Project, CRISP). While computerization was achieved in a majority of districts, the project had only a marginal impact on the efficiency of these agencies because the administrative reforms required to take advantage of computerization stalled.[46] (See chapter 5 for a detailed discussion of the basic components of e-government applications.)

Cultural factors and resistance to change also play a role in the success of e-development projects. Two factors in particular that cause resistance are (i) loss of control and jurisdiction and (ii) lack of clarity concerning agency mandates. Productivity increases associated with ICT applications can create redundancies, adding an additional element of tension to project deployments.[47] The potential for staff redundancies necessarily implies resistance and a corresponding need to ensure the buy-in of different stakeholders (see box 1.7). Political patronage and the legacy of state planning have created bureaucratic and administrative cultures in many countries that place a premium on information as a source of power. ICT implementation challenges current hierarchies by demanding horizontal communication between government institutions. To achieve increased community participation, decentralization is required. Corruption (with the added cost it imposes on technology diffusion), dependency on government cycles, political partisanship and bureaucracy can all create additional obstacles to ICT-enabled projects.[48]

ICT projects as part of a broader strategy

As mentioned earlier, there is mixed evidence on the contribution of ICT to economic development and equitable growth. ICT may help bridge the North-South gap or it may exacerbate it; much depends on the strategies that governments follow to explore the potentialities of ICT. In order to fully take advantage of the opportunities created by new technology, an integrated vision must incorporate the following key elements:

1) A conducive legal and regulatory policy framework. If such a regime is not already in place, regulatory reform can be undertaken in parallel with ICT deployment. Without such reforms, countries have faced such problems as redundant efforts and costs; the inability of the ICT sector to thrive in a monopoly telecommunications climate; failure to provide "proof of concept" for significant new public investments; and lack of internal buy-in and sustained funding on the part of different government stakeholders.[49]

2) Recognition of the links between different sectors. For example, in the case of e-commerce, the interdependency of the postal and transport sectors as well as the need for a developed and well-functioning financial system, must be considered. Trade restrictions, moreover, may affect access to technology or the free circulation of e-commerce goods.[50]

Box 1.7 Local obstacles to information sharing

An ICT project in the Indian state of Andhra Pradesh provides a good illustration of the importance of involving stakeholders in the planning, design, implementation and maintenance of computer-based systems. Lack of such involvement can seriously thwart, and even derail, IT initiatives.

In 1998, the Government of Andhra Pradesh set up the Andhra Pradesh Value-added Network (APVAN) with a consortium of public sector IT companies from Singapore. APVAN was positioned as India's first value-added network for the delivery of online services. The network was intended to enable businesses, citizens, and the government to interact with one another over electronic networks. McKinsey and Co. was engaged to prepare a business plan for rolling out APVAN. While spelling out the value propositions for the project, McKinsey made a number of observations on the potential to reduce and relocate existing staff. These observations quickly caused a serious controversy with government employee associations and the project was temporarily shelved.

In contrast, the CARD (Computerized Administration in the Registration Department) project introduced computers into more than 200 sub-registrar offices to streamline the registration of land sales. Despite subsequent shortcomings, project implementation went smoothly, as channels of communication were kept open with Registration Department employees, who were involved in each stage of the planning and implementation process.

Source: Sudan. 2002. "Towards SMART Government."

Box 1.8 Indonesia and the need for accountability of ICT expenditures

Indonesia currently lacks the fiscal and comprehensive internal management systems that government policymakers need to analyze and report ICT usage throughout the country. Information on the number of PCs, software applications and networks, for example, can only be obtained through laborious investigation of manual records and incongruent electronic data fields.

Although the national parliament has stringent internal controls over the budgetary process, its accounting methodology does not have a single line item for ICT goods and services. Requests for such goods and services at the planning stage are often simply categorized as "supplemental" or "miscellaneous" expenditures by both the central government and the decentralized governorates. Nor are shared databases maintained to keep critical information needed to monitor, evaluate and control the ICT industry in a transparent and efficient manner.

In the area of basic composite ICT information, Indonesia stands apart from its neighbors in South and East Asia (Singapore, Malaysia, Myanmar, or the Philippines), where information on ICT expenditures and information are readily available. This obstacle to e-development may, however, soon be overcome as a result of the reorganization of the Indonesian Ministry of Communication and Information and the implementation of the a new treasury system in 2006.

3) The right incentives (e.g. attractive fiscal policy for investment in IT and innovation) and institutions that are strong enough to act on them.

Achieving this integrated version requires an appropriate institutional framework and the definition of clear responsibilities for implementing an ICT strategy. This may be achieved by creating a dedicated organization with responsibilities to establish a vision for ICT, and strategies to achieve that vision[51] – possibly within the Ministry of Telecommunications, or under the prime minister's office. It may also be done through utilizing existing institutions. Whatever the model used, it is essential that the different institutions co-ordinate responsibilities as to minimize contradicting and inconsistent policies, and unnecessary overlap.

Continuously monitor and evaluate ICT projects

It is essential to ensure that appropriate evaluation methodologies are implemented during the lifecycle of any e-development project, including management systems that can track ICT expenditures (See Box 1.8. For an in-depth description of monitoring and evaluation frameworks, see Chapter 3).

Conclusions

While e-development and networked computing are particularly powerful tools in the struggle for broad-based development, the potential for using ICT to leapfrog stages of development should not be overplayed. E-development solutions can be both costly and risky—the path to successful implementation is filled with obstacles. Before embarking on any initiative, particularly before scaling up an existing project, it is essential to pose hard questions about sustainability, replicability and scalability.

Ensuring the success of e-development programs requires emphasizing the two "I"s, namely, institutional aspects (e.g., an enabling policy environment and regulatory framework that promote fair competition; skilled human resources; collaboration between institutions; respect for the rule of law; leadership; etc.) and infrastructure aspects (e.g., telecommunications, power, hardware, software, etc.). One without the other usually leads to failure.

In addition to focusing on an enabling environment, governments should begin with smaller projects, embarking on larger projects only when evidence of impact becomes available. Indeed, government strategies for e-development should be "no-regrets" policies: projects should have controlled costs (e.g., e-commerce legislation), be justifiable on grounds unrelated to the presence of the Internet (e.g., financial sector reform) or based on a careful micro-level analysis of the expected return on investment. Given our current level of knowledge, blanket support for subsidies, tax incentives or government ICT investments cannot be justified.[52] Policies designed to encourage investment in the ICT sector should take into account the track record of similar policies in other countries and the relative comparative advantages of a given country and its labor force.

Despite the examples of difficulties and failures cited in this chapter, e-development and its applications have a potentially huge role to play in supporting sustainable economic growth. Careful strategic and implementation planning can build on the enthusiasm and creativity that surround e-development to open up significant opportunities. In this area, international organizations can play a key role by facilitating dialogue and partnerships in e-development (see Chapter 7).

Notes

[1] Dutta, S., B. Lanvin and F. Paua, eds. 2004. Global Information Technology Report 2003–04. Oxford University Press., http://www.weforum.org.

[2] In 1987, for example, Nobel laureate Robert Solow said, "We see computers everywhere but in the productivity statistics." (R. Solow, "We'd Better Watch Out," New York Times Book Review, July 12, 1987.) Thirteen years later, Solow subsequently declared: "You can see computers in the productivity statistics." (L. Uchitelle, "Economic View: Productivity Finally Shows the Impact of Computers," New York Times, Section 3, March 12, 2000, 4).

[3] The Human Development Index is a composite index that measures average achievement in three basic dimensions of human development: a long and healthy life (as measured by life expectancy at birth), knowledge (as measured by the adult literacy rate and the combined primary, secondary and tertiary gross enrollment ratio) and a decent standard of living (as measured by GDP per capita).

[4] The Networked Economy Index is a composite of three components: the enabling environment for ICT; the readiness of a key community stakeholders (individuals, businesses and governments) to use ICT; and the usage of ICT among these stakeholders. See Dutta, S., B. Lanvin and F. Paua, eds. 2004. Global Information Technology Report 2003–04. Oxford University Press.

[5] Piatkowski, M. (International Monetary Fund) World Bank Seminar, December 7th, 2004, Washington D.C., The Potential of ICT for Development in Transition Economies – Technological Leapfrogging or a Growing Digital Divide.

[6] In 1999, for example, a Paris-based group called Reporters without Frontiers awarded Vietnam the dubious distinction of being among the "Twenty Real Enemies of the Internet" because of its policy of restricting Internet access. Today, the Vietnamese government actively makes Internet connections available to large sections of the population through public facilities. (S.R. Chidamber, "An Analysis of Vietnam's ICT and Software Services Sector," The European Journal on Information Systems in Developing Countries 13, no. 9 (2003):1–11).

[7] IDC and Business Software Alliance on-line Newsletter (2002) www.infobalt.lt/docs/aut_klausimai.pdf9 Committee on Vision 2020 for India, 22nd May 2001. India's trade in 2020: A Mapping of Relevant Factors: Nagesh Kumar

[8] NASSCOM. 1996. The Software Industry in India, 1996: Strategic Review. New Delhi: NASSCOM and Heeks, R.

1996. "India's Software Industry". New Delhi: Sage Publications" 1996. 11 World Employment Report 2001; Developing countries in international division of labour in software and services industry: Lessons from Indian experience. http://www.bib.ulb.ac.be/cdrom/wer_lawtie/back/ind_2.htm

[9] C. Qiang, G. Clarke, and N. Halewood, "The Role of ICT in Doing Business," in ICT Trends Report, edited by C. Qiang (Washington, DC: World Bank, 2005).

[10] K. Lal, "e-Business and Export Behaviour: Evidence from Indian Firms," Discussion Paper No. 2002/68, United Nations University, World Institute for Development Economics Research, Helsinki, Finland, 2002. The paper identifies and analyzes the factors that influence the export performance of firms in the post-liberalization era of the Indian economy, based on primary data from 51 firms located in the national capital region.

[11] After endogenizing Internet use by using the instrumental variables of national regulation of data services and Internet provision. G. Clarke and S. Wallsten, "Has the Internet Increased Trade? Evidence from Industrial and Developing Countries," World Bank, Washington, DC, 2004.

[12] S. Chowdhury and S. Wolf, "Use of ICTs and the Economic Performance of SMEs in East Africa," Discussion Paper No. 2003/06, World Institute of Developing Economics Research, United Nations University, Helsinki, Finland, 2003.

[13] The so-called NIEs are Hong Kong SAR, South Korea, Singapore and Taiwan Province of China.

[14] See World Bank, "Chile: New Economy Study," volume II, Report No. 25666-CL (Washington, DC: World Bank, 2004).

[15] An enterprise cannot, for example, buy one-half of a computer, and thus can end up purchasing "too much" ICT equipment. This "over-investment" shows up as a decrease in labor productivity because the corresponding output is lower than average, given the value of the input (in this case, the ICT equipment).

[16] Chowdhury and Wolf, "Use of ICTs," 2003.

[17] In the case of Estonia, for example, three jobs are typically created in the broader economy for every person directly employed in the software industry; workers in the software industry earn 85 percent more than the national average wage; and each software worker generates 15 percent more revenue for the economy than does the average IT worker. Datamonitor, "The Growth of the Software Industry in Estonia," Datamonitor, 2001, http://www.bsa.ee/download.php3?file_id=81. Last accessed 15th July 2005.

[18] See S. Dutta, B. Lanvin, and F. Paua, eds., Global Information Technology Report 2003–04 (Oxford and New York: Oxford University Press).

[19] Ivar Odrats, ed., "IT in Public Administration of Estonia: Yearbook 2002," trans. Kadri Podra, Estonian Information Center, Tallinn, Estonia, http://www.ria.ee/english/2002 Last accessed 15th July

[20] World Bank, Chile: New Economy Study, 2004; Yusuf, Innovative East Asia, 2004.

[21] C. Kenny, "The Internet and Economic Growth in Less-Developed Countries: A Case of Managing Expectations?" Oxford Development Studies 31, no. 1 (March 2003): 99-113

[22] J. Grace and C. Kenny, "A Short Review of Information and Communication Technologies and Basic Education in LDCs—What is Useful, What is Sustainable," International Journal of Educational Development 23 (2003):27–36.

[23] S. Yusuf, Innovative East Asia: The Future of Growth (New York: Oxford University Press, 2004).

[24] See R. Heeks, "Information Technology, Government and Development," Report on the IT, Government and Development Workshop (26 November 1998), Manchester, England, 1999, http:www.man.ac.uk/idpm/itgovsem.htm; and C. Kenny and C. Qiang, "ICT and Broad-Based Development," in ICT and Development (Washington, DC: Global Information & Communication Technologies Department, World Bank, 2003).

[25] Income per capita is, for example, a significant determinant of PC use; recent research has shown that each US$1,000 increase in per capita income is associated with more than a one percentage point increase in the number of PCs per capita. M. Chinn and R. Fairlie, "The Determinants of the Global Digital Divide: A Cross-country Analysis of Computer and Internet Penetration," National Bureau of Economic Research (NBER), Working Paper 10686, NEBR, Cambridge, MA, USA, 2004.

[26] Kenny, "The Internet and Economic Growth," 2003.

[27] Chowdhury and Wolf, "Use of ICTs," 2003.

[28] L-H Röller and L. Waverman, "Telecommunications Infrastructure and Economic Development: A Simultaneous Approach," American Economic Review 91, no. 4 (2001):909–23.

[29] Studies do also suggest that where poor populations do have access to ICT, telephony can play an important role in income generation and improving services related to the quality of life E. Forestier, J. Grace, and C. Kenny, "Can Information and Communication Technologies be Pro-poor?" Telecommunications Policy 26, no. 11 (2002):623–46.

[30] See M. Chinn and R. Fairlie, "The Determinants of the Global Digital Divide," 2004. In Africa as a whole, new forms of ICTs (e.g., the Internet, fax, and computers) have touched only 2 percent of low-income households, mostly in urban areas. There is also low computer penetration, particularly in government institutions. (M. Pigato, "Information and Communication Technology, Poverty, and Development in Sub-Saharan Africa and South Asia," Africa Region Working Paper Series, no. 20, World Bank, Washington, DC, 2001, http://www.worldbank.org/afr/wps/wp20.pdf).

[31] R. Schware and A. Deane, "Deploying e-Government Programs: The Strategic Importance of 'I' before 'E'," Info, The Journal of Policy, Regulation and Strategy for Telecommunications 5, no. 4 (October 2003): 10–19(10), Emerald Group Publishing Limited, London, UK.

[32] Lal, "E-business and Export Behaviour," 2002.

[33] See Pigato, "Information and Communication Technology," 2001.

[34] M. Chinn and R. Fairlie, "The Determinants of the Global Digital Divide," 2004.

[35] Qiang and Ayers, "Contribution of ICT to Growth," 2003.

[36] For most regions of the world, however, regression analysis suggests that the effect of lower education levels may have only roughly half the impact that differences in regulatory efficiency have on e-development. M. Chinn and R. Fairlie, "The Determinants of the Global Digital Divide," 2004.

[37] M. Chinn and R. Fairlie, "The Determinants of the Global Digital Divide," 2004.

[38] Firms in the Dominican Republic, for example, have found that residents are not ready to take advantage of e-commerce offerings, largely because credit card fraud in the country is the seventh highest in the world. (Kirkman et al., "The Dominican Republic Readiness for the Networked World," Information Technologies Group, Center for International Development, Harvard University, Cambridge, Massachusetts, 2002.)

[39] Yusuf, Innovative East Asia, 2004.

[40] ITU, "The Application of Information and Communication Technologies in Least-developed Countries for Sustained Economic Growth," ITU, Geneva, Switzerland, 2004.

[41] J. Oxley and B. Yeung, "E-Commerce Readiness: Institutional Environment and International Competitiveness," Journal Of International Business Studies 32, no. 4 (2001):705–23. See also UNCTAD (2000), 'Building Confidence: E-commerce and Development' http://r0.unctad.org/ecommerce/docs/edr00_en.htm (last accessed 20 July 2005).

[42] For example, if two projects are co-located, they could consider sharing a VSAT link.

[43] G. Boyle, "Putting Context into ICTs in International Development: An Institutional Networking Project in Vietnam," Journal of International Development volume 14, issue 1, (2002):101–112.

[44] See World Bank. Reaching the Rural Poor - Annexes (Washington, DC: World Bank, 2003), for a case study of a Russian e-development project, in which the incorporation of these elements resulted in success.

[45] See the Cap Gemini Consulting, "Does e-Government Pay Off?" European Public Administration Network, http://www.eupan.org/index.asp?option=documents&section=details&id=19, n.d.

[46] Pigato, "Information and Communication Technology," 2001.

[47] See Kenny and Qiang, "ICT and Broad-Based Development," 2003.

[48] In one ICT project in the Dominican Republic, for example, requests for parts had to be signed by 24 people. See Peace Corps Online, Directory: Dominican Republic, September 15, 2002, http://peacecorpsonline.org/messages/messages/467/2014175.html Lat accessed 15th July 2005. It should be noted, however, that ICT can also be successfully used to counter corruption within government institutions. See also Luc de Wulf (2005), Customs Modernization Handbook, World Bank http://www.thattechnicalbookstore.com/b0821357514.htm (last accessed 20 July 2005).

[49] Schware, R. and Deane, A. "Deploying e-Government Programs," 2003.

[50] Interestingly, unlike many other empirical studies of economic growth, Chinn and Fairlie find that openness to international trade does not appear to be an important factor in PC use or Internet penetration, after including an explicit measure of regulatory efficiency in their analysis. The fact that other studies find a positive effect of trade openness may thus reflect the omission of a regulatory and/or policy variable from those studies, such as the one included in the regression analysis in annex 1. Chinn and Fairlie, "The Determinants of the Global Digital Divide," 2004.

[51] Schware, R., "Information and communications technology agencies: functions, structures, and best operational practices", 2003

[52] World Bank, "Financing Information and Communication Infrastructure Needs in the Developing World: Public and Private Roles," 2005.

Chapter 2

Creating the "Right" Enabling Environment for ICT

by Boutheina Guermazi and David Satola[1]

For ICTs to deliver on their promise of economic and social development, it is critical that countries adopt enabling legal and regulatory environments that support e-development. "Enabling environment" in this chapter means policy, legal, market, and social considerations that interact both at domestic and global levels to create fertile conditions for ICT-led growth. The importance of this enabling environment was recognized in the Declaration and Action Plan of the first phase of the World Summit on the Information Society (WSIS), which emphasized that a trustworthy, transparent, and non-discriminatory environment was essential for the use and growth of ICTs in the developing world.[2]

In most cases, creating the "right" environment is a daunting task for policymakers.[3] While best practices are emerging from countries that have successfully crafted policies to facilitate digital opportunities, there is no single blueprint that can be followed in every case. Given the context of the convergence of telecommunications and in-formation technologies, successful reforms must take into account the need for comprehensive changes that cut across traditional technological and commercial boundaries. In addition, the role of regulators and regulation itself must be re-evaluated. Some areas where regulatory reform will be important are the regulation of communications services and infrastructure, data privacy protection, security, intellectual property rights, public infrastructure, Internet governance (including domain name registration), and general principles of competition.[4]

Based on international experience, the ideal framework for maximizing the contribution of ICT to development consists of public policies that apply to different layers of the ICT market (infrastructure, applications, and consumer confidence). The basic goal of regulatory reform is to create a stable, open, and future-proof environment that encourages confidence in the ICT market.[5] A major step towards this goal is to establish clear and transparent governance structures and respect for the rule of law. Basic principles that support regulatory reform include encouraging market-based approaches and ease of market entry; promoting business confidence and clarity; enhancing transactional enforceability; ensuring interoperability (of systems, standards, networks, etc.); and protecting intellectual property and consumer rights. All regulatory policies should, moreover, be neutral regarding both the use and type of technology.

The policies undertaken by governments and the manner in which they are reflected in law will affect how ICT infrastructure and services develop and are used. Because of the global nature of the information and knowledge economy, minimum common international standards have long been recognized as important. Such common standards contribute to the interoperability of national legal regimes and develop truly global commerce.

Based on success stories from a wide range of countries (both developed and developing), this chapter provides pointers for policymakers on how to create the requisite environment for promoting ICT-led growth. Such an enabling environment requires not only ICT-specific considerations, but macro-level improvements in the business and political environment, among other factors. This chapter focuses primarily on the policy, legal, and regulatory conditions needed to advance the e-development agenda at the national level.[6] The chapter follows a three-layered approach to the enabling environment, which emphasizes improving:

- access to ICT tools (the access layer);

- access to e-development applications (the application layer); and

- consumer confidence and trust (the trust layer).

At each of these layers, the sequencing of reform will vary from country to country. All successful reforms, however, share common elements of broad stakeholder consultation, transparency, and strong local ownership. Unfortunately, difficult policy choices that influence the reform process and its implementation are often not addressed early on, causing delays or unanticipated outcomes.

For developing countries, some of the issues covered in this chapter (e.g., digital signatures or the security of online transactions) may not appear immediately relevant to their concerns. However, these issues may be encountered much earlier than anticipated in the development process. For example, successful operation of telekiosks or Internet cafés—both cost-effective ways to provide access to the Internet and advanced ICT applications—requires a legal framework that addresses the protection of intellectual property rights and consumer privacy. Understandably, developing countries are likely to concentrate first on creating an enabling environment for private investment in their basic ICT infrastructure, a demanding task in and of itself. Yet as their ICT networks grow and begin to provide advanced applications that promote development (e.g., in the education and health sectors), these countries will soon need to expand their policy and regulatory frameworks to address the full spectrum of issues outlined in this chapter.

Part I. The access layer: Creating the enabling environment for access to ICT tools

Without adequate access to "the common essentials for plugging into the online age," developing countries risk missing out on the promise of the information revolution.[7] This section discusses the enabling environment needed to improve access to ICT infrastructure and IT hardware and software, a prerequisite for the propagation of ICT-for-development (ICT4D) applications.

Enabling access to ICT infrastructure

For most developing countries, lack of adequate ICT infrastructure remains a major obstacle to the uptake of ICT. Lack of investment in infrastructure and networks, coupled with inefficient provision of services, undermines the development of networked economies. The lessons accumulated in this sector indicate that success is principally market driven. However, creating a predictable legal and policy environment is crucial for attracting investors. A predictable and certain policy framework requires an overall investment climate that is friendly to domestic and foreign investors (the macro level) and ICT-specific policies to promote competition and market entry, expand networks and the boundaries of service provision, reduce prices, and improve service quality (the micro level).

Enabling investment climate: Increased foreign direct investment (FDI) holds a particular promise for ICT in developing countries. FDI allows developing countries not only to relax capital constraints to network build-out, but to channel technology transfer and know-how into their economies. Guaranteeing a proper investment climate and establishing investor confidence is undoubtedly the first step towards attracting FDI.

While a considerable amount of private capital is available for telecommunications projects, attracting such capital is an extremely competitive endeavor. When choosing where to invest, the degree of political stability in the host country and legal and regulatory regimes that guarantee foreign investment against specific risks (political interference, arbitrary regulation, or regulatory "capture" by a single enterprise, for example) are key considerations for investors.[8] The basic legal environment should include clear contract and intellectual property regimes, as well as dispute resolution mechanisms for commercial ventures.

Private participation in infrastructure development has grown tremendously in recent years in both developed and developing countries.[9] Given that public sector financing has shrunk since the 1980s, the private sector, both domestic and foreign, has been called on to assume responsibility for funding infrastructure development. Despite a noticeable decline of overall North-South investment flows in the last few years (following the end of major privatization efforts and spectrum license auctions),[10] continued rollout of physical infrastructure suggests that these flows have been replaced by a combination of South-South FDI flows, domestic private financing, and other sources (see Box 2.1). As the example of Vietnam makes clear, however, not all countries are initially open to establishing a legal environment conducive to foreign investment in the ICT sector (see Box 2.2).

Many countries are now revising their regulations on foreign investment in telecommunications to facilitate capital expansion. These regulatory reforms are part of a global wave of telecommunications sector liberalization, driven by the World Trade Organization (WTO) Basic Telecommunications Agreement (BTA). Under a binding multilateral framework, liberalization can create a stable environment for investment that benefits both the foreign investor and the host country. Foreign investors are more confident when investing because host countries cannot withdraw or change their offers without referring to WTO rules. By the same token, host countries are better off because multilateral rules enhance reciprocity and reduce market distortions.

Enabling a pro-competitive ICT regulatory framework: For many developing countries, a poorly planned regulatory reform process will scare away potential investors and exacerbate the digital divide. Effective frameworks ensure

Box 2.1 Growing private investment in telecommunications infrastructure

Private investments in telecommunications infrastructure projects in developing countries were valued at US$372 billion during the period 1990–2003. Foreign direct investment represented roughly 60 percent of this sum (approximately US$172 billion). Of the 130 developing countries that received private investments, 53 were low-income countries. The countries of Latin America and the Caribbean, Europe and Central Asia, and East Asia, and the Pacific regions collected the greatest share of capital flows: 48, 21 and 15 percent, respectively, of total FDI. Brazil, Mexico, and Argentina were the largest beneficiaries overall, receiving US$76 billion, US$38 billion and US$24 billion, respectively.

Foreign investors acted both alone and in consortium arrangements with domestic private and public investors. The involvement of foreign investors spurred broader interest in the sector, prompting local investors to put money into telecom infrastructure development as well. As investment has slowed in recent years due to the downturn in the telecommunications market, private investors from the South have taken the place of foreign investors from developed countries. Mobile telephony has also become the leading growth sector, overshadowing traditional businesses in fixed and long-distance telephony.

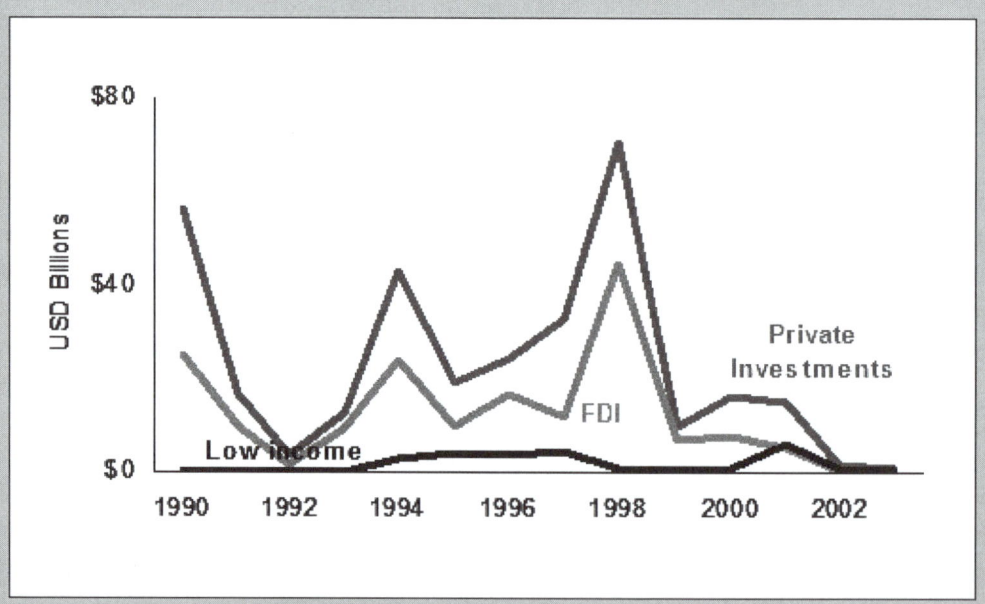

Source: World Bank. 2005. Private Participation in Infrastructure (PPI) database; Qiang, Christine and Pierre Guislain. 2005. "Foreign Direct Investment in Telecommunications." *World Information and Communication for Development Report 2006.* World Bank: Washington, DC.

proper competition, guard against market abuse by dominant market players and balance the goals of market efficiency, flexibility and innovation.

Countries may adopt sector-specific rules or rely more heavily on a general competition law.[11] While a competition law may prove effective in

---

Box 2.2 Vietnam's business corporation contracts

Under Vietnam's investment law of 1992, as amended in 2000, foreign companies are allowed to provide services to Vietnam's telecommunications market only under a Business Corporation Contract (BCC). A BCC is, in essence, a partnership agreement between a foreign and a Vietnamese party in which private investors provide investment capital and receive a negotiated return on their investment for a prescribed number of years. Foreign investors are not allowed to own equity stakes in Vietnamese telecommunications companies and the Vietnamese party is the only party permitted to hire and manage a workforce. A foreign company must be present in Vietnam for at least two years before entering into BCC negotiations.

In most cases, such schemes discourage foreign investors because they have no operational control over their investments. Lack of ownership rights and limits on management control increase investor risk and consequently, increase the cost of capital, reduce its availability, and impede the transfer of management expertise to firms in the host country. Since a BBC arrangement de-links management from investment risks, the incentives for effective, profit-oriented management are also reduced.

Unsurprisingly, as the Vietnamese telecommunications market gradually opens, resistance among foreign investors to BBCs is growing.

Source: European Union, Asia IT&C Program. 2004. "Promoting Internet Policy and Regulatory Reform in Vietnam: Assessment Report 2004." GIPI Vietnam.

---

some cases, certain specific rules (for example, those setting the parameters for interconnection) are likely to be needed, especially in telecommunications sectors where competition has not yet taken hold. Regulators and policymakers will also need to revisit the regulatory framework from time to time to respond to changes in market conditions.

A key determinant of an enabling environment for ICT is the elimination of barriers to entry and the introduction of competition in the ICT sector (see Box 2.3).

As mentioned earlier, the WTO has played a pivotal role in telecommunications liberalization and encouraging regulatory reform in developing countries. In addition to market access and na-

tional treatment commitments, WTO members have adopted a Reference Paper on regulatory principles. The paper is a set of common guidelines to guarantee effective market access and foreign investment. These guidelines represent the regulatory component of the WTO Basic Trade Agreement (BTA) and provide policymakers in developing countries a road map for establishing (or reforming) a regulatory framework. The Reference Paper compiles in one short document the experience of long years of regulatory practice.

Early evidence of the impact of liberalization under the BTA shows that growth in telecommunications revenues as a percentage of GDP is higher in countries that have made GATS commitments in telecommunications (see Figure 2.3).

Box 2.3 Lack of competition leads to high prices

Competition in the ICT sector leads to lower prices, as well as improved quality and availability of services. Lower prices for international telephone calls, for example, are highly correlated with the level of competition. In Africa, one of the regions of the world where competition in long-distance telephony is lowest, prices for both international telephone calls and broadband services are much higher than in other regions of the world (see Figures 2.1 and 2.2 below).

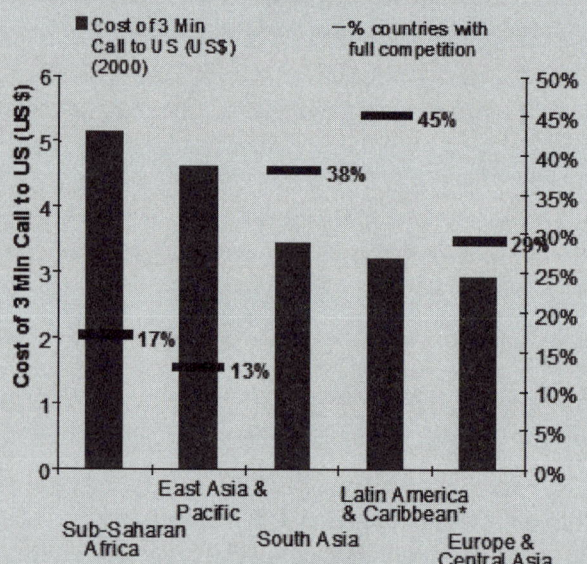

Figure 2.1 Cost of international calls, selected regions of the world, 2003

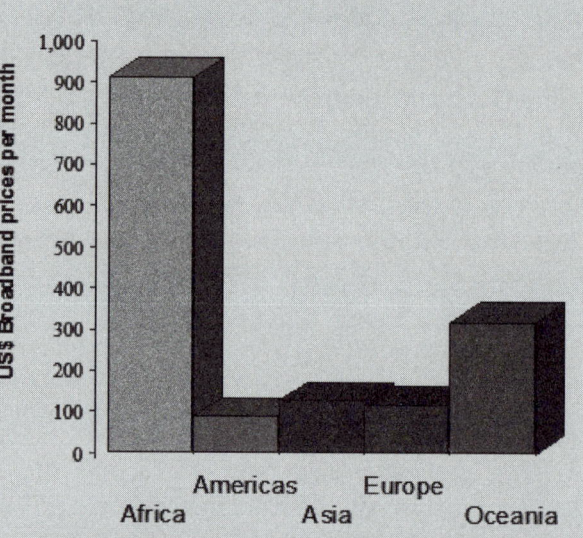

Figure 2.2 Cost of broadband services, selected regions of the world, 2003

Source: Global Information and Communication Technology (GICT) Department. 2005. "Connecting Sub-Saharan Africa: A World Bank Group Strategy for ICT Sector Development." World Bank Working Paper, no. 51. GICT, World Bank: Washington, DC.

Investors are thus likely to be more willing to commit capital and technology in countries with WTO telecommunications commitments, as they are likely to be rewarded with higher revenues. As expected, countries in sub-Saharan Africa without WTO basic telecom commitments initially earned higher telecommunications revenues (as a percentage of GDP), but were overtaken by countries that had made such commitments. Uganda, for example, reformed its telecommunications sector and enjoyed healthy revenue growth, while Ethiopia, which had not reformed its own sector, experienced much lower revenue growth.

Building strong institutional capacity: In addition to substantive rules of the game, proper implementation of policies requires independent regulatory institutions that are empowered to enforce regulations and suitable processes by which regulatory decisions are adopted and enforced (see Table 1.1). A transparent, participatory regulatory process guards against the capture of regulatory agencies by stakeholders and acts as an important guarantee for private investment. While there is no one-size-fits-all model for institutional organization, the credibility of regulatory institutions, including the independence with which they perform their regulatory roles, is supported through clearly defining their competencies and functional responsibilities *vis-à-vis* other sector stakeholders.

In many developing countries, the creation of an independent telecommunications regulatory agency has brought about a sea change in the relationship between business and government. However, mechanisms such as consultations have not yet become part of these governments'

regulatory efforts. Greater consultation on the part of regulators can impart greater stability to the sector and generate confidence in the ability of regulators to regulate fairly and predictably. In addition, efficient dispute resolution mechanisms are another important element for promoting growth and creating a favorable investment climate for prospective investors.[12]

Emerging regulatory approaches for broadband deployment and converged services: A regulatory emphasis on improving access solely to traditional telephony would be out of tune with the development potential of modern information and communications technologies. The risk

---

Box 2.4 WTO Reference Paper on regulatory principles

Under Article XVIII of the General Agreement on Trade in Services (GATS) of the WTO, parties are allowed to schedule "additional commitments" in addition to market access and national treatment commitments.[a] In principle, these additional commitments are binding on the countries that make them and enforceable through WTO dispute procedures. The drafting of the Reference Paper on regulatory topics was driven by a need to guarantee effective competition in the basic telecommunications sector, especially the need to prevent major suppliers from abusing their dominant market positions. WTO member countries that adopt the Reference Paper commit to:

- establish a regulatory authority that is independent of all suppliers of telecommunications services and networks;

- adopt measures that prevent and safeguard against anti-competitive practices by major suppliers;

- require major suppliers to interconnect with other suppliers at any technically feasible point on a non-discriminatory, cost-oriented basis following transparent procedures and subject to dispute settlement by an independent body;

- administer universal service programs in a transparent, non-discriminatory, and competitively neutral manner; and

- allocate and assign the use of scarce resources, including the radio spectrum, numbering blocks, and rights of way, in an objective, timely, transparent and non-discriminatory manner.

[a] The article allows WTO members to negotiate commitments with respect to trade in services that are not subject to scheduling under Articles XVI (market access) or XVII (national treatment) of GATS, including commitments regarding qualifications, standards and licensing. These commitments are then inscribed in a member's schedule.

Source: WTO. 1996. "Reference Paper." WTO Negotiating Group on Basic Telecommunications, Geneva.

Figure 2.3 Telecommunications revenues and WTO telecommunications commitments in Sub-Saharan Africa, 1997–2002

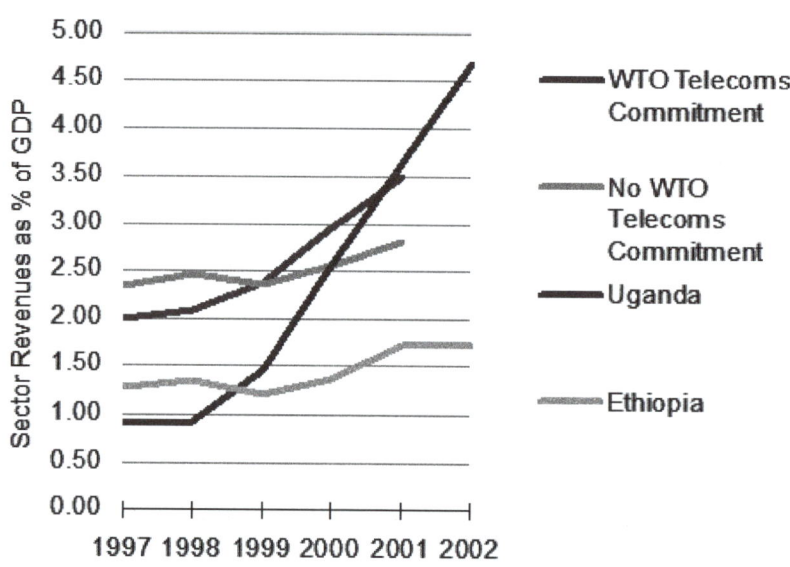

Source: Analysys, Harris Wiltshire & Grannis LLP. 2004. Telecommunications Trade Liberalization and the WTO, Final Report for the GICT Department. World Bank.

inherent in a narrow, traditional regulatory approach is that it could inadvertently widen the digital divide. While the basic tenets of an enabling environment in the pre-broadband era remain valid for today's environment, countries need to adapt their legal and regulatory frameworks to make them better suited to support broadband services, given that most e-applications require higher bandwidth and permanent Internet connections.

There is a growing consensus that broadband[13] is "[of] strategic importance to all countries because of its ability to accelerate the contribution of ICT to economic growth, and facilitate innovation."[14] Broadband not only satisfies communication needs between individu-

als, it provides a needed platform for many applications and offers a wide range of positive externalities which have the potential to support and accelerate development (e.g., in health, education and commerce).

In parallel with the emergence of broadband services, the convergence of communications, computing, and media brought about by digital technologies has revolutionized not only the telecommunications sector, but has also blurred lines between technology and the economic sectors and industries built around them. Converged licensing, for example, encourages market entry by a full range of operators, including small-scale and medium entrepreneurs, and gives these operators sufficient flexibility

Box 2.5 Morocco: Effective regulation attracts investment

The case of Morocco demonstrates the importance of an effective regulatory framework for attracting foreign investors and improving connectivity. Because of the confidence of foreign investors, the auction of a second GSM license in 1999 stimulated the country's mobile market and acted as a catalyst for neighboring countries (Algeria, Tunisia, Mali, Mauritania), which followed Morocco's lead in awarding competitive GSM licenses. The National Agency of Telecommunications Regulation (ANRT), the new Moroccan regulatory agency, emerged as a world-class regulator, setting the standard in the Middle East and North Africa region for transparency and appropriate design and auction of GSM licenses.

Morocco's mobile sector has since achieved spectacular development. From being the country with the lowest teledensity in the region, Morocco has become the country with the highest teledensity. (The number of mobile subscribers grew from 150,000 in 1999 to over 8 million by year-end 2004.) The ANRT is now being encouraged by the World Bank to build on this success and ensure continuous, effective regulation of the sector in the context of improved competition and new technologies.

Sources: ITU. 2002. "The Role of Effective Regulation: Morocco Case Study." ITU: Geneva.; and B. Wellenius, C. Rosotto and A. Lewin. 2004. "Morocco: Developing Competition in Telecommunications." CITPO Working Paper, GICT Department, World Bank: Washington, DC.

to embrace technological developments and tailor their services to market demand.

Regulators and policy makers should seek only that level of regulation necessary to promote the rapid growth of new services and applications and to minimize barriers to entry. Globally, the trend is to minimize licensing hurdles (by establishing general authorization regimes) and to adopt technological neutrality—allowing for greater competition between different delivery platforms and greater end-user access. Many countries are accordingly moving away from service-specific licensing regimes to embrace converged licensing approaches, relieving investors from restrictive and burdensome licensing rules.[15]

New regulatory approaches, for example, need to be crafted to harness the power of radio tech-

nologies, including new approaches to spectrum management. To cite one possibility, allowing unlicensed utilization of 2.4 MHz spectrum for locations with low-density traffic, especially in rural and/or remote areas, could facilitate the growth of school and rural community networks. The most appropriate regulatory approach may differ from country to country. In countries where the infrastructure is already in place, one of the challenges for policy makers and regulators is to deal with legacy regulation and existing access platforms and established models when designing policies to encourage competition and encourage the use of alternative infrastructures. One area of growing concern for both regulators and policy makers is how to deal with technologies like Voice over Internet Protocol (VoIP), which challenge existing business models. Early attempts to ban the service have largely been in-

Table 1.1 List of possible impediments to regulatory effectiveness

Issues	Impediments
Relationship between policy maker and regulator	▪ Political interference in running of regulator ▪ Function ambiguity between regulator and policy maker ▪ Function ambiguity between regulator and competition authority ▪ Function ambiguity between regulator and universal service agency ▪ Lack of political commitment ▪ Interventions in regulatory decisions by policy maker overly-influenced by its relationship with operators
Accountability of regulator	▪ Inadequate mechanisms for holding regulatory members accountable for their decisions
Autonomy of regulator	▪ Over-reliance on government/external bodies for funding ▪ Political interference in remuneration, appointment and dismissal of regulator's members ▪ Regulatory capture or excessive influence by a particular group
Participation in decision-making processes	▪ Inadequate consultation mechanisms for involvement of external parties in processes ▪ Over-reliance on informal (non-orthodox) lobbying of regulator
Transparency of decision-making processes	▪ Lack of explanations provided in public and to operators for decisions
Predictability of decision-making processes	▪ Poor enforcement of license conditions and/or legislation ▪ Lack of consistency in decision-making
Effectiveness of regulatory policy tools in key areas	▪ Policy tools do not achieve their objectives (e.g. ineffective price caps, universal service targets, licensing procedures, ineffective dispute resolution procedures etc)
Regulator's organizational structure and resource requirements (human, financial)	▪ Inappropriate organizational structure ▪ Inadequate financial resources ▪ Inadequate regulatory/administrative/business management skills of key staff

effective, with a gray market flourishing in many developing countries. There is even a growing recognition on the part of policymakers that this application offers the benefit of cheaper access (see Box 2.6).

Addressing access gaps: Going beyond the market: Evidence across the world demonstrates that the market has been the main driver for improved access to ICT. In many areas, however, the upfront investment needed may be too high to be justified on purely commercial grounds.

Box 2.6 VOIP in call centers

Togo recently overcame the "bifocal" approach to VOIP and became the first African country to establish a VOIP call center. The innovative call center allows entrepreneurs to tap into the rapidly growing, lucrative trend of call center outsourcing. The driving forces behind such outsourcing are low labor costs, better-quality Internet services and government support. Given the potential for growth in outsourcing and adequate access to ICT, call centers could potentially be a new business for developing countries.

Source: Jacques Rostenne. 2005. "Togo: First VOIP Call Center in Africa." *Balancing AcT*, no. 47. Available at http://www.balancingact-africa.com/news/back/balancing-act47.html; and ITU. *2004/2005. Trends in Telecom Reform: Licensing in an Era of Convergence.* ITU, p.15.

Table 2.2 Minimum subsidy auctions for public rural telephones, selected countries, 2004

	Chile	Columbia	Dominican Republic	Peru	Nepal
Projects	200	6	1	7	1
Bidders	numerous	2 to 7	2	2 to 5	2
Average subsidy per locality	US$3600	US$4600	US$6800	US$9500	US$11200
Localities served	6509	7415	500	4420	1064
Population served (millions)	2.2	3.7	1.0	1.6	4.0

Source: Navas, Juan. 2005. "Universal Access and Output-Based Aid in Telecommunications and ICT." GICT, World Bank: Washington, DC.

Especially in areas that require significant investment, incur high operating costs and feature limited or uncertain demand, there may be a role for complementary government initiatives that fill the access gap.[16]

Some form of incentives or funding support may need to be considered for more remote, unserved locations with low-income populations. One approach is to have coverage requirements linked to license obligations. Another approach is to offer explicit financial incentives for servicing locations that are "beyond the market." Such areas need to be carefully identified, so that limited subsidy or incentive programs do not crowd out private investment in areas where greater policy and regulatory flexibility could enable market forces to provide increased access on their own.

Among the possible approaches to funding investments in remote and poorer areas is a universal access fund. The purpose of such funds is to collect potential subsidy resources (whether from within the sector, the government or outside sources) into a central, independent account that is managed on a non-discriminatory, transparent basis and distributed according to clear criteria and procedures. Allocation of the funds can be achieved through minimum-subsidy auctions (see Table 2.2 and Box 2.7 for examples). This approach has many advantages in terms of flexibility and avoids unwarranted favoritism toward incumbent players.

An access gap also exists between dial-up and broadband users of the Internet. The question of whether similar approaches would be justified to

Box 2.7 Output-based subsidies in Chile

The impact of public support can be maximized by leveraging competitive private investment through minimal, well-targeted ("smart") subsidies allocated under an output-based aid (OBA) scheme. Such an OBA system has been used in Chile to finance rural universal service obligations. Chile first created a rural universal service fund in 1994 to provide subsidies to private investors to provide rural pay phones. Chile is now a leading example of how cost-effective solutions can reduce access gaps in basic telecommunications in developing countries: the fund reduced the proportion of the population without access to a telephone from 15 to 1 percent in five short years.

Subsidies were allocated through competitive tenders and financed by the national budget. In the period 1995–2000, the telecom regulator Subsecretaria de Telecommunicaciones (SUBTEL) held auctions for 7,850 localities, specifying a maximum amount of subsidy for each locality. Operators and service providers were invited to bid for the amount of subsidy they needed to build pay phones in these localities, provided that the subsidy did not exceed the maximum specified amount. Based on lessons learned from this program, the government is now applying the same scheme to bring Internet access to 750 towns in rural Chile. An estimated investment of US$38.7 million will require a government subsidy of US$9.0 million, meaning that the private sector will provide US$2.6 dollars for every US$1 dollar of government funding. The towns slated to receive Internet access have been selected based on their poverty level and lack of current service.

Source: Bjorn Wellenius. 2001. "Closing the Gap in Access to Rural Communications: Chile, 1995–2002." *info*Dev Working Paper, World Bank: Washington, DC.

encourage broadband deployment is a hot subject in policy discussions today. Some argue that it is too early, and that countries should wait for the normal uptake of technology. Some countries, however, are considering direct intervention in the broadband market and devising Public Private Partnership (PPP) schemes to speed up the roll out of the broadband networks.

Different rationales are presented to defend the role of public funding. Some argue that direct funding is needed to correct market failure resulting from the fact that investment in backbone infrastructure requires high sunk costs. Others argue that broadband enjoys the fastest takeup rate of all communications services and that a delay in the availability of broadband for rural users should not be taken to be an automatic

sign of market failure.[17] Rather, public funding is needed because of the strategic nature of broadband for economic development and the need to speed up deployment rather than wait for the market to fully mature. It should be noted that while direct funding of broadband deployment has been provided in many cases, alternatives include demand aggregation and ensuring that a government will be a principal user of broadband services (e.g., via e-government applications).

A key lesson emerging from different initiatives being attempted today is that public support for the expansion of coverage and use of broadband services should not pre-empt private sector initiatives or hinder competition. Promoting access to rural and underserved areas by extending backbone infrastructure is, of course, contingent on the existence of a proper regulatory and policy framework. One of the challenges of governments is to prevent monopoly control over the telecommunications backbone network. Some countries have opted to transfer management of this network to a third company in order to promote open access. In most cases, such companies provide only wholesale services and are prevented from offering retail services to end-users.[18]

If a government opts for third-party management, the award of a management contract should be based on open, transparent procedures. The third party should, moreover, be required to meet specified operating requirements and provide open access to the network. Public-private partnerships that involve community investment in and ownership of local infrastructure that is managed by professional private-sector partners have proven effective in developing rural telecommunications infrastructure in a number of countries

Table 2.3 Alternatives for supporting the deployment of broadband services

Models of Intervention	Characteristics	Issues
Infrastructure provision	Public sector subsidizes investment in or procures the network or network elements for use by both public and private sectors.	<ul><li>Uncertainty regarding the rules of state funding</li><li>Deploying current-generation versus next-generation broadband in rural areas</li></ul>
Demand aggregation	Procurement by the public sector provides a demand stimulus for private sector provision.	<ul><li>Potential for anti-competitive, exlusive supply agreements</li><li>Impact on current initiatives</li><li>Procurement at regional level may reduce local partnering opportunities</li></ul>
Public-private partnerships	Multiple partners from both the public and private sector cooperate to share network investment and operational risks. These projects often combine supply-side initiatives with demand stimulation.	<ul><li>See "Demand aggregation" issues</li><li>Spreads risk between public and private partners</li><li>Relationship with demand aggregation schemes</li></ul>
Subsidized broadband pilots	Demand subsidies used to pilot broadband technology; supply subsidies provided to community broadband networks to trial new technologies.	<ul><li>Need rules on the use of public sector networks to deliver commercial services</li><li>Long-term viability of public-sector backhaul for community networks</li></ul>
Promotion and content commissioning	Demand registration schemes; marketing and promotion events; public broadband centers; commissioning of content.	<ul><li>Persistent lack of awareness of (i) benefits of broadband services and (ii) available technologies</li></ul>
Community network projects	Delivered through "grassroots' community action; receive minimal or no public sector assistance.	<ul><li>Long-term viability in the absence of strategic approach to broadband technologies and business models</li></ul>

Source: Ecorys Research and Consulting. 2005. *Best Practice Options for Improving and Extending Access to Electronic Communications in Lithuania, a publication for GICT.* p.41. Available at http://www.worldbank.org/ict.

Box 2.8 Locally owned broadband networks

Andhra Pradesh is the first state government of India to finance a statewide broadband project. The fiber optic network will link 23 districts, 210,000 villages and 40,000 government offices. The project promises to provide effective e-government services to rural areas, increase the capacity of the private sector and provide the lowest broadband tariffs in India. Total estimated cost of the network is about US$90 million and will be funded by a public-private partnership.

The consortium includes entities with complementary strengths, including a broadband provider, the Railway Corporation and cable network providers. The state government is a key player in the project, providing an equity investment of US$5.5 million, right-of-way permissions, and serving as the anchor client (with a fixed annual usage fee). In this case, the network operator is expected to provide both wholesale and retail services.

Source: Fiber Optics Weekly update. "Andha Pradesh to be connected with fiber this year." January 7, 2005. Available at http://www.findarticles.com/p/articles/mi_m0NVN/is_1_25/ai_n8699107. Accessed July 2005.

(e.g., the NTCA experience in the US) and can also be used in areas with regional autonomy.

Enabling other "access tools"

Adequate access to ICT infrastructure, although a major first step, does not guarantee a country's capacity to participate fully in the global digital economy. In Africa, for instance, Internet growth in the near future could be limited by the market penetration of personal computers (there are only 1.05 PCs per 100 inhabitants in Africa).[19] Currently, computers remain unaffordable to most households in developing countries. In the case of India, the cost of a PC is equivalent to two year's average per capita income.

While an enabling legal and regulatory environment cannot guarantee a computer in every home, general taxation laws and import duties can help control end-user costs. Many countries still maintain tax structures that inhibit growth of the IT sector. Vietnam, for instance, requires hardware manufacturers to pay a VAT tax larger than the price they can charge buyers for components.[20] For many countries, import duties on IT-related products can be very high (see Table 2.4), constituting an impediment to the development of e-business.

On a global level, many countries are considering joining the WTO Information Technology Agreement (ITA) negotiated during the Singapore Ministerial Meeting in 1997. The ITA seeks to move to zero duties on IT products such as computers and telecommunications equipment.

In addition to reducing customs duties on computers, countries can also implement fiscal incentives to encourage wider ownership of PCs. Korea, for instance, launched a subsidy scheme that enabled one million households to buy a PC for under US$900. The economic rationales for such initiatives remain questionable and the implications of such subsidy schemes remain to be tested. Other countries especially in the Middle East and North Africa region have encouraged public-private initiatives involving local banks, PC vendors, and telecom operators to increase PC ownership amongst households (see Box 2.8).[21]

Table 2.4. Tariffs and taxes on computer hardware and software, selected African countries, 2003

	Tariff on computer hardware	Tariff on computer parts	Tariff on computer software	Other taxes
Cameroon	5–30%	5–30%	5–30% (	18.7% VAT applied on CIF value + duty; 25% excise tax (indirect tax on consumption goods covers specific categories of goods defined by ministerial ordinance) is applied on the CIF value.
Cape Verde	5–50%	5–50%	5–50% (	7% fixed rate (wholesale value of exporting plus CIF charges); 5–60% consumption tax (non priority goods)
Eritrea	25%	25–30%	2% (	3%, 5% and 12% sales tax on CIF + duty (on most goods)
Guinea	20-60%	20-60%	20-60% (	18% turnover tax; 15% combined customs charges applied on CIF value; 2% processing fee; 20–60% surtax on some luxury items

Source: U.S. Office of Technology and Electronic Commerce (USOTEC). 2003. "Africa: Tariffs and Taxes on Computer Hardware and Software." USOTEC, International Trade Administration, U.S. Department of Commerce: Washington, DC.

In many cases, in order to enable access, governments have opted to support community rather individual PC access. Multi-purpose telecenters, for instance, offer consumers access to numerous ICT applications, including public telephony, fax, Internet, tele-education, and telemedicine. International organizations, including UNESCO, the World Bank and the ITU, have initiated pilot telecenter projects in a number of countries, providing both facilities and technical support. The sustainability and scalability of such initiatives can, however, prove to be an issue.

Part II. The applications layer: Creating the enabling environment for improved e-development applications

E-business has changed the way business is conducted at the international level and is becoming a driving force of the global economy.[22] E-business also offers the potential for economic develop-ment, promising increased productivity and increased access to the global market.[23] E-commerce generates many important opportunities, including better availability of information, global distribution and customer service, reduced transactions costs, lower barriers to entry, and new sources of revenue.

Commerce can also have important impacts on individual economic sectors, such as finance and tourism, as well as on macroeconomic performance and policies. According to one recent study, e-commerce can cut distribution costs by 5 percent; companies using e-commerce in the study achieved efficiency gains valued at 0.75 percent of GDP.[24] The projected growth of business conducted over the Internet is impressive. According to the United Nations Conference on Trade and Development (UNCTAD), the number of websites using secure socket layer protocol (SSL, a protocol used mostly for e-commerce, e-payments and e-banking transactions) grew more than 55 percent between 2003 and 2004.[25]

Box 2.9 The family computer initiative of Tunisia

A "one-computer-per-family initiative" was launched in Tunisia by presidential decision in November 2000. The initiative aimed to enable low-income families to purchase computers at reasonable prices (less than 1,000 Tunisian Dinars, or US$750) via loans provided by the national solidarity bank. The bank offers soft loans (supported by the Ministry of Finance) at an interest rate of 5 percent; terms include a possible grace period of over 3 months. The local press reports that Phase I of the initiative has largely met its initial target of connecting 10,000 families per year. Additional elements could expand the current initiative by:

- opening the computer supply to an international competitive bidding process, thus procuring cheaper computers. (The initiative began by trying to link two policy goals: improving PC penetration and supporting the nascent local IT industry. Roughly 48 percent of computers sold in Tunisia are made and/or assembled locally.); and

- giving end-users a choice of ISP (in most cases the PCs came bundled with a pre-determined Internet service package.).

A decision of the Council of Ministers of December 2004 initiated Phase II of the initiative, which intends to provide 20,000 PCs per year. This phase will use an open competitive process and hopes to offer consumers a product that is 10 to 15 percent cheaper.

Sources: Babnet Tunisie. 2005. "Ordinateur familial: Rude et...douloureuse sera la concurrence." Available at http://www.babnet.net/cadredetail.asp?id=2549. Accessed July 2005.; and Serene Zawaydeh. 2003. "Tunisia Internet & Datacomm Landscape Report." Arab Advisors Group, Strategic Research Service: Amman, Jordan.

The lack of an enabling framework to support e-business is a significant roadblock to a country's fuller participation in the global economy. Many countries have not yet adapted their legal frameworks (designed for physical, paper-based commercial transactions) to an environment where transactions are conducted over electronic platforms. Electronic transactions raise a number of legal issues unique to the "virtual" world, ranging from acceptance of digital signatures to contract formation to the admissibility of electronic evidence to jurisdiction, to name a few.[26] The emerging legal framework is based on a mix of industry standard-setting, voluntary accreditation of certificate authorities, and possibly some government approval of technologies that will have a presumption of legal validity. But these approaches are sometimes subject to the overriding principles that parties may choose their own technological methods, and that no electronic signature can be denied effect solely on the grounds that it is not supported by a cryptographic system or does not comply with an accredited or otherwise favored scheme. This flexible framework is reflected in the EU Directive on Electronic Signatures, for example.[27]

Model laws, conventions, and regional laws from a variety of sources contribute to the emerging body of international best practices available to developing countries. Too often, however, there is a tendency to adopt international precedent (whether a model law, directive, or other precedent) wholesale, without adapting it to local dynamics. Certainly there is value in learning from the experience of others, but adopting model laws verbatim, without a holistic approach to regulatory reform, can be as ineffective to the growth of ICT4D as reform that does not take the international dimension into account at all.

In the East Asia and Pacific region, research on 23 countries shows that harmonization of legal frameworks to ensure cross-border interoperability is necessary for applications associated with the Internet (i.e., e-commerce); isolated activities of individual countries were ineffective in addressing this challenge.[28] Even with regulatory reform, if the financial system is not sophisticated enough to support electronic transactions such as inter-bank electronic payments and bank credit cards, a country will find it difficult to reap the benefits of e-business. In the Middle East, for example, only 18 percent of banks (most of which are foreign) offer e-bank-

ing services. The absence of digital certification laws and the low level of credit card penetration in Arab countries are major factors that discourage banks from going online. In the case of Jordan, the total transaction volume of Visa credit cards in 2004 was estimated at US$258 million, of which online payments accounted for only US$2.5 million, not even 1 percent of the total.[29]

Part III. The trust layer: Creating the enabling environment for improved consumer confidence and trust

The development of a digital environment is predicated on the security of electronic networks and communications. In the converged world of ICT infrastructure, digitzation of information into bits of data has given rise to new online applications and efficiencies, whether these transactions are

---

Box 2.10 Cybercafes in Algeria

Given the scarce diffusion of personal computers in Algeria (less that 1 percent of the population owns a PC)[a] and the high relative costs of Internet subscriptions,[b] people predominantly access the Internet at cybercafés. In 1999, the Government of Algeria launched an initiative to create 100 cybercafés in the capital. Three years later, the number of cybercafés had jumped to 4,000. The rapid growth of cybercafés between 1998 and 2000 resulted from the gradual liberalization of the telecommunications sector. Reforms simplified the licensing process and made it extremely affordable (US$13) to obtain authorization to provide Internet service.

The telecommunications reform has generated more than 120,000 Internet-related jobs in the last four years, many of which are in cybercafés, multi-service kiosks, and sales points. As of December 2004, Algeria had 29 active ISPs and more than 500,000 estimated Internet users, of which 50,000 were ADSL subscribers. Broadband Internet access has been available since November 2003.

[a] In 1999, the number of PCs in Algeria reached 180,000, a penetration rate of 0.60 percent. Between 1999 and 2001, this number increased by 20,000 PCs annually and is expected to reach 650,000 by 2008, a penetration rate of 1.89 percent.

[b] The cost of a full-day Internet connection can reach US$463 per month.

Source: Serene Zawaydeh. 2004. "Algeria Internet & Datacomm Landscape Report." Arab Advisors Group, Strategic Research Service: Amman, Jordan.

Box 2.11 Chile moves from a paper-based to online tax system

In 1998, Chile's Internal Taxation Service (SII) launched an online taxation system. Its aims were to (a) reduce the cost and increase the accuracy of tax collection; (b) equip Chile's tax authority with the resources it needed for the foreseeable future; and (c) offer taxpayers throughout the country better service, along with swift and easy access to vital tax information.

Three years after project launch, the online taxation system has racked up impressive statistics. Over 400,000 taxpayers have checked their assessments online, some 183,548 sworn returns and 89,355 income tax returns have been received, and the Chilean exchequer has collected US$1.943 billion in taxes. Managers at SII are now preparing the online system to process a potential 1.8 million tax returns per annum, plus 950,000 VAT returns every month.

E-governement applications often require changes in the legal code in order to fully utilize their potential. In Chile, the popularity of the online tax system spurred citizen demand for legal changes that would facilitate the transfer of information between SII and taxpayers. The government responded by speeding an amendment to the tax code through parliament; the change authorizes taxpayers to present their annual reports, accounts and tax returns on media other than paper.

Source: World Bank. 2005. "Chilean Tax System Online," abstract, E*Government. GSPR net (Governance and Public Sector Reform Sites). Washington, D.C., n.d. Available at http://www1.worldbank.org/publicsector/egov/chile_taxcs.htm. Accessed at July 2005.

---

commercial (traditional e-commerce) or between citizens and a government (e-government). However, data in digital format, as well as the networks and storage devices that use this data, are increasingly vulnerable to theft and unauthorized use. Securing the integrity of data and infrastructure is thus imperative to build user confidence.[30] During any activity carried out over the Internet, a user "opens a window on his privacy." Lack of privacy protection means that the online market will not reach its full potential.

Promoting confidence in the online world (e.g., by protecting consumer privacy and preventing unsolicited e-mail) is needed to create trust and increase the use of digital networks. Research indicates, for example, that many people are still reluctant to conduct business online.[31] Identity thieves steal personal and financial data from data brokers, banks and retailers and use the stolen data to engage in illicit activities. It is not only the consumer who loses from "breaches" of personal privacy on the Internet; according to e-Marketer, companies lost US$5.5 billion in online sales in 2001 due to poor security and could lose more than US$24 billion by 2006.[32]

In April, 2005, the UNDP Asia Pacific Development Information Programme (APDIP) published a summary analysis of a recent regional survey on Internet governance priorities for the Asia Pacific region. Survey results revealed an overwhelming, near universal concern over virus attacks, online fraud, cyber-crime, and spam.[33] More than 90 percent of respondents from all stakeholder groups and from almost all countries surveyed regarded the solution to these problems as somewhat important, important, or very important. These issues by far evoked the strongest sense of concern among those surveyed.

The following subsections will examine six major issues that affect the trust and confidence of digital networks: network security, consumer protection, privacy, cyber-crime, protection of intellectual property rights, and dispute resolution.

Protecting critical infrastructure

In an environment where more and more "public" services are provided over networks that are privately owned and operated, governments must address how best to protect critical information infrastructures.[34] Many countries are developing cybersecurity policies and programs, including the creation of national Computer Emergency Response Teams (CERT). These programs are part of multi-stakeholder information-sharing efforts aimed at creating the capacity to assess and manage cybersecurity risks. Such programs are generally a combination of bottom-up, industry-led programs, and top-down, government-led initiatives. All such initiatives focus on the process of sharing information on security issues among various actors and stakeholders; they do not, however, focus on the institutional arrangements for this process. One key issue that public policy makers must consider is how information about potential threats should be escalated and addressed. Thus, the establishment of a well-functioning collaborative information-sharing framework is essential to infrastructure security at both national and international levels.[35]

Implementation of a national CERT and related Computer Incident Response Teams (CISRT) in key government agencies not only includes training and emergency alert and response services, it also provides risk analysis to ensure continuity of critical government systems and applications. Responsibility for critical information infrastructure protection (CIIP) programs should

---

Box 2.12 Tunisia launches e-commerce without credit cards

A recent study of the ICT sector in Tunisia revealed that while the financial system is no longer a major roadblock to the effective use of ICT, there is still important room for improvement. An early success was the introduction of the e-dinar, a rechargeable pre-paid card available for purchase at most post offices in denominations of 20 to 500 dinars. This innovative mechanism allowed Tunisia to initiate e-commerce without the use of regular credit cards. Only recently did the Tunisian Agency for the Internet launch a Secure Socket Layer (SSL)-based secure-payment server called e-Tijara for users of MasterCard and VISA credit cards (the server is operated by Agence Tunisienne de l'Internet ATI in cooperation with major Tunisian banks).

Tunisia now needs to exploit existing global network externalities. Currently, international financial transactions are made more costly and more difficult by relying solely on the government's own certification agency. In addition, the e-dinar initiative, which proved to be a very beneficial first step, needs to be phased out in favor of a wider use of credit cards (which yield superior outcomes for the retail market).

Source: Catherine L. Mann. 2004. "Information Technology and e-Commerce in Tunisia: Domestic and International Challenges and the Role of the Financial System." Available at http://tunis.usembassy.gov/wwwftunisia_report.pdf. Accessed July 2005.

be given to government agencies or other bodies that will give this issue the attention and the priority it requires. Any CIIP program should identify critical infrastructures, assess the vulnerabilities of key systems and raise awareness of security concerns. A permanent structure should then be created to coordinate program development and implementation, a process that should involve the government and the private sector. A complementary approach to reduce cybersecurity risks is to develop corporate risk management capabilities in both public and private institutions.

Any cybersecurity program must take a multifaceted approach to information security. In addition to setting standards and building the capacity of government agencies, adequate policies and regulation should be devised to promote a safe and trusted environment for electronic transactions.

Consumer protection

Many countries are in the process of crafting guidelines for protecting consumers who participate in online transactions. At a global level, many countries use the EU consumer protection guidelines as the basis for their own consumer protection legislation.[36] The approach to consumer protection varies among countries. In the United States, for example, the government relies on a hands-off approach that focuses on industry self-regulation, while countries of the European Union have adopted laws and regulations that limit the purposes for which companies can use personal data. Data collection in Europe, for example, cannot proceed unless the data subject has unambiguously given his or her consent (with certain exceptions).[37] Current variations in laws among countries is prompting policy makers to contemplate harmonizing such standards.

Data privacy protection

Creating trust and confidence is not only about protecting consumer privacy, it also extends to protecting the privacy of individuals against unreasonable government intrusions. The online environment poses particular issues with respect to unauthorized use and manipulation of data. Moreover, legitimate public order, security and related government concerns require investiga-

---

Box 2.13 Ghana banned from e-commerce: The cost of late reform

An FBI investigation of global credit card internet fraud revealed that over 5 million of online shopping fraud was detected to have generated from Ghana. The report shows that even if credit card usage is not very common in Ghana, the offenders managed to hack into credit card accounts in Ghana to conduct online transactions.

Ghana is in the process of updating its legal environment to respond to such fraudulent activities. The lack of laws protecting against cyber fraud simply means that perpetrators of such crimes can still get away. The implications for the lack of reform can be very costly for Ghana. First as a result of the FBI report, Internet shopping was banned for Ghana, credit card holders in Ghana can no longer use their cards to buy online. The implications for the banks can also be onerous as the combination of lack of an adequate regime for compliance with security procedure and for deterrence of cyber fraud threatens to scare away potential business with wider economic implications for the country.

Source: "GISP calls on Ghanaian Govt to help reserve Internet shopping ban Balancing Act." Balancing Act's News Update 247 of 3 March 2005. Available at http://www.balancingact-africa.com/news/back/balancing-act_247.html. Accessed July 2005.

tion and disclosure of such data. In many jurisdictions, privacy protection has been assured as a basic right, with the need or wish of an online user to maintain anonymous communications respected. The legal framework thus needs to strike a delicate balance between protecting privacy and preserving a government's right to protect the public interest against illegal and criminal use of cyberspace.

Since the mid-1990s, the EU has used a general directive on personal data privacy protection.[38] More recently, it adopted special privacy rules applicable to electronic communications. [39] As is the case with the EU directive, data privacy protection frameworks often require the establishment of institutional mechanisms to regulate compliance with privacy statutes.

Cyber-crimes

Laws establishing penalties for unauthorized use of data, computers, and networks are often referred to as "cybercrime" laws.[40] While some aspects of these legal frameworks deal with crime, others deal with tort or civil law issues. Collectively, legal frameworks and laws provide a range of civil and criminal penalties and enforcement procedures. In civil or tort law, penalties are applied in a range of situations, including liability for copyright and trademark infringement, financial loss, compromise of data, violation of network integrity, content violations, and false or misleading advertising. In the criminal area, penalties are levied for such transgressions as unauthorized access to or interference with systems (computers or networks), unauthorized interception of or interference with data, misuse of devices (e.g., unauthorized eavesdropping), fraud, forgery, and conspiracy. On the procedural side, "cyberlaws" generally include provisions for the discovery or production of electronic evidence.

Protection of intellectual property rights

It is axiomatic that the protection of intellectual property rights (IPRs) is part of an enabling legal and regulatory framework.[41] The UN Working Group on Internet Governance has noted that the Internet poses new possibilities for low-cost, global dissemination of information, but also makes protected property more vulnerable to unauthorized use.

There is no dispute that protection of IPRs can provide incentives for growth and development. What has emerged in the development debate over the last decade is how property rights can be exploited, by whom and for whose benefit.[42] This debate revolves around whether the protection of IPRs should benefit a few rights holders (primarily from developing countries), or whether a balance can be struck that both provides necessary incentives (i.e., protecting intellectual property) for innovation while at the same time does not exclude potential users in less developed countries (i.e., granting access). To some extent, the debate has centered around the use of free and/or Open Source software, which some development specialists see as a tool to promote development while avoiding transfer payments (via software copyright license and royalty payments) to existing rights holders.

Alternative dispute resolution[43]

Competitive markets inevitably produce disputes, and competitive telecommunications markets are no exception. These disputes may involve failures to fulfill contractual obligations, non-compliance with regulatory requirements or a wide range of other issues. Successful dispute resolution is increasingly important to attract investment, spur competition and develop the global ICT sector. Dispute resolution mechanisms, moreover, need to be as speedy as the networks and technologies that they serve.

Disputes in which service providers have enough power in the market to resist liberalization, or even abuse their power, are particularly relevant for regulators, especially when such disputes distort the functioning of competitive markets. Interconnection provides many examples of this type of dispute, such as when a service provider with exclusive control over essential infrastructure facilities fails to reach a reasonable agreement to interconnect with competitors or to provide access to its network facilities.

In the Internet's early years, the ethos behind dispute resolution, including domain name disputes, was based on informal procedures and community consensus. These informal procedures have since evolved into more formal (if still alternative) processes, including the referral of domain dispute resolution and related intellectual property rights issues to the World Intellectual Property Organization (WIPO).[44] New domain name dispute resolution rules and procedures have also been established by the Internet Corporation for Assigned Names and Numbers (ICANN).[45] The Internet itself has spawned new technological approaches to resolving disputes, including so-called "online dispute resolution" (ODR), for use in both the online and physical worlds.

Policy makers and regulators should use minimal but well-focused regulatory intervention to create an environment where industry players have incentives to resolve disputes constructively. This framework should also recognize that dispute prevention is as important as dispute resolution. Reducing contentiousness and reliance on destructive dispute processes enhances prospects for investment and growth. Use of consensus-building measures by policy makers and regulators can engage parties in the sector and identify mutually beneficial commercial opportunities.

Ultimately, the test of successful dispute resolution, as of regulation in general, is its impact on investment, growth, and development in the sector. Successful dispute resolution is important for all countries that seek to facilitate the rapid diffusion of new communications infrastructure and ICT services. It is particularly crucial for countries that have historically not experienced high ICT investment and growth, as rapid and effective dispute resolution helps such countries bridge the digital divide.

Conclusion

Given the interdependent nature of the global information society, cross-national common standards are needed to achieve interoperability, both of legal frameworks and physical ICT networks. This chapter focused primarily on the role of governments and the actions they can take to create appropriate policy, legal, and regulatory conditions to advance the e-development agenda. While many of the issues explored in the chapter may appear more relevant to highly developed countries, which rely on highly evolved and sophisticated communications networks, services, and broadband applications to provide economic and social services, contemporary technology makes it possible for developing nations to rapidly deploy sophisticated ICT networks and applications. This chapter therefore attempted to present the full spectrum of policy, legal and regulatory issues that enable ICT-led growth, giving policy makers an idea of the progression of issues that they will eventually address as their ICT networks and capabilities grow.

Notes

[1] The authors wish to thank Juan Manuel Galarza Tohen, Zaid Safdar, Rachele Gianfranchi and Isabel Neto for their research input.

[2] See World Summit on the Information Society (WSIS). 2003. "Declaration of Principles" and "Plan of Action." WSIS, International Telecommunications Union: Geneva, Switzerland.

[3] Indeed, the World Bank has acknowledged that "policy reform is hard work." World Bank. 2004. "Operations Evaluation Department Report 2003." World Bank: Washington, DC.

[4] Depending on the context of a given country, the use of competition policy or the exercise of regulatory forbearance in the presence of active market forces may be appropriate to spur competition.

[5] "Future-proofed" implies an environment that makes it easy to introduce new technologies and services. Laws drafted today, if based solely on today's technology, may prove inadequate for new technological innovations.

[6] The WSIS Declaration of Principles and Action Plan deals with an enabling environment at both the national and international level. At the international level, these documents address Internet governance. Although not the focus of this paper, clearly Internet governance will involve both an international and national level. To the extent that such governance deals with national-level concerns (e.g., building consultative mechanisms to ensure management of core Internet resources and developing national capacity to participate in national and international governance mechanisms), this chapter addresses the topic. For a broader discussion of Internet governance, see "Working Papers" prepared by the Working Group on Internet Governance (WGIG) in preparation for the WSIS Summit in 2005, available at http://www.wgig.org/working-papers.html. (July 2005).

[7] ITU. 2002. *World Telecommunications Development Report: Reinventing Telecoms.* Geneva: ITU, p.20.

[8] See H. Singh and K.W. Jun. 1995. "Some New Evidence on Determinants of Foreign Direct Investment in Developing Countries." Policy Research Working Paper, No. 1531. World Bank: Washington, DC.

[9] Global Information and Communication Technologies Department (GICT). 2005. "Financing Information and Communication Infrastructure Needs in the Developing World: Public and Private Roles." GICT, World Bank: Washington, DC.

[10] Qiang, C. and Guislain P. 2005. "Foreign Direct Investment in Telecommunications." *World Information and Communication for Development Report 2006.* World Bank: Washington, DC.

[11] Different countries have chosen different models, with varying degrees of success. See D. Geradin and M. Kerf. 2003. *Controlling Market Power in Telecommunications: Striking the Right Balance Between Antitrust and Sector-Specific Rules and Institutions.* New York: Oxford University Press.

[12] See, World Bank, ITU. 2005. *Dispute Settlement in Telecommunications: Current Practices and Future Directions.* Washington, DC.

[13] There is no single definition of broadband. The notion is a moving target and differs from country to country. At a minimum, broadband means a permanent connection and transmission capacity with sufficient bandwidth to permit combined provision of voice, data and video.

[14] OECD. 2003. "Broadband Driving Growth: Policy Responses." DSTI/CCP92003, Final. OECD: Paris. Also see ITU. 2002. *The Birth of Broadband.*

[15] Examples include member states of the European Union, India, South Africa, Tanzania and Zambia.

[16] Navas-Sabater, J., Dymond, A., and Juntunen, N. 2002. *Telecommunications and Information Services for the Poor: Toward a Strategy for Universal Access.* World Bank: Washington, D.C.

[17] Leighton, W. A. 2001. *Broadband Deployment and the Digital Divide, A Primer.* OECD Policy Analysis.

[18] The city of Amsterdam, for example, has taken the responsibility for setting up an independent legal entity, Citynet Amsterdam, that will own the city network. Private partners have been invited to supply the infrastructure equipment and operate the network. Peter Smith and Hien Tu Thiu, Summary of selected Municipal Backbone initiative, a GICT mimeo August 2004.

[19] ITU database. 2005.

[20] Elmer, L. 2002. "Vietnam's ICT Enabling Environment: Policy, Infrastructure and Applications." USAID: Washington, DC.

[21] In cases like Egypt, Algeria and Tunisia local banks offer soft consumer loans for the purchase of home computers. Algeria had introduced "Ostratic," a family PC initiative in July 2005. See Abderrafic Khanifsa. 2005. "Ordi-densite." *IT-mag.* July 2005. Available at "http://www.itmag-dz.com/article.php3?id_article=248&. Accessed July 2005.

[22] E-business refers to e-commerce, e-banking, e-insurance and any other economic activity conducted over the Internet.

[23] There is a vast growing literature on the development dimension of e-commerce. See, for example, A. Goldstein and D. O'Connor. 2002. "E-commerce for Development: Prospects and Policy Issues." Development Centre Studies, OECD Development Center, OECD: Paris.; and OECD. 1999. *The Economic and Social Impact of Electronic Commerce: Preliminary Findings and Research Agenda.* Paris: OECD.

[24] Cisco Systems and University of Texas. 2001."Measuring the Internet Economy." University of Texas, Austin. Available at http://www.smartecon.com/articles/internet_economy.pdf. Accessed July2005.

[25] UNCTAD. 2004. *E-Commerce and Development Report 2004.* New York and Geneva: UNCTAD.

[26] Digital signatures is used to refer to generic electronic, digital means of authenticating the identity of a party to an electronic transaction. While it is recognized that the term "digital signature" is most commonly associated with key public-private infrastructure, it is intended to be technology neutral in this text.

[27] Directive 1999/93/EC of 13 December 1999 on Electronic Signatures.

[28] The study also showed that e-commerce laws adopted by a number of countries in the region, based on the UNCITRAL model law of 1996, did not enable cross-border interoperability. (Satola, D., Sreenivasan, R. and Pavlasova, L. 2004. "Benchmarking Regional e-Commerce in Asia and the Pacific and Assessment of Related Regional Activities." in *Harmonization of Legal and Regulatory Systems for E-Commerce in Asia and the Pacific: Current Challenges and Capacity Building Needs.* United Nations: New York.

[29] Arab Advisor Group. 2005. "An Analysis of e-Commerce Adoption in Jordan and the Gulf Region based on Reported Figures from Visa International." Arab Advisor Group: Amman, Jordan.

[30] This fact was explicitly recognized in the WSIS Declaration of Principles, which states that, "Strengthening the trust framework, including information security and network security, authentication, privacy and consumer protection, is a prerequisite for the development of the Information Society and for building confidence among users of ICTs." (WSIS. 2003. "Declaration of Principles.")

[31] According to the U.S. Federal Trade Commission, for example, identity theft has ranked as the top consumer fraud compliant for the past five years. The cost of identity theft including its impact on business, is estimated to exceed US$52 billion. Christopher Caldwell. 2005. "The price of privacy is high." *Financial Times.* April 16/17 p. 7.

[32] Op.cit

[33] Summary Analysis of the ORDIG Survey on Internet Governance Priorities in Asia-Pacific Available at http://igov.apdip.net/ORDIG.Survey.Report.pdf. Accessed July 2005.

[34] See M. Dunn and I. Wigert. 2004. *International CIIP Handbook 2004: An Inventory and Analysis of Protection Policies in Fourteen Countries.* edited by Andreas Wenger and Jan Metzger. Swiss Federal Institute of Technology, Zurich.

[35] T. Glaessner, T. Kellerman, and V. McNevin. 2004. "Electronic Safety and Soundness: Securing Finance in a New Age." World Bank Working Paper, no. 26. The World Bank: Washington, DC.

[36] See OECD. 1980. "Guidelines on the Protection of Privacy and Transborder Flows of Personal Data (Privacy Guidelines)." OECD: Paris.; and OECD. 2003. "Privacy Online: Policy and Practical Guidance." OECD: Paris.

[37] See "Working Papers" prepared by the Working Group on Internet Governance (WGIG) in preparation for the WSIS Summit in 2005, http://www.wgig.org/working-papers.html; and Dispute Resolution in the Telecommunications Sector: Current Practices and Future Directions; A Joint Study Undertaken with the International Telecommunication Union, *infra* note 12.

[38] EU. 1995. "Directive 1995/46/EC of 24 October 1995 on Personal Data Privacy Protection." *Official Journal of the European Communities.* Brussels.

[39] EU. 2002. "Directive 2002/58/EC of 12 July 2002 on Privacy and Electronic Communications." *Official Journal of the European Communities.* Brussels.

[40] See, for example, G. Sadowsky et al. 2004. *Information Technology Security Handbook.* Washington, DC: *info*Dev, World Bank and Global Internet Policy Initiative.; and Dunn and Wigert. 2004. *International CIIP Handbook.*

[41] IPR law distinguishes between three types of intellectual property: trademark, copyright and patent.

[42] See "Working Papers" prepared by the Working Group on Internet Governance (WGIG) in preparation for the WSIS Summit in 2005, http://www.wgig.org/working-papers.html. Accessed July 2005.

[43] This section is adapted from Dispute Resolution in the Telecommunications Sector, infra note 12.

[44] See, for example, the alternative dispute resolution procedures of the WIPO Arbitration and Mediation Center, Geneva Switzerland, n.d., http://arbiter.wipo.int/center/index.html. Accessed July 2005.

[45] See ICANN. 2005. "Domain Name Dispute Resolution Policies." ICANN: Marian Del Rey, California. Available at http://www.icann.org/udrp#udrp. Accessed July 2005.

Chapter 3

E-Strategies for Development

Efficient e-strategies require strong monitoring and evaluation

by Bruno Lanvin

The "Plan of Action" of the World Summit on the Information Society (WSIS) calls for more e-strategies as a way to build information societies on a global scale. However, the energy to pursue "e-agendas" sometimes appears to be diminishing, as some of donors and aid recipients come to regard e-strategies as a distraction from other, more fundamental development objectives. Indeed, it is striking that internationally agreed development objectives such as the Millennium Development Goals (MDGs) make so little reference to information and communication technologies (ICTs) and their application in such sectors as health, education, governance, and more generally, poverty reduction.

This chapter attempts to explore two possible reasons for the apparent reduced interest in national strategies for e-development, namely:

- absence of a well-structured body of evidence linking e-strategies both to broad development goals (e.g., the MDGs) and national development objectives; and

- lack of data and measurement tools that donors, analysts, and policy makers could use to evaluate the development impact of resources invested in ICTs, particularly in e-strategies.

This chapter will attempt to show the critical role monitoring and evaluation (M&E) efforts in the design and implementation of e-strategies, relying on recent work in this area by the World Bank. It does not attempt to define a "good" e-strategy, how it should be sequenced, or how resources should be allocated among its various components. Rather, it seeks to identify ways in which upstream linkages (i.e., with national development objectives) and downstream accountability (i.e., measuring results with proper M&E tools) can enhance the validity and efficacy of e-strategies. It is the author's firm belief that the exploration of proper M&E methodology for e-strategies will generate a few lessons about the measurement of broader development goals.

Box 3.1 An operational definition of e-strategies

Despite the fact that the WSIS "Action Plan" mentions e-strategies, the plan (as well as other basic WSIS documents) does not provide a definition of the term. This remarkable absence of an agreed definition, which affects most of the e-strategy literature, indicates that the practice of such strategies has preceded their conceptualization. E-strategies are sometimes considered plans for applying ICTs to national development or shorthand for policies and strategies that use ICTs to promote national development. In this context, an e-strategy is a *national* strategy (although the definition can be adapted *mutatis mutandis* to other geographic or institutional contexts, leading to sub-regional or regional e-strategies).

The *formulation,* or design, of an e-strategy takes the priority development objectives of a particular country as a starting point. This means that development objectives, or "d-goals," must be defined and adopted prior to e-strategy objectives, or "e-goals." Although most definitions of e-strategies include references to both ICTs and development, the reality is that such plans, particularly their architecture and components, demonstrate only a loose relationship between the two. For example, ICT is considered both a component of e-strategies and one of its objectives. This conceptual ambiguity becomes more striking when local champions of an e-strategy are close to the ICT field, as many staff from ministries of telecommunications or similar structures have technical and/or engineering backgrounds.

Why analysts have shied away from defining e-strategies is fear of promoting a "one-size-fits-all" approach. This fear is reinforced by the fact that most of the early e-strategies were formulated and implemented in more advanced countries (typically, members of the OECD), triggering additional caution about exporting Northern thinking to Southern realities.

Existing knowledge about e-strategies has now reached a higher level of maturity. Best practices have started to emerge, and common bottlenecks and stumbling blocks are more easily identified. Based on the experiences of developing countries, the following operational definition of e-strategies is proposed here: ***an e-strategy is a set of coordinated actions and policies that seek to accelerate the social, economic, and political development of a given country (or region) through the use of telecommunications, information networks, and the technologies associated with them.*** This definition will, most likely, be refined in the future through exchanges between analysts and practitioners in the field.

E-strategies can be a risky challenge

At the end of the first phase of the WSIS in December 2003, political leaders made a commitment to develop national e-strategies by the time of the second WSIS meeting in November 2005.[1] This task is a major challenge, as well as a major risk, for many countries. The first risk is that individual e-strategies will be launched in the absence of a common framework, which will make it difficult to evaluate their impact, compare their achievements, and consolidate them at sub-regional or regional levels. The second risk is that errors of the past might be repeated: over the past decade, many countries have spent significant time, energy, and resources to design e-strategies which often remained blueprints, or white elephants, because no systematic set of indicators had been established to monitor and evaluate their implementation.

It is therefore of paramount importance that monitoring and evaluation ("M&E") should not be an *ex-post facto* component of e-strategies, but a vital part of their design and implementation. Developing M&E components of an e-strategy ensures that the strategy will be explicit, realistic, and that its implementation will be regularly assessed and realigned. Such assessments allow scarce resources to be used efficiently, particularly given the opportunity cost of deploying such resources in other poverty reduction interventions, such as healthcare or non-ICT infrastructure projects.

Prerequisite #1. E-Strategies should fit into the bigger development picture

No e-strategy can be a substitute for a development strategy (d-strategy). From an M&E point of view, this reality has important practical consequences, including:

- *Formulation.* Certain indicators (especially those that measure "impact") must be formulated at a level of decision making higher than that of the e-strategy. In other words, impact indicators must be derived from a country's overall development strategy (d-strategy) or even its socio-economic policy. Designers and promoters of e-strategies should thus refrain from re-inventing the wheel and focus on making existing M&E indicators a fully integrated component of their own efforts.

- *Linkages.* M&E indicators should be related to each other in a way that reflects the se-

quencing of strategy objectives. For instance, if an e-strategy includes distance education initiatives, it is important that such activities (and their outputs) be connected not only to broader e-strategy objectives (e.g., promoting e-literacy or enhancing the use of ICTs in education), but also to d-strategy objectives (e.g., promoting general educational goals or developing general ICT usage) and more generic policy objectives (e.g., diversifying a traditional economy). The sequence of decision making involved in selecting M&E indicators is illustrated in Figure 3.1.

E-strategies versus information societies

An increasing amount of international effort has been devoted to building information societies over the past few years.[2] Nevertheless, there is limited awareness among development specialists and national leaders about the potential role of ICT in the fight against poverty.[3] Despite the significant cross-sectoral intellectual effort that mobilized the Millennium Declaration, ICTs appear in the document either as a second thought or a relatively minor tool to reach the MDGs. In spite of the myriad of findings regarding the development impact of ICT projects in the field, such evidence has not yet been aggregated in a way that can easily convince decision makers at the policy level. To a large extent, the case for ICT for development (ICT4D) still needs to be made.[4] M&E indicators and processes can play a crucial role in educating policy makers about the potential of ICTs. This role will not, however, be fully realized unless the following objectives become clear development priorities at both the national and international levels:

- *M&E integration.* Designers of e-strategies should make M&E tools and indicators as compatible as possible with those established for general development objectives and targets.

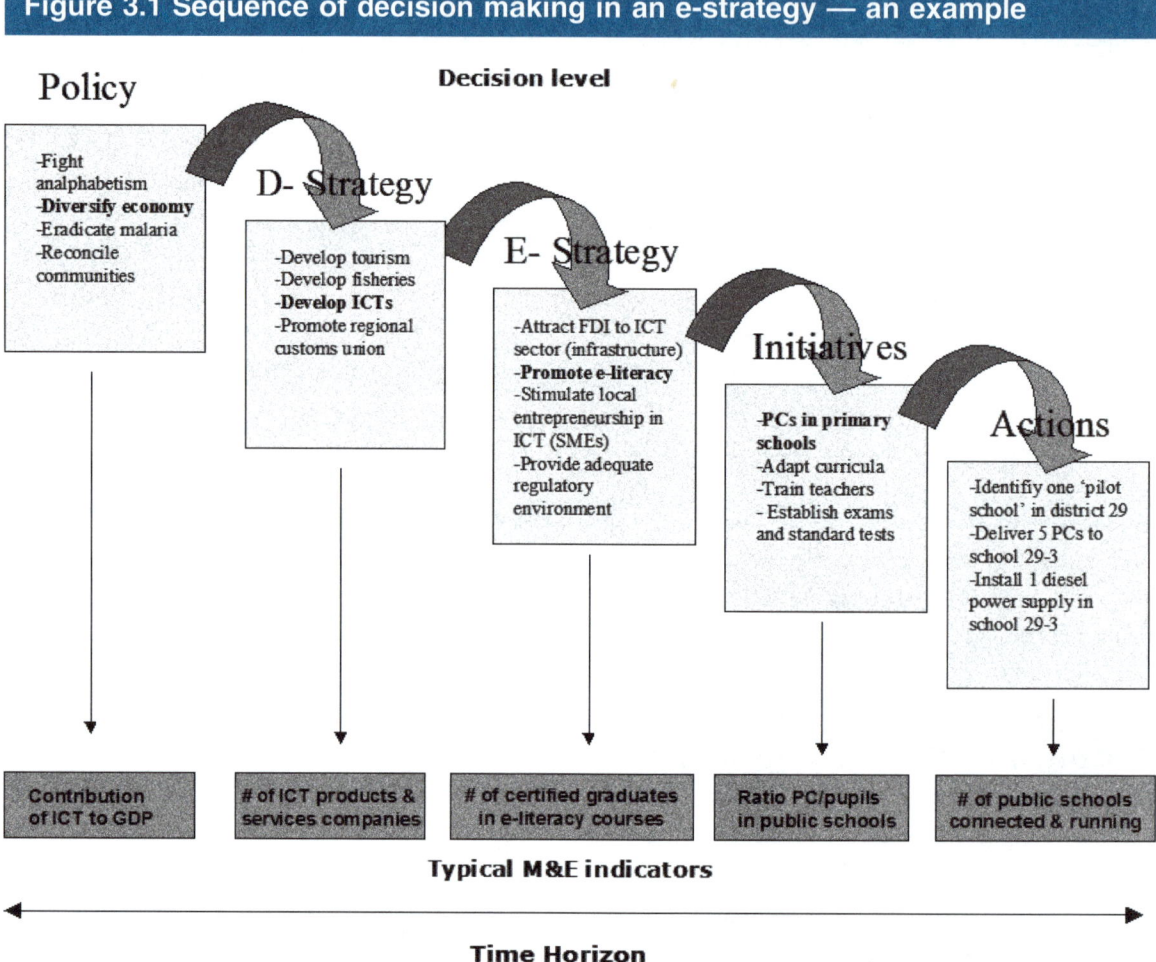

Figure 3.1 Sequence of decision making in an e-strategy — an example

This implies a search for homogenous terminology or, more importantly, the need to establish causal linkages between objectives and indicators. Such linkages enhance the ability of M&E indicators to garner international support and benefit from best practices in the field.[5]

- *Indicator quality.* Every effort to enhance the quality, coverage, and detail of ICT and e-economy indicators should be pursued. Major gaps currently exist between data on applications and usage. Indicators today do not measure much beyond physical teledensity, connectivity, equipment, and information traffic flows. In most cases, the first step in im-

proving indicator quality will be to strengthen local statistical and data collection capacities.[6]

- *M&E compatibility.* As mentioned above, M&E instruments attached to e-strategies should be made as compatible as possible with existing M&E instruments for traditional d-strategies. Compatability is necessary to (a) achieve consistency in pursuing overall national policy objectives and (b) obtain the support of those parts of government and civil society that might otherwise see e-strategies as a fad or a distraction from more fundamental development objectives.

E-readiness versus access and usage

The M&E component of an e-strategy should reflect the fact that ICT is only a tool, not an end, of development. In other words, the number of telephone lines, personal computers, or even Internet hosts available in a given country are not the ultimate indicators of whether or not an e-strategy has been successful. On the other hand, while the economic and social value that people derive from greater use of ICTs is clearly a better indicator of such success, this value is much more complex to measure, monitor, and evaluate.

Although usage may be a better indicator than access, there is no usage without access. More-

over, both access and usage depend heavily on the legal, regulatory, economic, and social frameworks within which information and information technology are used. They are also dependent on whether government, business, schools, and individuals are interested and able to access and use ICTs. These elements are generally understood as components of "e-readiness."

E-Readiness: Most business strategies begin with a review or assessment of the current state of a business, focusing on such key elements as the customer base, operations, and product line. A business strategy also describes the past achievements of a business and highlights areas of relative strength, weakness, and opportunity.

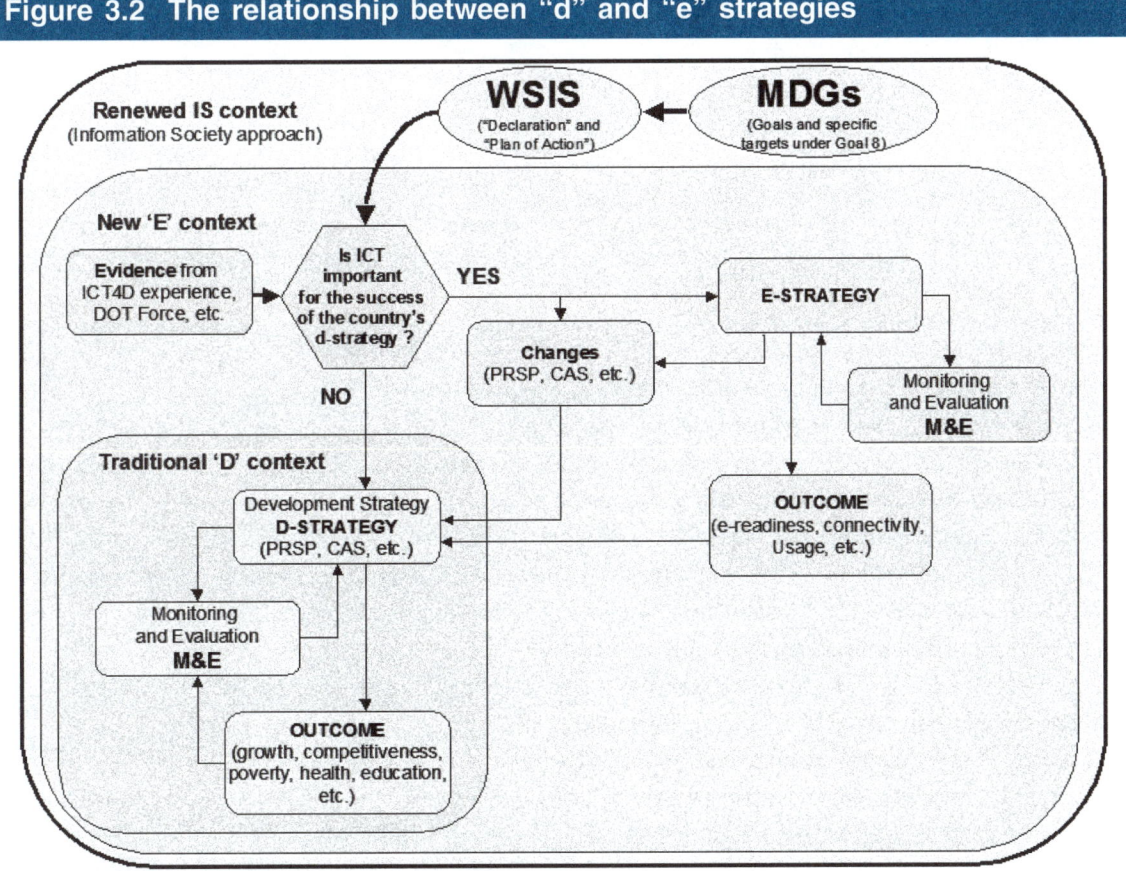

Figure 3.2 The relationship between "d" and "e" strategies

The assessment of how well (or badly) a business is operating will drive the degree of future change. A similar approach is required for the development of national e-strategies. Understanding where a country stands with regard to key elements of its ICT development agenda is the basis of a national e-strategy. Some 137 countries have already conducted e-readiness assessments.[7]

E-readiness assessments provide policy makers with two key pieces of information:

- *What to do.* E-readiness assessments determine the themes or sectors that will be the focus of a country's e-strategy. Often these themes and sectors are identified through comparisons with other, similar countries.

- *How much of it to do.* E-readiness assessments help a country decide how far to pursue each key objective. In other words, once a country has decided *what* to do, it must decide *how much* of it to do (set specific targets). Such assessments also provide baseline data against which the progress of a national e-strategy can be measured.

Country comparisons play an important role in selecting strategic ICT priorities and establishing growth targets. If a comparator country is considerably more ready in a given area (e.g., ICT infrastructure), strategists may choose to emphasize this area. Such comparisons also provide a foundation for growth targets. For example, if a comparator country has expanded its infrastructure (as measured by teledensity) at a rate of X percent per year, strategists may chose to establish the same or a slightly more ambitious target for their own ICT infrastructure development. Depending on the specific context of different countries, an e-readiness strategy will give a different emphasis to such issues as security, privacy and consumer protection.

Access and usage: Access (both physical and economic) is only one dimension of the digital divide.[8] In fact, "access" encompasses a number of conditions, including whether or not the connectivity and equipment provided to businesses, local governments, schools, hospitals, community access points, and individuals will be used in a productive and sustainable fashion that contributes to local and international development objectives.

Measuring e-readiness, access and usage: From an M&E point of view, it is important to link evaluation indicators to e-readiness, access and usage—the three categories against which the probable success of an e-strategy can be rated. In many respects, the credibility and efficiency of e-strategies in fact will depend on having a strong M&E spine. Possible indicators for these three components are listed below.

Readiness:

- legal, regulatory, and overall institutional framework (e.g., rule of law, international property rights regimes, trade and investment openness, regulatory framework, competition framework, etc.);

- society's support (at all levels) for innovation, reform and ICT;

- human resources (education in general, e-literacy in particular, etc.);

- perceptions of security and privacy[9]; and

- digital divide issues (e.g. rural/urban disparities).

Availability/Access:

- infrastructure (e.g., telecom) and network penetration; and

- equipment (e.g., computers in business, administrations, schools, homes, etc.).

Usage:

- applications (e.g., e-government, e-business, e-education, e-health);

- specific usage modalities (e.g., community access points); and

- specific sectoral or policy objectives (e.g., export competitiveness).

The more such indicators are compatible with internationally agreed objectives and targets (such as those used to measure progress in achieving the MDGs),[10] the easier it will be to generate international support for particular e-strategies, benchmark national efforts vis-à-vis those of other countries and encourage foreign direct investment.

Prerequisite #2. E-strategies need a strong monitoring and evaluation component

In order to facilitate ongoing assessments of e-strategies and ensure that such assessments are internationally comparable, the World Bank recently launched the *E-strategies Monitoring and Evaluation Toolkit* (METER, see figure 3.3). This toolkit is organized as a series of modules on the background, methodology, and themes of a national e-strategy.[11] The M&E framework of the toolkit addresses the process of how an e-strategy is actually formulated, including the development of policy goals, strategic priorities, and key initiatives.

Figure 3.3 Structure of World Bank METER Toolkit

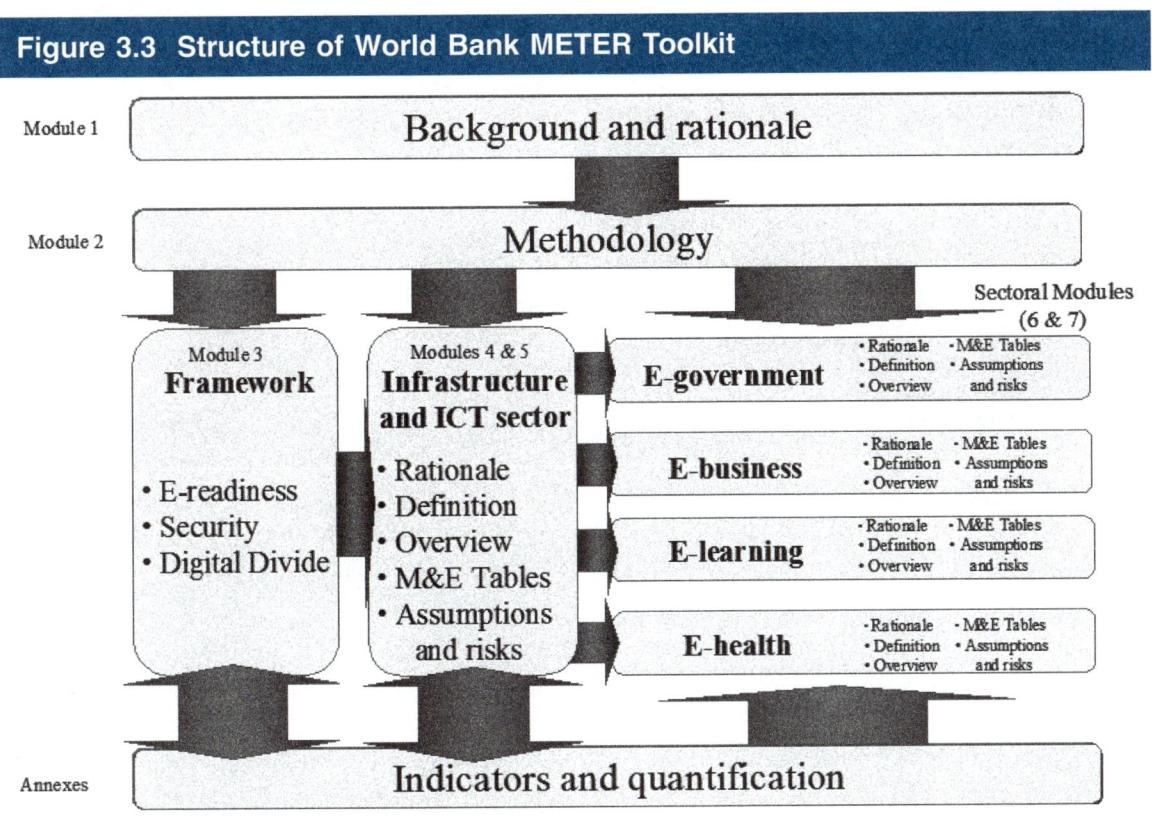

Source: Adamali, Lanvin and Schware. 2005. *Monitoring and Evaluation Toolkit for E-strategies Results.* Washington, DC: GICT Department, World Bank.

Each thematic or sectoral module of the METER toolkit is based on a common format and consists of the following elements: rationale, definition, overview, M&E tables, and assumptions and risks. M&E tables form the heart of each module and are designed to be applied to selected strategic interventions undertaken under the theme considered. Matrices from past interventions are used as examples.

The choice of themes is driven by: (a) common strategic priorities of developing nations and (b) the complexity of the M&E challenge (i.e., where possible, tables are developed for areas that are more challenging to monitor and evaluate than others). No formal value judgment is attached to the selection process. However, there is an implicit acceptance that such priorities are at least useful; no tables are developed for initiatives that the authors think potentially ineffective.

A simple framework to monitor and assess e-strategies

Based on the *Logframe Handbook* developed by the World Bank (2001), the METER toolkit uses a simple pyramid framework to consider the inter-relationship between policy, strategy, and the implementation of an e-strategy (see figure 3.4). At the top level (apex of the pyramid), the overall development policy of a specific country will determine the strategic priorities of its e-strategy (second level). At the third and fourth levels, the implementation of the e-strategy is divided into "key initiatives" and "actions" (which are specific to one area of responsibility, such as individual institutional or geographic goals).

The fifth level considers the inputs and resources required to implement the e-strategy, whether these resources are institutional structures, staff, or financial resources (a clear understanding

of resource requirements links the strategy and its implementation and constitutes the foundation on which all elements of the strategy depend.). Finally, the sixth level identifies the assumptions and risks on which the e-strategy is based, setting the parameters for measuring its success or failure. This level offers a means by which risk-mitigation measures can be developed and, where possible, incorporated into the e-strategy itself.

Integrating M&E into a logical framework

M&E applies to all levels of the e-strategy pyramid. Each level of this pyramid will require different types of indicators (see Figure 3.4). For example, policy objectives, which are typically broader and longer term, have traditionally been measured in rather unquantified ways. One of the ambitions of the METER toolkit is to offer simple ways to attach indicators to such objectives.[12] Strategic priorities have proved more amenable to quantification, although such quantification has often remained limited to broad aggregates (e.g., percentage of the national population that has reached a certain level of ICT education), instead of society-wide indicators. By the time the implementation layers of key initiatives and specific actions are reached, M&E indicators are easier to design and use, referring respectively to outputs (e.g., number of computers installed in classrooms) and deliverables (e.g., the number of computers installed and connected in a certain number of schools in a specific region).

Whatever the level of the e-strategy pyramid, each indicator is the potential basis of an M&E component. An efficient M&E approach will, however, also account for local specificities. The thematic and sectoral modules of the METER toolkit provide countries practical ways to exercise such selectivity.

Figure 3.4 Logframe pyramid for a national e-strategy with M&E indicators

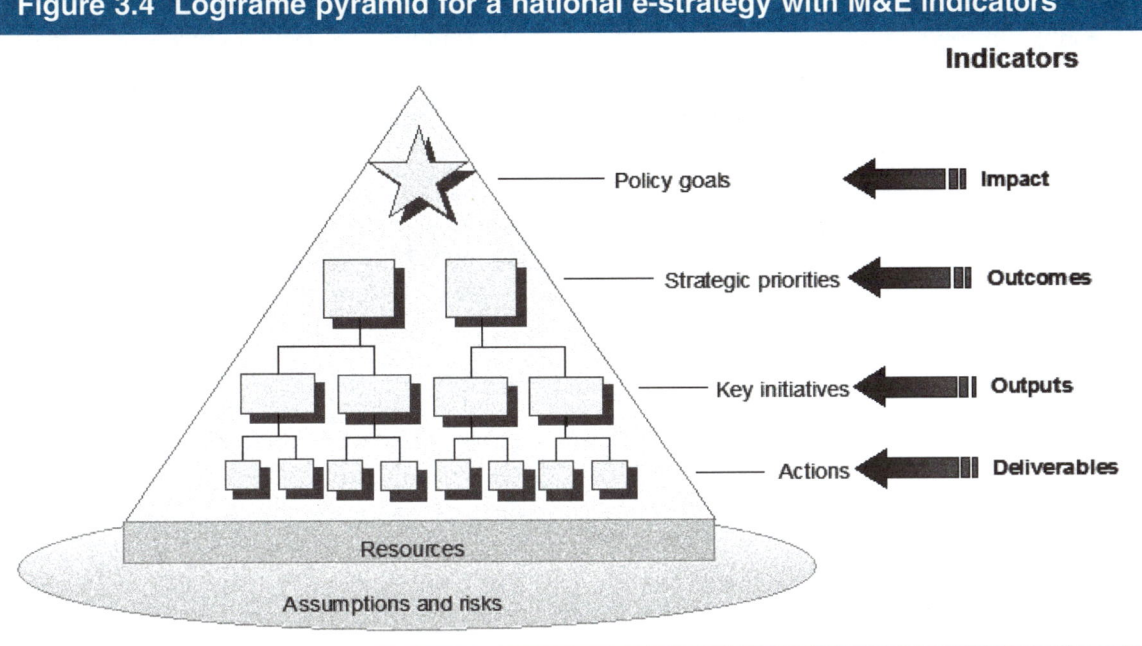

Source: Adamali, Lanvin and Schware. 2005. *Monitoring and Evaluation Toolkit for E-strategies Results.* Washington, DC: GICT Department, World Bank.

Monitoring and evaluation as a strategic tool

As mentioned earlier, the way in which an M&E model and its indicators are incorporated into an e-strategy will influence the strategy's feasibility and, hence, its credibility and wider application. It is therefore important that an M&E system be designed so that it is comprehensible and usable by domestic participants (e.g., the government, ministries, enterprises and civil society), as well as by external stakeholders (e.g., investors, donors, partners). Understood in this context, M&E ceases to be a mere component of e-strategies and becomes a powerful instrument to make such strategies more meaningful and convincing to those who will implement it.

When designing the M&E component of an e-strategy, methodological and institutional issues are paramount. The term methodology refers mainly to the tools that will be used to monitor

and evaluate progress at the various levels of the logframe pyramid and their expected results. The institutional and strategic context refers to the means by which these tools are best adapted to local constraints, thus encouraging "buy-in" on the part of the various stakeholders involved.

Policy goals and impact indicators

At the top of the strategy pyramid is the policy or vision that the e-strategy ultimately attempts to fulfill. The indicators by which such policy goals are measured are generally development-focused, pertaining to a country's economy and society as a whole. For example, a policy that seeks to expand a country's ICT sector to make it a leading factor in economic growth may choose to measure this objective by growth in GDP, total employment, or total productivity. Indicators at this level are considered *impact indicators*.

Impact indicators are often the most difficult to assess due to:

- *Time horizons.* Impact indicators are often only applicable after a considerable time lag, often years after the e-strategy has been launched. Due to this time delay, such indicators are seldom monitored on a regular basis.

- *Unclear causal links.* Establishing causality between e-strategy interventions and the changes in an impact indicator is difficult; many other factors come into play, making it hard to establish whether or to what degree an ICT intervention is responsible for change in an impact indicator. For example, GDP growth is clearly driven by a vast array of factors, of which the ICT sector is just one.

Strategic priorities and outcome indicators

Converting a policy or vision into tangible change on the ground requires choosing which initiatives to undertake and establishing goals for each particular initiative. This process also requires establishing indicators to track achievement of the core objectives and clarify the tangible outcomes. For example, if a country identifies growth of its ICT sector a policy goal, it will have to make choices among a number of potentially viable strategic objectives, such as:

- develop ICT infrastructure;

- develop high-bandwidth technology parks;

- encourage foreign direct investment (FDI) in the ICT sector; and

- increase the stock of locally trained ICT professionals.

Should a country choose to increase the stock of ICT professionals, it will require *outcome indicators* to assess its progress towards this objective. These indicators could include, for example, the number of people graduating from tertiary and professional education institutions or the number of people employed by the high-tech sector (the latter indicator could be segmented by domestic or foreign firms to provide meaningful data for FDI-related strategic objectives.). Outcome indicators are easier to monitor than impact indicators, as they are likely to show results over a shorter time horizon than impact indicators. Causality is thus somewhat easier to determine. However, it remains important to assess to what degree interventions are responsible for a certain outcome and what the outcome would have been had the intervention not occurred. In the above example, the stock of locally trained ICT professionals may only increase some time after the strategy is initiated, yet such a delay should not exceed more than a few years.

Key initiatives and output indicators

To meet strategic objectives, a number of distinct initiatives are undertaken. For each initiative, an e-strategy should identify specific a key deliverable, or *output indicator*. For example, increasing the number of qualified ICT workers will require a variety of initiatives, all of which will generate outputs or products measured in terms of quantity and quality. If we take the example of an objective such as 'increasing the stock of ICT professionals' (see Table 3.1 below), required interventions may include the following :

- improving the capacity of ICT-focused learning institutions;

- increasing demand for ICT education and training; and

- improving the quality of ICT education at the tertiary and vocational levels.

In addition to establishing output indicators, assessing the success or failure of these initiatives may require measuring the capacity, demand, and quality of ICT-focused education.[13]

Table 3.1 Output indicators for increasing the stock of ICT professionals

Models of Intervention	Characteristics	Issues
Improving the capacity of ICT-focused learning institutions, e.g., measurable improvement of teacher qualifications in such institutions and quantified support to teachers responsible for introducing computers in classes and curricula. Similar output for on-the-job training in the business sector	■ Increase the number of teachers and vocational schools trained in basic ICT skills and using ICT in teaching by X% ■ Increase in-service training of managers in the use of ICT in educational settings by X% ■ Increase the design and application of training programs and materials for in-service training staff by X % ■ Increase funding to specific institutions by X% ■ Increase number of professional teaching staff by X% ■ Increase number of students graduating by X% ■ Increase % of women graduates	■ Increase rating of graduate capabilities by private sector by X points ■ Increase rating of institutions by standards agency by X points
Increase demand for ICT education and training	■ Increase number of students applying to technical institutions by X%	■ Adapt secondary curricula to place greater emphasis on ICT-focused subjects
Improve quality of ICT education improved at tertiary and vocational levels	■ Form X number of partnerships with private sector ■ Form X number of partnerships with foreign institutions ■ Extend access to a full curriculum of distance	■ Include market-leading techniques and knowledge in curricula of tertiary and vocational educational institutions ■ Create an information environment that provides a range of ICT-based support ■ Establish hot-line services to support teachers and advisors in their use of hardware and

Aside from measuring the quantity and quality of outputs, initiatives should be assessed on how effectively they have been undertaken, both during and immediately after implementation. This process entails conducting periodic assessments of distinct initiatives, allowing the implementation team to understand areas of comparative strength on which the e-strategy can build further and, hopefully, incorporating these comparative advantages into other elements of the strategy. Periodic assessments also allow the team to address areas of relative weakness and make necessary adjustments, perhaps even bringing them to an early close. Mid-stream evaluation plays a key role in ensuring that a strategy is implemented well and that resources are spent efficiently. Ultimately, this helps ensure that a strategy meets its intended goals.

Actions and interim deliverable indicators

An e-strategy should present an overview of the actions involved in each initiative, as well as key milestones by which the progress of such actions can be gauged.[14] At this layer, indicators are *interim deliverables,* or sub-products, generated by each key task of the initiative. Such indicators track the progress of the project through its various stages and have shorter completion timeframes than impact, outcome, or output indicators. For example, building the capacity of ICT learning institutions requires a number of interrelated activities. These activities may comprise a single initiative or be part of separate initiatives aimed at a larger capacity-building objective. Depending on how a project is structured, activity indicators could include:

- assessing the capacity needs of higher educational and technical institutions, completing X percent of institutional assessments by month A;

- establishing a program to provide grant funding of amount $X to educational institutions by month B;

- disbursing X percent of grant facility funds to eligible institutions by month C;

- defining recruitment criteria for staff; and

- staffing X percent of institutions by month D.

Many initiatives undertaken as part of national e-strategies are related to creating institutions or building the capacity of those that exist. For example, an ICT infrastructure component may focus on establishing a regulatory agency to ensure an open and competitive telecommunications market. Monitoring and evaluating the success of this initiative should focus on the key elements of creating and operating a well-functioning organization. These elements can range, for example, from choosing and/or developing a physical location for the institution to its staffing to the sustainability of its financing.

Resources and input indicators

The resources required to undertake e-strategy projects and, ultimately, meet strategic and policy objectives, should be specified in the strategy. These *input indicators* take a variety of forms and can include institutional structures (e.g., mechanisms required to implement initiatives or supervise the strategy) and staff (often highly skilled professionals with expertise in ICTs as

well as in a specific area such as e-education or e-health). Financial resources are, of course, another key input. A clear understanding of required financing and the source of this financing is the basis for implementation.

Assessing the outputs of an e-strategy and, therefore, its success, cannot be done in absolute terms. It also requires integrating the resources dedicated to the strategy into the indicators themselves. For example, performance measures for an ICT business incubator may include the number of firms launched that are financially sustainable after a certain number of years. However, these indicators should also assess how many financially sustainable businesses were launched for a given amount of money invested.

The definition of required resources facilitates communication with regard to the e-strategy. Many e-strategy initiatives will have little precedent to go by, making it difficult for stakeholders to grasp the scale of required activities. Financial resource requirements, however, are the most basic means by which a variety of stakeholders can understand the scope of an e-strategy.

Assumptions and risks

ICT development is dependent on a number of factors over which the formulators of a national e-strategy have little control. Many of these factors relate to the political, economic and social environment in which the strategy exists. These environmental factors are often prerequisites, or assumptions, that strategists take for granted when developing targets and goals. The most general assumption is that a country will remain politically stable.

A change in assumptions on which a strategy is based will require re-evaluating its goals. Such a re-evaluation need not be negative. A strategy

Box 3.1 M&E requirements and costs

The coordination required for monitoring and evaluation costs money, time, and energy. It also creates new sources of conflict, such as turf battles and competition for power within organizations. In many respects, any coordination attempt initially exacerbates the difficulties it hopes to address. This may even be its only tangible result, unless an M&E effort receives adequate human, financial, and institutional resources.

Direct costs. The institutional *visibility* and perceived *neutrality* of an M&E team is important. The team may not require sizeable financial resources, apart from remuneration of staff. However, assigning junior or low-level staff to certain tasks may diminish the impact (and institutional commitment) of M&E efforts. M&E should not be an additional task thrown on management and staff; it should be assigned to a small but dedicated staff whose status should be firmly established at the initial stages of e-strategy implementation.

Training of relevant personnel is also crucial to the success of M&E efforts. The cost of such training can be significant and should not be underestimated. *Specific equipment and tools* (e.g., software) and, in some cases, external expertise, may also need to be acquired. When analyzing the cost-benefit ratio of such acquisitions, relevant authorities should consider possible externalities and economies of scale (e.g., it may be possible to share equipment for other management tasks).

Indirect (and hidden) costs. Achieving the buy-in of all relevant stakeholders in an M&E effort requires significant time, communication and training. Information and training sessions, for example, will need to be organized both at the level of ministries and specific departments. In many cases, the cost incurred will diminish over time as practices start to sink in and attitudes change. The use of on-line tools (e.g., self–training, shared information resources and M&E instruments) should minimize such costs. One of the major sources of indirect costs (and benefits) of a strong M&E effort is the re-engineering or re-sequencing of strategic tasks that such an effort will identify.

that focuses on ICT sector development for export purposes, for example, may assume an export market of a certain size with revenues of $X million. Should the market suddenly boom, however, the country may revise its revenue targets upward.

While many assumptions on which an e-strategy is based are outside the control of the strategy, this is not always the case at the component level. For example, ICT sector development initiatives may be dependent on the advancement of e-government programs, based on the assumption that the government will be a major source of demand for locally developed ICT products and services. Reductions or delays in e-government initiatives will therefore adversely impact the development of the sector.

Similarly, the ICT sector is dependent to a large extent on the establishment and enforcement of an intellectual property rights (IPR) regime to safeguard investments in knowledge-intensive products. Creation of an IPR regime may thus become a component of legislative reform. However, policy makers may choose to make the development and enforcement of an IPR regime a component of an ICT sector strategy, thereby wielding better control over the outcome of related initiatives and internalizing the risks associated with them.

Incorporating activities on which the success of an e-strategy is dependent into the strategy itself is one way to mitigate risk. However, the ability to do this is usually limited and such an approach is inadvisable, as the strategy will become excessively fragmented. Risk mitigation measures such as monitoring progress or change in certain key areas on which the success of the strategy depends may be all that can reasonably be done.

The institutional and strategic context of monitoring and evaluation

M&E mechanisms and institutions

All major initiatives of a national e-strategy must be clearly defined in the strategy. The strategy should also specify which agencies will take lead responsibility for each project and estimate the resources required to complete the projects. Unambiguously stating implementation responsibilities and resource requirements in a strategy increases the probability that the projects will actually be implemented. Alternatively, lack of clarity regarding project responsibility and budgets reduces the chances of strategy implementation.

The same reasoning applies to M&E activities. An e-strategy should clearly define the roles, responsibilities and financing of planned M&E efforts. The choice of institutions that will take primary responsibility for the M&E effort depends on the layer of strategy being addressed and existing national M&E capacity.

In general, as one moves down the strategy pyramid from the apex to the base of the logframe pyramid (see figure 3.4), the location of M&E activities should move closer to the agencies responsible for project implementation. In some cases, there may be an existing agency that can take primary responsibility for M&E-related activities, while in others, a team may have to be established for this purpose. Selecting the agency that will take lead responsibility, or alternatively, deciding where to locate a new M&E team, should be done in a way that balances ownership, access and capacity.

- *Ownership.* M&E activities are conducted to inform and guide e-strategy decision making and implementation and to encourage the accountability and transparency of public institutions. Agencies responsible for the implementation of e-strategy objectives should view M&E information-gathering and analysis as an integral component of their work and develop a sense of ownership for that component. Should M&E be conducted by an external agency, there is a risk that the agency will be perceived as an external auditor. It may then face resistance that will impair its ability to gather data and information and, even worse, encourage parties responsible for implementation not to act on M&E findings. The benefit of being able to make adjustments and improvements to an e-strategy mid-stream would therefore be lost.

- *Access to data.* The ability to conduct good M&E is dependent on access to data. Gathering and analyzing national data can be effectively done by a national organization. (This applies more to policy and strategic objectives, that is, to impact and outcome data). Some of this data may be the responsibility of a National Statistical Office (NSO) or a line ministry. For example, an NSO may

Table 3.2 Responsibility for M&E at each level of the logframe pyramid

Pyramid Layer	Objective	Indicator	Responsibility for Gathering and Analyzing M&E data
Policy goals	Expand the country's ICT industry	■ Total sector revenues ■ % contribution to GDP growth	NSO or Ministry of Trade and Industry
Strategic priorities	Increase stock of locally trained ICT professionals	■ Number of people graduating with ICT-related qualifications ■ Number of people employed in ICT sector	Ministry of Education
Key initiatives	Improve capacity of ICT-focused learning institutions	■ Increase funding of educational institutions by X% ■ Increase number of professional teaching staff by X% ■ Increase graduates by X%	Ministry of Education or Project Team
Actions	■ Conduct capacity needs assessment ■ Create grant program ■ Establish staff recruitment	■ Complete assessments of X% of institutions by month A ■ Establish fund to provide grant funding by month B	Project Team

have data on the growth of the ICT sector (a policy objective), while a ministry of education may have information on the number of locally trained ICT professionals (strategic objective). Lower down the pyramid, relevant M&E data is more likely to reside in the project team responsible for implementation.

- *Capacity leverage*. The most efficient means to conduct M&E activities may be to leverage the capacity of established M&E agencies and institutions, such as National Statistical Offices (NSOs). However, depending on the country, little data may exist on ICT access and use and analytic capabilities in this area may not be developed.[15]

It is clear that the institutional location of the team responsible for formulating and discharging M&E responsibilities will have a significant impact on its ability to do so. On one hand, the operational entities involved in the e-strategy should not see the team as a remote judge and censor. On the other hand, if the team is too close to implementation tasks, it runs a distinct risk of becoming both judge and juror and will lose its credibility.

To perform efficiently, an M&E team also needs to derive its legitimacy from the highest levels of government. This means that it must be supported above the level of specific ministers involved in the strategy.[16] It will also need to exercise its responsibilities in a visible and transparent manner. The pre-existing institutional framework of a given country and the work habits of its government, business and civil society will largely determine whether a centrally-located government unit is created or a more flexible network of individuals involved in the e-strategy is established. Whatever the case, the work of the M&E team must be based on highest technical and methodological standards.

Conclusion

Considered a central part of national development strategies, e-strategies have the potential to stimulate many changes in the way governments, businesses and other stakeholders function and contribute to growth, competitiveness and development. However, to achieve their potential, e-strategies must not be designed (or implemented) in isolation from other strategies and policies that address fundamental development priorities (e.g. health and education). Rather, they should be conceived as a means to pursue such development objectives, including those of transparency and good governance.

Finally, such strategies must incorporate monitoring and evaluation components at the earliest stages of design and implementation. Only M&E will allow a country to measure progress made, assess the efficiency with which resources are being used and take corrective action as required. E-strategies conceived within this context will take full advantage of local and global digital opportunities, as well as international experience and best practice, to address the major challenges of development and poverty.

Notes

[1] Article 8 of the WSIS "Plan of Action" states that the "[d]evelopment of national e-strategies…should be encouraged by all countries by 2005." See WSIS, "Action Plan," WSIS, International Telecommunications Union, Geneva, Switzerland, 2003.

[2] Chief among these efforts are the European Union's "e-Europe Initiative," the G-8 Digital Opportunity Task Force (DOT Force), the United Nations ICT Task Force (UNICTTF), and the process surrounding the World Summit on Information Society (WSIS).

[3] A recent survey carried out by the Development Assistance Committee (DAC) of the OECD underlined the remarkably small proportion of Poverty Reduction Strategy Papers (PRSPs) mentioning ICTs. See OECD. 2004. "Role of Infrastructure in Economic Growth and Poverty Reduction—Lessons Learned from PRSPs of 33 Countries." DCD/DAC/POVNET(2004)16, OECD, Development Co-operation Directorate, DAC, Paris.

[4] See, for example, K. McNamara. 2004. *Information and Communication Technologies, Poverty and Development—Learning from Experience.* Washington, DC: *info*Dev, GICT Department, World Bank.

[5] Not to mention the significant impact that causal linkages would have on the ability of countries to benchmark their efforts against one another.

[6] Capacity building at the local and national level is a priority. Considering the expected cost of such efforts, coordination at the international level (such as that advocated by members of the "Partnership on Measuring ICT for Development" launched during the June 2004 UNCTAD XI meeting) is likely to attract increasing attention.

[7] In a number of cases, one can consider such efforts excessive or, at the very least, redundant: 55 countries have been assessed for e-readiness at least 5 times and 10 countries, at least 8 times. See bridges.org. 2005. "E-Readiness Assessment: Who is Doing What Where." Updated February 28, 2005, Cape Town, South Africa and Washington, DC, http://www.bridges.org/ereadiness/where.html. One of the positive outcomes of the over-abundance of assessments is a significant improvement in the approaches and methods used, especially with respect to the specific characteristics and needs of developing countries. Such improvements were necessary to address concerns about "one-size-fits-all" and "e-readiness for the sake of e-readiness" policies. See, for example, Choucri et al. 2003. "E-readiness for What?" MIT Working Paper, MIT, Cambridge, Massachusetts. The paper points out that: "A wide range of studies on e-Readiness, undertaken over the past several years, constitutes the 'first generation' in our understanding of e-Readiness. These are pioneering efforts and have begun to chart unknown terrain. Their contributions are commendable. But, as with all pioneering efforts, these studies are fraught with uncertainties and ambiguities in both theory and practice and lack robust foundations for empirical analysis. As such, they provide little guidance for business and government, thus obscuring the realities as well as the opportunities. For example, current e-Readiness studies and attendant indices assume a fixed, one-size-fits-all set of requirements, regardless of the characteristics of individual countries or the demands for specific applications. Most e-Readiness studies provide little information on how their indices were constructed and why, or how they might be adjusted to analyze particular e-Business opportunities."

[8] Digital divide here refers to disparities among various groups of the national population, for example, between urban and rural areas.

[9] Security concerns have received increasing attention in the recent past. Such concerns are no longer restricted to digital signatures, encryption, consumer protection or intellectual property issues. Topics such as cyber-crime, identity theft, phishing and spam are progressively finding their way into e-strategies. E-security is thus expected to be addressed as a separate item in future editions of the World Bank toolkit for evaluating the results of e-strategies (METER, see figure 3.3).

[10] In order to reach the targets set by the MDGs, countries can either increase the resources they allocate to specific objectives, or increase the efficiency with which they use available resources. At the core of the discussion about ICTs and the MDGs is the question of whether ICTs can assist countries to achieve the MDGs more efficiently.

[11] See annex 2 for a list of the 50 national and regional e-strategies that were reviewed by the authors of the METER toolkit.

[12] If a country adopts a policy objective (e.g., "to become a knowledge society within twenty years" or "to stimulate the growth of the national ICT sector") various strategic goals will need to be articulated to assess progress towards this objective. Such goals could include, for example, providing primary education to 80 percent of a class age by a certain date or generating a certain percentage of national income through the ICT sector by a certain date.

[13] Appropriate indicators will be both quantitative and qualitative.

[14] This is particularly important in the case of ICTs, as many proposed initiatives will be unfamiliar to policy makers and reviewers. Details of the actions required to implement such initiatives will make the initiatives more tangible and, therefore, comprehensible.

[15] Building the capacity of National Statistical Offices is clearly a priority for future M&E activities related to e-strategies. This objective is complementary to the current efforts of such institutions as the ITU and World Bank to maintain worldwide databases on connectivity and ICTs. Capacity-building efforts will require significant financing. One way to optimize the use of resources and available knowledge is to enhance coordination and cooperation among various multilateral agencies. This is precisely the purpose of the "Partnership on Measuring ICT for Development" that was launched during the UNCTAD XI meeting in June 2004 by the ITU, OECD, UNCTAD, UNESCO's Institute for Statistics, the U.N. Regional Commissions (UNECLAC, UNESCWA, UNESCAP, UNECA), the U.N. ICT Task Force and the World Bank. See the website of the UNCTAD E-commerce Branch, "Measuring the Information Society: ICT Indicators for Development," UNCTAD, Geneva, http://measuring-ict.unctad.org.

[16] The issue of 'e-leadership' is addressed in the next chapter.

Chapter 4

The Elusive Quest for E-Leadership

What can we learn from the champions?[1]

by Bruno Lanvin

The search for internationally replicable best practices in e-strategies[2] often leads to two central questions: What is the single most important success factor in designing and implementing e-strategies? What is the main obstacle that prevents e-strategies from (fully) succeeding? When asked these two questions, a remarkably broad majority of decision makers, managers and implementers involved in e-strategies gave the same response: leadership.[3]

Among the factors that explain the importance of leadership in the design and implementation of e-strategies are:

• No specialist in any one policy area or social sector naturally emerges as a leader recognized by all organizations involved in an e-strategy.4 Strong leadership is thus necessary to transcend the unavoidable differences of views (and possible conflicts) among these component organizations;

• Leadership is also vitally important to overrule possible resistance to change and, more importantly, to communicate a vision that offsets the loss of particular interests by increased collective benefits to the community. Any agenda for change should expect to meet resistance at all levels, which will be proportional to the interest and/or powers affected by the implied changes; and

• The presence of a leader is also critical because the fast pace of technological evolution increases the uncertainty of e-strategies. This implies that many stakeholders and e-strategy players will be expected to take a leap in the dark. Under such circumstances, a leader has the responsibility for articulating a vision that is credible and inspiring in its principles and priorities, even if its details, modalities and implementation change over time.

For all these reasons, the e-agenda is a contentious one, making e-leadership a vital ingredient for success. The concept of e-leadership has, in fact, emerged more from practice than theory. Over the last decade or so, a certain number of countries, regions and cities become success stories in e-readiness and e-competitiveness. When one attempts to identify what these success stories have in common, the recipe for success seems to be an e-leader.

How is an e-leader different from a leader?

An e-leader is either a leader who has proved able to adapt to the challenges of the '*e-world*', or someone who has emerged as a leader because he or she helped a community address the challenges of the '*e-world*'. Both kinds of e-leaders have contributed to driving the e-agenda. In some countries, such leadership has been provided mainly by institutions (e.g., Singapore, UK, Tunisia); in others, largely by consensus (e.g., Finland, Switzerland, Ireland), and in still others, by personal engagement (e.g., Estonia, Bolivia, Mozambique, Senegal). Certain border cases have combined these elements (e.g., USA, France, Italy).

With few exceptions, however, the process that led to the emergence of an e-leader has generally been heuristic, providing few easily identifiable best practices. Much of what e-leaders have learned appears to have been learned on the job, with experience progressively becoming their best asset. For this reason, the present chapter relies on a series of interviews that were conducted with internationally recognized e-leaders, that is, individuals who, by choice or fortune, have played a significant role in moving their respective countries and regions along the path to successful ICT sectors, information services and e-strategies of various kinds.[5]

IT affects both the functions and roles of government

The advent of information-intensive societies and networked economies has affected the roles of government leaders in at least three major ways. It has (i) changed the functions and roles of government,6 (ii) empowered new segments of societies, and (iii) globalized the policy agenda.

On one hand, ICTs have been instrumental in changing the ways in which governments and administrations operate. Informatization, decentralization and the advent of e-government all reflect the impact of ICTs on how governments function. On the other hand, the information revolution has encouraged and enabled governments to accept new roles. In addition to traditional government roles in such spheres as economic and social policy, education, diplomacy, defense and justice, ICTs have prompted governments to articulate a vision of major socio-economic change and to facilitate this change by example. At the same time, civil society has become an organized player in local and global issues, globalization has become a major force in world affairs and new market efficiencies have arisen. The elements of this new context of governance are summarized in Figure 4.1.

IT has deeply changed the way in which government functions, for example, through office automation and the growing ubiquity of Web-based services. The advent of e-government and e-procurement, in particular, has allowed greater transparency and accountability across governmental agencies. To some extent, these applications have even pushed governments and their leaders closer to "real time" management, that is, indirect, but more continuous, management, frequently intermediated by IT. One danger of this management is that governments may be tempted to make online services (which citizens can use and appreciate immediately) a priority, instead of longer-term and less visible efforts to increase government efficiency via back-office

Table 4.1 The relationship of ICT to the role and functions of government

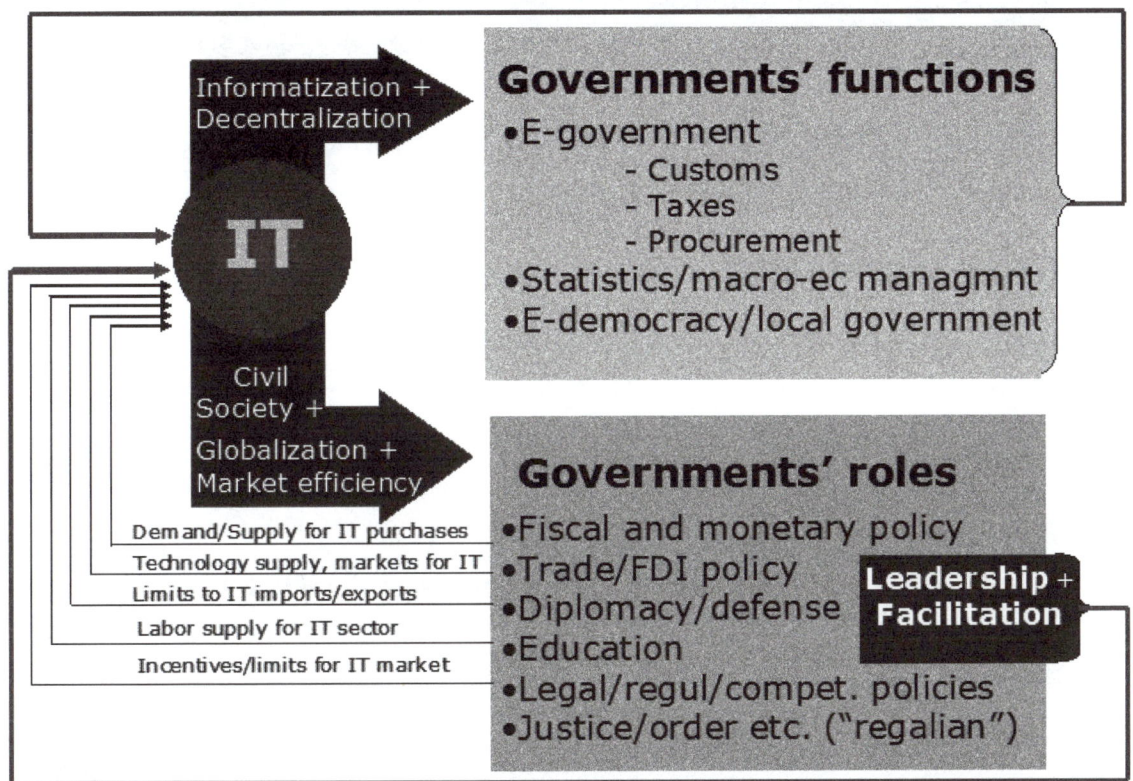

Demand for IT solutions/leading through example

Informatization + Decentralization

IT

Civil Society + Globalization + Market efficiency

Demand/Supply for IT purchases
Technology supply, markets for IT
Limits to IT imports/exports
Labor supply for IT sector
Incentives/limits for IT market

Governments' functions
- E-government
  - Customs
  - Taxes
  - Procurement
- Statistics/macro-ec managmnt
- E-democracy/local government

Governments' roles
- Fiscal and monetary policy
- Trade/FDI policy
- Diplomacy/defense
- Education
- Legal/regul/compet. policies
- Justice/order etc. ("regalian")

Leadership + Facilitation

E-strategy, national ambition/social project pursued through IT

Source: Lanvin, "Leaders and Facilitators," 2003.

re-engineering. Leaders of e-strategies have to maintain an appropriate balance between these two sets of objectives.

IT has had an even more significant impact on the role of leaders (and, consequently, e-leaders) by changing the roles of governments. In all types of economic systems, governments around the world have tried to directly influence the determinants of ICT supply and demand. Governments exert such influence less and less as producers (or buyers), and more and more as facilitators, seeking to create the proper environment for innovation and growth in ICTs and

to mobilize financial and human resources for the ICT sector. Government leaders have accordingly established ICT as a national priority, provided a national vision of network readiness, launched large ICT projects and accelerated the adoption of ICTs by government departments. It is the ability of e-leaders to combine these two roles—leading and facilitating—that allows them to become "champions."

Using a two-dimensional graph (see figure 4.2 below) in which the vertical axis denotes growing leadership and the horizontal axis, growing facilitation, one can ideally represent five areas in which governmental e-leadership has a critical role to play. These roles (and corresponding sets of activities) are to provide access (G1), an enabling environment (G2), an ICT-friendly education policy (G3), vision (G4) and e-government applications (G5).

Access (G1)

In the past, building fixed infrastructure has generally been the responsibility of national monopolies. Often, these monopolies also produced terminals and various switching equipment for the telecommunications network. Research and development were often publicly subsidized, or carried out through large public projects, both civil and military.[7] More recently, public projects have continued to be important in China, Korea (broadband roll-out), Malaysia (Multimedia Super Corridor) and Singapore (Singapore One), although such projects often involve public-private partnerships. Where large government initiatives are undertaken, they generally span the whole spectrum of ICT environment, ICT readiness and ICT usage.

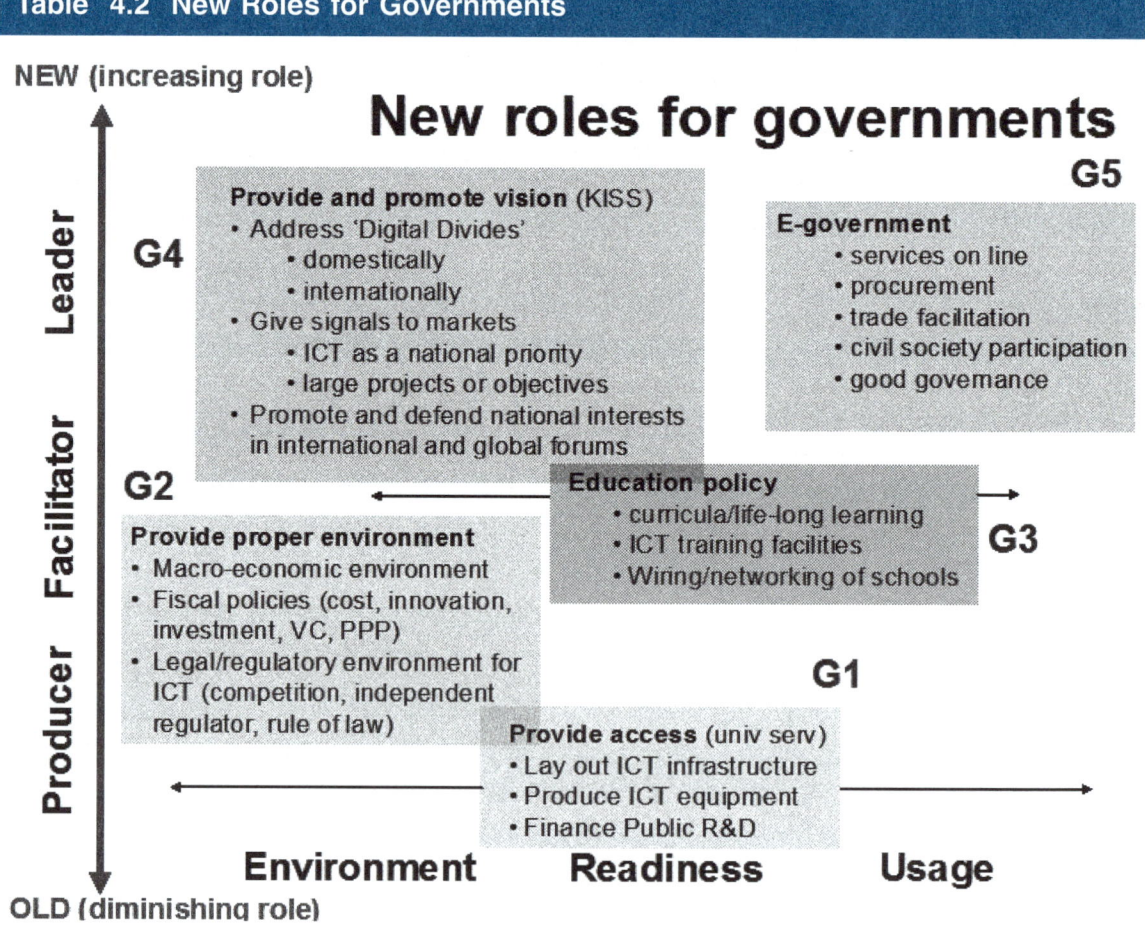

Table 4.2 New Roles for Governments

Source: Lanvin, "Leaders and Facilitators," 2003.

> *"The ideal e-leader?* *The younger the better, as a young person won't see a dichotomy between the terms "leader" and "e-leader. It will be only a matter of time until the young generation, which grew up with computers and the Internet, will be in leadership positions. For them, this won't be an issue anymore. Meanwhile, one can qualify who is willing to adapt to the challenges presented by technological innovation.*"
>
> Markus Kummer, former E-Envoy
> of the Swiss Government

Enabling environment (G2)

Providing a macro-economic, legal and regulatory environment conducive to economic growth and development is a traditional responsibility of governments (see chapter 2). In the digital age, however, these functions imply new responsibilities specific to the ICT sector, such as spectrum management. "Environmental" tasks thus have significant spillover effects on e-readiness. Their effects on usage are not necessarily tangible in the absence of e-government applications.

Education policy (G3)

Providing the right amount and quality of human resources for a network-ready economy is closely linked to the long-standing involvement of governments in education. In this area, the emergence of a digital economy requires original approaches. For instance, changes in basic and advanced education curricula (see chapter 6) require that schools be adequately equipped

and connected. Constant changes in technologies and applications also require that life-long learning and vocational training capacity be established. Although most enterprises consider education policy to be an "environmental" or e-readiness measure, the business sector can enjoy significant benefits from this policy should, for example, a country adopt a national policy of equipping and connecting schools.

Vision (G4)

Large public initiatives in the area of ICT, as well as governments' ability to provide a society-wide vision of ICT development, differ from traditional public infrastructure programs financed by governments (G1). In the area of ICT, the role of governments as "vision providers" cannot be underestimated. It is the nature of the budget allocation process to pit different ministries and departments against each other. It is thus important that ICT be established as a priority at the highest levels of decision making, not simply at the level of an IT ministry.[8] Providing an overall vision of ICT development (G4) overlaps other, more traditional roles of governments, such as ensuring social justice and equity through universal service programs.[9]

> *" What is the ideal profile of an e-leader? Experience? Position? Origins? Training? Profile?. . . These things are not important. What is really important is that he/she be open and ready to change him/herself, that he/she should be curious and interested to learn.*"
>
> Mart Laar, former Prime Minister of Estonia

Another new aspect of this group of governmental responsibilities is the growing importance of global issues. Governments increasingly find it difficult to address ICT issues without considering their global underpinnings. This is the case for intellectual property (e.g., WIPO and WTO treaties and agreements), Internet governance (ICANN) and norms and standards (e.g., ISO, ITU, W3C). Last but not least, over the last few years, governments have taken a leading role in formulating international plans of action to bridge the digital divide and create digital opportunities for all.10 Although such broad initiatives are not expected to generate massive amounts of external financing in the immediate future, their importance should not be underestimated, as international initiatives often constitute the "think tanks" that generate the guiding principles on which future actions and international agreements are based.

E-government (G5)

The last group of new governmental responsibilities is very closely linked to e-usage objectives. By promoting the use of ICTs in its own services (i.e., e-government), a government can acquire

> " E-leadership is the capacity to see the potential of ICT for development and the capacity to use it both as tool for change and as a tool to deliver better services to the large majority. It is the commitment to advance even when the constraints are very large. It is also the ability to create a common vision between all stakeholders. "

Lidia Brito, former Minister of Higher Education and Research, Mozambique

> " One thing one learns to do in the private sector is to observe closely what your competitors are doing, and to be quick in adopting emerging best practices. In Italy, the implementation of various components of a national e-strategy benefited from knowledge ... of the experiences of several other European countries, such as the United Kingdom (especially with regard to the importance of stimulating usage, rather than just increasing the number of government online services) and France (for example, facilitating students' ability to acquire a computer). "

Lucio Stanca, Italian Minister of Innovation and Technology

both experience and credibility, while leading through example. By focusing initially on activities that can generate significant savings, governments have been able to broaden the legitimacy of ICTs and generate important externalities. For example, online procurement, trade facilitation and customs automation not only generate resources, but enhance transparency in specific government operations, thus contributing to the fight against corruption, This specific externality may even encourage foreign investors to participate in a country's network readiness efforts. Offering government services online with some degree of interactivity also strengthens the democratic process by engaging individuals and civil society in public-sector activities and reforms.

" *E-leadership is not fundamentally different from leadership. Since ICT is only a tool and not an end in itself, the objective of an e-leader must be to use ICT to generate change. In the public sector, such change could mean a change of model; in the business sector, it could mean a change of product, for example. An e-leader is hence a person who can drive such a change; to do so, he/she must have a clear idea of the change to be implemented (some would call it a vision), and be able to communicate the reasons why such a change is desirable.* "

Lucio Stanca, Italian Minister of

IT changes the structures of power

It has been expected that increasing reliance on ICT networks by both private and public organizations would empower younger people. Extensive social science and business literature has, in fact, focused on the nature, extent and consequences of this power shift.11 Much of the academic debate has focused on whether or not the 'e' in e-development was displacing the locus of leadership. Such a possibility has important consequences both at the micro- and macro-economic level. For example, the development of virtual teams across national borders requires specific management abilities.

The international dimensions of outsourcing, however, have significant economic and social consequences. Efficient e-leaders must be able to master both dimensions. For example, a few years ago a leader (whether in business or government) could joke about his or her ignorance of information technologies. Today, the concept of an "e-illiterate" leader would no longer be acceptable.

IT contributes to the globalization of national policies

Because information is the most internationally mobile factor of production, and because information networks have a natural (almost organic) tendency to spread across national borders, ICTs have contributed to a rapid acceleration of globalization, resulting in a growing inter-relationship between domestic and regional and/or global policy issues. This phenomenon has necessitated a reshuffling of policy agendas in all countries. Outsourcing, for example, began with information-intensive services such as call centers, but rapidly spread to other economic sectors.12 In such a complex political and intellectual framework, no up-to-date textbook can guide the actions of leaders and managers. Rather, the abil-

" *The public sector is a much more complex environment, with a different time scale. In the public sector power, is not enough, a leader needs to invest time and effort to convince rather than just instruct and command. Negotiating skills are key.* "

Lucio Stanca, Italian Minister of Innovation and Technology

> " *E-reforms depend on good coordination, which is not possible when the coordinator does not have enough authority.* "
>
> Mart Laar, former Prime Minister of Estonia

ity of e-leaders to look around and find inspiration in the examples of others, as well as their ability to make and explain decisions against the background of global trends, has become the key to their effectiveness.

Driving the e-agenda

In some cases, traditional leaders have proved capable of becoming e-leaders. In other cases, e-leaders have emerged from other circles to replace or complement existing leadership. In still other situations, countries and e-strategies are waiting for a leader to emerge.

> " *To a large extent, this kind of leadership can only be established through experience, and experience includes success and failure, excitement and frustration. With hindsight, maybe, I would have invested more time in politics in the early stages of my ministry. It took me time to realize that technical competence was only a part of the equation.* "
>
> Lucio Stanca, Italian Minister of Innovation and Technology

What have e-leaders brought to the e-agenda so far? In their own judgment, and that of a number of observers, their input has been critically important in three major areas: vision, change management and communication.

Vision

In the face of globalization, as well as significant changes in citizens' everyday lives (e.g., employment uncertainties, cultural changes, etc.), a leader is currently expected to provide future-looking guidance and adhere to clear principles, providing citizens a minimum level of predictability, and thus psychological comfort, on which to base their own decisions. Such a role is particularly important whenever change accelerates.

In the field of ICT and information-intensive services, change is a way of life. As the intensity of ICT usage continues to increase total output, employment and affect virtually all aspects of

> " *A national e-strategy always reflects the underlying political structures of a country. In a centralized country with a strong executive office, the decision of a political leader to put a new issue such as a national e-strategy on the political agenda can make a difference. There are many success stories in countries where political leaders have embraced ICTs and adapted government policy to the new technological environment.* "
>
> Markus Kummer, former E-Envoy of the Swiss Government

people's daily lives, it is vital that a leader be able to formulate an overall vision of e-development. Such visions should, however, refrain from portraying all benefits as future-oriented and all changes as positive and beneficial. Successful e-leaders have been able to generate visible and positive change in the short term as they worked to bring about longer-term structural changes, but they have never ignored the downside of the vision that they were proposing.[13]

Managing change

One major difference between the field of ICT and that of most other human endeavors is the pace of change, from fundamental research to it's the application of this research in everyday life. It is hence no surprise that applying the potential of ICTs to any area of human activity will result in significant and cumulative changes in the way individuals and communities operate and

"I should have been stronger in organizing and controlling the project management ... IT-projects start to live their own life and create delays due to bad management."

Errki Liikanen, former EU Commissioner for Enterprise and Information Society

interact. It is a law of nature and of organizations that when changes occurs, resistance to change also occurs. Such resistance can come from the top (where people's authority, ability to control and legitimacy is challenged) or lower hierarchical layers (where people may encounter higher levels of job insecurity, such as when new skills must be acquired or more efficient processes are implemented). In such situations, it is the role of an e-leader to articulate a set of core values that help various stakeholders understand the cost and benefits of such changes.[14]

"In countries with decentralized government structures, there are many different levels of decision making. Switzerland, for example, has a strong tradition of subsidiarity and delegating decision-making power to the lowest possible level. A national e-strategy will therefore have to include all levels of decision making in order to be successful. This bottom-up cooperation, based on a shared political approach, is not necessarily fast, but it has led to good results."

Markus Kummer, former E-Envoy of the Swiss Government

"We can learn a lot from civil society. Their increasing importance in international cooperation to a large extent is due to their networking techniques through the Internet. Their distributed decision-making process and their culture of dialogue can be seen in many ways as new partnership models that can inspire all of us."

Markus Kummer, former E-Envoy of the Swiss Government

" A good e-leader must be able to assess risks and opportunities and be an enthusiastic agent of change. He must also be a good communicator, a good listener, and have the ability to be respected by his government colleagues, his fellow politicians (in cities, regions) and the private sector, whose role is key in the ICT field. "

Lucio Stanca, Italian Minister of
Innovation and Technology

One pitfall that e-leaders should avoid when managing change is to ignore or underestimate the inertia and rigidities of the public sector. Coordination remains essential, however, e-leaders must also have sufficient power and authority to implement decisions across multiple government departments.

Communicating with and engaging civil society

From an institutional point of view, most modern nations are significantly more complex than traditional nation-states. On one hand, local governments have taken on growing importance in the management of national objectives. On the other, civil society as a whole, including the private sector, has accepted—sometimes demanded—increasing responsibility in formulating and pursuing national objectives. E-leaders therefore must communicate their vision across multiple layers of society, often in very different institutional, cultural and political contexts.[15]

Can e-leadership be taught?

Based on practical experience, it appears that the answer to this question is a qualified yes. By and large, successful e-leaders have all embraced the objectives of conveying a vision, overseeing its implementation as a change management process and communicating the vision to relevant stakeholders. These three dimensions lend themselves well to the identification of best practices and knowledge sharing. Other fundamental principles outlined earlier, such as linking an e-agenda to a nation's fundamental development agenda

" Common to all attempts to define the term is the notion that e-leadership is about operating in a new environment and adapting leadership techniques to that environment ... The good e-leader makes the best possible use of the opportunities offered by ICTs. The key words in this regard are sharing of information and knowledge and empowering subordinates to cooperate actively and efficiently in these emerging new structures, which are networks rather than the traditional hierarchical leadership structures ... the successful e-leader is more a coach or mentor, someone who convinces rather than gives instructions and tells subordinates what to do. "

Markus Kummer, former E-Envoy
of the Swiss Government

and avoiding excessive involvement in technology issues, relate as much to traditional leadership as to e-leadership and can also be codified and disseminated as knowledge:[16]

Other aspects of e-leadership are, however, less amenable to codification and have to be learned on the job. Successful e-leaders are not shy about recognizing their mistakes and are eager to correct them when they can. Many e-leaders interviewed for this chapter noted that there was no substitute for experience, observing that failure was often the only way to learn. These leaders were eager to listen to others' point of view, while remaining enthusiastic about their own tasks. In addition, they sought to adapt their approaches to local conditions and to grasp opportunities when they arose, rather than to force change.

Conclusions

The fundamentals of e-leadership are not radically different from those of leadership in general. Certain differences exist, however, regarding the relevant chain of command and ways of reaching out to specific stakeholders. Common points and differences between the two types of leadership are summarized in table 4.1.

" an e-leader needs mostly to be a person willing to learn, sometimes to unlearn and learn again, because ICT brings major changes in the work culture, transparency, accountability, and the capacity to reach citizens. An e-leader must also be capable of inspiring people and taking actions that convince more and more people to support the processes of change. We need leaders with different kinds of experience, in different positions, coming from all sectors of society and from different professional profiles, because e-strategies should be people-centered and an important tool for the development of the society in general."

Lidia Brito, former Minister of Higher Education and Research of Mozambiquet

Table 4.1 Circumstances and tactics of leaders and e-leaders

Issues	Impediments
Pyramid organizations	Flat (virtual) teams, multiple organizations
Command	Convince
Demonstrate good practice	Find/adapt best practice
Public monopolies	PPPs (new business models)
Inspire/influence (vision)	Inspire/influence (vision)
IT an "extra" (specialty knowledge)	IT as basic knowledge
Communication with stakeholders preferred	Communication with stakeholders is essential
Agent of change	Agent of change

The experience of e-leaders interviewed for this chapter offers several practical lessons in e-leadership:

- The ability to listen is a key to efficiency. E-strategies are complex and multi-sectorial endeavors, in which no leader can claim exhaustive knowledge or competence. Gathering advice from government (central and local), business (large and small) and civil society is essential to allow e-leaders to make strategic choices and maximize the possibilities of buy-in by all stake holders;

- There is no "one-size-fits-all" approach to e-leadership. Fresh thinking will always help, and it may need to come from outside the government. Governments may find inspiration abroad in best practices or in the experiences of civil society, various government agencies and local governments at home;

- Linking local objectives to global trends and concerns safeguards against parochialism and obsolescence. Developing countries and the international community may find it particularly important to explore possible linkages between national e-objectives and internationally agreed development objectives such as the MDGs;

- Technological neutrality and technological knowledge are not incompatible. E-leaders have to be e-literate, but they must stay above the fray by encouraging e-strategies and not e-tactics. There is more than one technological response to any socioeconomic objective; e-leaders should not attempt to second-guess the market or base their decisions on technical solutions that may soon be outdated; and

> _" Leadership is the critical factor in the public sector [due to] lack of market pressure or market incentives. The adoption of ICT requires major changes in administration and processes. Without strong leadership, the bureaucracy always fights back and defends the administrative legacy. ICT projects will then end up maximizing costs and minimizing benefits. "_
>
> Errki Liikanen, former European Commissioner for Enterprise and Information Society

- Last but not least, e-leaders should not underestimate the elements that have allowed successful information societies to thrive: strong independent regulators, competition (which drives prices down and enhances access) and private-public partnerships.

In the end, e-leaders will be judged more on what they have done than what they have encouraged. To a large extent, e-leaders must lead by example. No e-leader has put it more clearly than Errki Liikanen, former European Commissioner for Enterprise and the Information Society, _"If the top is not working in the way they teach, no change will take place."_

Notes

[1] 'Champions' refers here to the governments recognized as having succeeded in turning ICT into an instrument of reform, growth and development. The term also conveys a meaning of advocacy, referring to the ability of individuals at higher levels of government to 'champion' such objectives, and convince various stakeholders of the value of their vision of what an information society should be. Various countries have adopted different approaches about creating such leadership, some creating 'e-envoys', others pusuing a 'Central Information Officer" approach, whereby a personality - often nominated from the private sector- is given high visibility and, sometimes, significant powers to promote a national e-strategy. One could valuably argue that, to implement e-strategies, leadership is required at many different levels of implementation. This chapter focuses on the critical role that top government leaders have played and can play in that context.

[2] See Chapter 3.

[3] The surprising part of this reaction was the response to the second question. Respondents did not answer "lack of leadership," but "leadership." In other words, leadership is considered a given. On one hand, the presence of supportive leadership is a critical factor in the success of certain e-strategies. On the other hand, the failure of some e-strategies can be explained by unsupportive leadership, rather than the absence of leadership. This point will be discussed later in this chapter.

[4] E-strategies are by nature multidimensional and multisectoral. They typically combine one or several policy goals (e.g., building a competitive knowledge society) with social and economic goals (e.g., stimulating the involvement a less densely populated region in a national economy or enhancing the trade competitiveness of a given country). Such strategies also involve a number of sectors, including education, health, justice, telecommunications, transport and tourism. See chapter 3 for more details.

[5] E-leaders interviewed for this chapter include Mart Laars, former Prime Minister of Estonia; Lidia Brito, former Minister of Higher Education and Research of Mozambique; Lucio Stanca, Minister of Innovation of Italy; Erkki Liikanen, former EU Commissioner for Enterprise and Information Society , currently President of the Central Bank of Finland; and Markus Kummer, former "E-Envoy" of Switzerland.

[6] A fundamental difference exists between the functions and roles of governments. The functions of governments correspond to what is delivered by governments once their roles have been defined and accepted. The roles of governments correspond to the missions with which governments have been entrusted by a democratic process, or which they themselves have selected or a higher authority has given them. For example, promoting social justice would be a role, whereas tax collection would be a function. For a lengthier discussion of these issues, see the following article, on which this sub-section is based: B. Lanvin, "Leaders and Facilitators—The New Roles of Governments," in *Global Information Technology Report 2002–2003* (Geneva: World Economic Forum, *info*Dev and INSEAD, 2003).

[7] As in the case of DARPANet, a U.S. Department of Defense project that laid the groundwork for the Internet.

[8] The same analysis applies to all levels of government, including local (e.g., regions, states, municipalities) and supra-national. The success of the European Union in launching certain technology programs (e.g., Eureka) has often been attributed to its ability to transcend such internal budgetary obstacles.

[9] When pursuing such objectives, governments must keep track of recent technological developments, as such developments may significantly affect the relative cost of the solutions selected. For example, mobile telephony and WiFi have considerably enhanced the possibilities for providing telecommunications access to rural areas.

[10] More noteworthy initiatives include the G-8's Digital Opportunity Task Force (DOT Force), which was created by the Okinawa Summit of 2000, and the World Economic Forum's Digital Divide Initiative, which was initiated a few months earlier. Multilateral institutions (e.g., the ITU, UNDP, World Bank) have also contributed to this effort, either through their regular work or through special bodies, such as the United Nations ICT Task Force.

[11] See, for example, B. Avolio, S. Kahai and G. Dodge, "E-Leadership: Implications for Theory, Research and Practice," *Leadership Quarterly* 11, no. 4 (2000):615–68; R. Hargrove, *E-Leader: Reinventing Leadership in a Connected Economy* (Cambridge, Massachusetts: Persesus Publishing, 2000); and D.Q. Mills, *E-Leadership: Guiding Your Business to Success in the New Economy* (Paramus, New Jersey: Prentice Hall Press, 2001).

[12] Discussions about the values conveyed by the proposed European constitutional treaty (especially in countries in which a national popular debate took place, such as France and the Netherlands) are one of the most recent examples of this spill-over effect.

[13] In some cases, changes in the e-side of societies are compounded by other rapid changes: being an e-leader in a transition economy of Eastern or Central Europe in the 1990s was certainly not an easy task. On the other hand, an "e-vision" in this region has the power to transcend some of the debates on societal change, especially if it is linked to an "upgrading process," such as joining the European Union. In such a context, the importance of the so-called "Lisbon approach" (with its e-Europe component) should not be underestimated. The experiences of Estonia or of the Slovak Republic come to mind in this respect.

[14] "Recognizing that people who need to cooperate are often separated by a gulf of potential divergent interests and potential mistrust, the best one can do is try to identify and promote a set of values to which most of the organization seems willing to conform." D.Q. Mills, *E-Leadership,* 2001.

[15] Communicating e-objectives and e-strategies is not limited to articulating the pros and cons of specific ICT applications and relating them to social and economic objectives, it sometimes requires addressing much more fundamental concerns, such as the fear of "Big Brother" (government intrusions on individual privacy). Concern over the misuse of private data, for example, caused France to create the *Commission national de l'informatique et des libertés* in 1978. The Commission has since been replicated in a significant number of other countries. (The *Loi relative à l'informatique, aux fichiers et aux libertés,* which underpins the work of the Commission was significantly updated in August 2004, see http://www.cnil.fr/index.php?id=301) (last accessed 28 July 2005).

[16] During the Spring of 2005, the World Bank Institute and a core group of external partners (private and public) organized a workshop around the issue of capacity building in e-leadership. Initial responses have been highly positive, making it likely that efforts will be pursued along those lines.

Chapter 5

The Basic Building Blocks of e-Government

by Randeep Sudan

Electronic government (e-government) is broadly understood as the use of ICTs by government to enhance the range and quality of government information and services provided to clients in an efficient, cost-effective and convenient manner, while making government processes more accountable, responsive and transparent.[1] The "e" in e-government is expected to eventually wither away as "government" rather than technology is at the core of e-government.

E-government applications can be useful tools for improving governance and the quality of life of citizens. Although not a digital-age panacea for government ills, e-government potentially offers a number of compelling benefits, including better-quality government services, increased citizen satisfaction, higher efficiency, reduced costs, a lower administrative burden, shorter processing times and reduced rent-seeking on the part of government employees. Such benefits can far exceed the costs of e-government applications and can thus justify corresponding investments in technology, provided that such projects are carefully identified and implemented.

In developing countries, the problems of poverty, hunger, deprivation and disease are so pressing that e-government almost seems to be a luxury that poor nations can ill-afford. As Bill Gates, Chairman of Microsoft Corporation, asked a conference on the digital divide in 2000, "Do people have a clear view of what it means to live on $1 a day?"[2] To a poor person struggling for existence, ICTs are at best irrelevant. When it comes to governments, public funds are both scarce and fungible. A dollar spent on ICT can well be spent on providing food or tackling disease.

ICTs are not merely expensive, they are also complex. The record of e-government projects in both developed and developing countries has thus been mixed. A survey conducted by Richard Heeks of the University of Manchester in 2003 found that 35 percent of e-government initiatives were total failures in developing and transitional countries, 50 percent were partial failures and only 15 percent were successes.[3] While the methodology used to arrive at these figures can be questioned, it must be noted that the e-government landscape includes impressive achievements, but also monumental failures.

Recent news stories on e-government projects in developed countries reveal that failures are also not uncommon in advanced industrial nations. The e-University project in the United Kingdom, for example, a joint venture between the government, universities and Sun Microsystems, was shelved in 2004 after spending £50 million for a mere 900 students.[4] The House of Commons Select Committee on Work and Pensions, in its assessment of an IT and telephony system of the Child Support Agency (UK) observed that the IT solution was "clearly over-spec, over-budget and overdue".[5] The Irish government made an investment of •50 million to introduce e-voting for local and European elections in June 2004, but abandoned the idea after a report of the Independent Commission on Electronic Voting raised doubts about the software.[6] The U.S. Federal Bureau of Investigation spent $170 million on a Virtual Case File System before it was determined that the system met only 10 percent of the FBI's own requirements for searching and accessing documents across all of its offices.[7]

While these examples should make us cautious, it would be wrong to dismiss e-government as prohibitively expensive or pointless. Chile is reported to have achieved savings of 7 to 10 percent on government purchases by using an e-procurement application.[8] In the Indian state of Andhra Pradesh, use of the e-Seva (e-Services) network allows citizens to access multiple government services across one counter. As of April 2005, transactions on e-Seva averaged 3 million a month.[9] In contrast to Ireland, Brazil successfully introduced an electronic voting system, deploying 406,000 electronic voting machines in October 2002 to register the votes of 115 million citizens.[10]

E-government readiness

While embarking on e-government many developing countries are keen to know what are the key areas that they should be focusing on to achieve success. One approach is to look at e-readiness frameworks and focus on those aspects that would make them more e-ready.

A number of e-readiness frameworks compare countries in terms of indicators that are aggregated into one overall value, which is then used for rankings and comparisons. *The Global Information Technology Report (GITR) 2004–2005,* for instance, ranked Singapore as the top networked economy according to a "Networked Readiness Index." Other public indices developed to measure ICT development include the World Bank Institute's Knowledge Assessment Methodology and the Knowledge Economy Index; Orbicom's index of "Infostates"; the Economist Intelligence Unit's e-readiness rankings and the ITU's Digital Access Index.

While most e-readiness frameworks deal with ICT development, the UN has constructed a composite index specifically for "e-government readiness" that combines indices for the Web, telecommunications infrastructure and human capital. Based on these indices, the United States is most e-government ready, followed closely by Denmark, the United Kingdom, Sweden and the Republic of Korea.

The methodology for measuring e-government readiness against a set of quantifiable, comparable variables suffers from a number of shortcomings. Leadership, organizational capacity, e-government architecture, financial resources, public-private partnerships and the regulatory environment are important elements in our view for e-government success, but are not captured by measures of Web presence, telecommunications infrastructure and human capital. It is difficult to measure and rank leadership for example, across countries in any meaningful way. Similarly, measuring organizational capability in precise terms is very challenging. E-government readiness frameworks while useful in focusing attention on some important parameters for success miss out on a range of other elements that do not lend themselves to quantitative measurement. We therefore present in this paper some of the basic building blocks for e-government that are often missed as part of readiness frameworks.

As developing countries begin adopting e-government, there is a tendency to focus on a few showcase applications that visibly demonstrate success and spur increased use of ICTs in individual departments. A few quick projects, even on a limited scale, can have a good demonstration effect and provide a launching pad for more ambitious projects. While such an opportunistic approach has much to commend itself in the short term, it is also important for e-government initiatives to focus on certain overarching issues crucial to long-term success.

This paper accordingly focuses on three key aspects of e-government. Firstly it spells out the importance of taking a "whole of government" cross-cutting approach while dealing with e-government, as often a narrow sectoral perspective can result in unnecessary duplication and waste. Secondly, the paper examines the entry points for developing countries with regard to e-government. It dwells on some of the limitations of evolutionary approaches and demonstrates how leap-frogging is possible. Finally, it focuses attention on the immense potential of m-government in developing countries, where the rapid proliferation of mobile phones offers an oppor-

tunity that has not been adequately seized by governments, for providing better access to information and services to citizens.

A "whole of government" approach

Governments are typically organized as a series of vertical silos in the shape of individual ministries, departments and directorates. Citizens and businesses consequently must deal with a daunting array of government entities, each with its own hierarchy, procedures and processes. ICTs potentially offer the possibility of dealing with government as a single entity by cutting across diverse organizational boundaries. To achieve such integration, a "whole of government" perspective must be kept in view when developing e-government applications. It is also important to have a cross cutting approach to economize on investments in services, infrastructure and applications development.

When the state government of Andhra Pradesh (India) decided to use electoral registration as a platform for a citizen database in the mid-1990s, it entrusted the work of digitizing the data to individual districts without defining a proper framework to standardize data across the state. In the absence of proper standards for capturing caste data for example, each district adopted a different approach and the government ended up with more than 28,000 caste categories in its database, when there were only 457 castes in the state. The cleaning up of this database proved to be a tedious and expensive exercise. Similarly in the absence of centralized coordination, when the state's Revenue Department began to build a citizen database, the Department of Health was building a comparable database in parallel. The Planning and Forests Departments were likewise found to be simultaneously digitizing maps of the state for GIS applications. Using common base maps instead, would have been far more economical.

When developing vertical e-government applications within individual departments, it is therefore important to think horizontally and organize IT governance structures accordingly. Some of the cross-cutting issues that need to be addressed include, the legal and regulatory framework, organizational structures for e-government, development of IT architecture, interoperability frameworks, provision of shared services and infrastructure, monitoring and evaluation systems and financing models including public-private partnerships. Legal and regulatory frameworks are explored in detail in chapter 2. This chapter will focus on other "whole of government" issues that are relevant to e-government applications.

Organizational structures

E-government is a major transformational exercise in change management. The European Commission argues that strong political leadership is needed for e-government applications "in order to overcome resistance and barriers, to change mindsets, to push through organizational change, to sustain investment, and to keep the long-term perspective in mind while insisting on concrete deliverables in the short term."[11] As the quality of political leadership is a given, it is important that developing countries establish organizational structures for guiding and facilitating the process of e-government.

It is of course difficult to prescribe an organizational framework that will work in all countries. However, a central coordinating agency can use scarce resources efficiently, avoid duplication of effort and provide government departments and agencies with technical advice on e-government. Many countries have established a governmental Chief Information Officer (CIO) and/or ICT agencies to perform the multiple organizational tasks needed to successfully deploy e-government applications, including:

- ICT strategies and policies;
- ICT governance;
- ICT architecture, standards and interoperability frameworks;
- Shared infrastructure and services;
- Unified procurement; and
- Strategies for common business applications.[12]

The examples that follow illustrate the range of organizational structures that have been used to implement e-government solutions.

Australia. Australia created a National Office for the Information Economy (NOIE) in 1997. The office was reorganized and renamed the Australian Government Information Management Office (AGIMO) in March 2004. At that time, functions relating to policy, research and programs were transferred to the Department of Communications, Information Technology and the Arts (DCITA). An Office for the Information Economy was created within the DCITA to present Australia's views on the information economy in international forums and to manage research and analysis.

AGIMO is headed by a CIO and focuses on promoting and coordinating the use of ICTs to deliver government programs and services. The agency reports to the Minister for Communications, Information Technology and the Arts and is tasked with developing standards to integrate services across agencies, developing e-procurement processes and managing the AusTender system. The office promotes "whole of government" telecommunications arrangements and volume software sourcing arrangements, is currently developing an e-government authentication framework and manages Gatekeeper, the Government's accreditation system for certifying digital signatures.[13]

While NOIE originally combined all three functions of policy, standards, and implementation support, these functions have now been split between two agencies: policy issues being transferred to the DCITA, and the remaining functions to AGIMO.

Singapore. Singapore established an Infocomm Development Authority (IDA) as a statutory board when it merged the National Computer Board and the Telecommunications Authority of Singapore in December 1999. IDA functions under the Ministry of Information, Communications and the Arts and is divided into five clusters that focus respectively on policy and competition development, industry, technology, government systems, and corporate development. While the policy function remains with the Ministry, IDA is now responsible for setting standards and providing implementation support.

United Kingdom. The UK previously established an Office of E-Envoy, which has now been transitioned to an E-Government Unit. The Head of e-Government is accountable to the Minister for the Cabinet Office and reports directly to the Cabinet Secretary. The country also has an e-Minister, who is responsible for e-government policy, while issues relating to standards and facilitation are vested in the E-Government Unit, which is tasked with:

* fulfilling public service agreement targets for electronic service delivery of the existing Cabinet Office;

* defining and driving implementation of a government-wide information systems strategy;

* defining architecture, requirements, and standards, as well as being the intelligent customer, for common government infrastructure and services;

* providing leadership and guidance to the government IT community; and

* acting as the Central Sponsor for Information Assurance.[14]

Hong Kong. Hong Kong established the Office of the Government Chief Information Officer (OGCIO) in July 2004, which centralized responsibility for governmental IT projects. The OGCIO was created by merging the functions of the former Information Technology Services Department and the IT-related divisions of the Communications and Technology Branch of the Commerce, Industry and Technology Bureau. The 640-strong OGCIO now deals with IT policy, strategy formulation and the implementation of pan-government IT initiatives. Hong Kong has also established a high-level e-government Steering Committee, chaired by the Finance Secretary, to coordinate interagency implementation.[15]

South Korea. In January 2001, South Korea formed a Special Committee for e-Government under the Presidential Commission on Government Innovation. The committee is charged with coordinating interagency collaboration across government and has oversight over major e-government initiatives. It reports directly to the President and by virtue of this connection, exercises great influence across various units of government.

Institutional approaches

The institutional framework within which the ICT agency is embedded is extremely important. In some countries the ICT agency reports to the Ministry dealing with ICT. Typically the Ministry for ICT is one among the many ministries in the government. Any attempt to impose standards or influence budgets and procurement by the Ministry/ICT agency is immediately perceived as a threat to the hegemony of individual ministries. In the absence of institutional mechanisms to draw on support from political leadership at the top, this can result in severely emasculating the effectiveness of the ICT agency. The potential benefits from a "whole of government" approach cannot be realized in this scenario.

Countries like South Korea and Sri Lanka have established institutional frameworks whereby the organization dealing with ICT has an organic link with the office of the President/Prime Minister. In the case of the US, the Office of Electronic Government is part of the Office of Management and Budget[16] and consequently exercises clear oversight with regard to ICT across the federal government through budgetary mechanisms.

At the risk of being prescriptive, it is important that institutional mechanisms be put in place to ensure that there are strong linkages between the ICT agency and the top political leadership as also with processes for budgetary control, in order to make the organization effective.

E-government architecture

One of the key lessons from the implementation of e-government initiatives is the need to avoid an "agency-centric" or "silo" approach to the use of ICTs. Avoiding such an approach requires an overarching architecture that can guide the development of applications across various ministries, departments and government agencies. The absence of such an architecture can lead to sub-optimal results and, often, conflicting and incompatible applications.

Enterprise architecture consists of four broad components: business architecture, information architecture, solutions architecture and technical architecture.

Business architecture. Developing an enterprise-wide architecture for government involves taking a detailed look at how a government is organized and identifying the various functions it performs. Such a functional analysis simplifies the complexity of government by breaking it down into its component elements. This process can be useful in re-engineering processes and developing applications that cater to the same function in more than one department or agency. Budgetary codes are often also aligned with functions as part of this process.

Information architecture. At the next level, information flows in the government must be mapped. The mapping exercise determines the type and ownership of data elements in use and provides a basis for deciding how to network and store this data. For example, if there is a need for synchronous access to a common database from geographically dispersed locations, data must be centralized.

Solutions architecture. At the third level, e-government specialists design meta-data repositories and define the components that can be reused across government. For instance the CORE.gov initiative in the US allows sharing of components that have been tested, approved and certified for reuse and enhancement.[17] The adoption of service-oriented architectures (SOAs) requires a deep understanding of business processes within and across agency lines so as to decompose them into services and then design and build services for reuse. This approach is consistent with the principle that public funds should be spent only once to develop a piece of software. An application for computerization of salaries of government employees for example, can be re-used by human resource systems in different government departments or agencies.

Technical architecture. Finally, at the fourth level, e-government specialists develop the technical standards for hardware, software, networks and security to ensure system interoperability. Data dictionaries also must be defined to ensure data interoperability.

The full benefits of ICT can often be derived only upon re-engineering of existing processes rather than by their mere automation. An Enterprise Architecture for e-government can play an important role in this regard. It was found by a study done jointly by McKinsey & Co. and the London School of Economics that use of IT alone by manufacturing companies did not yield significant benefits unless accompanied by sound management practices.[18] This conclusion is equally valid for e-government.

Developing an e-government architecture can be a complex and challenging exercise. While developing countries will require considerable time and effort to develop the overall architecture for e-government, there is an immediate need for them to define and commit to an interoperability framework for technical architecture.

Interoperability frameworks

An interoperability framework must not only be established, but adhered to by the different government entities that participate in e-government applications. According to the European Commission, "interoperability is not just a technical issue of linking up computer networks: it also concerns organisational issues, such as coordinating processes that not only span intra-organisational boundaries, but also interwork with partner organisations that may well have different internal organisation[s] and operations."[19]

Technical platforms built on open standards can greatly facilitate the integration and interoperability of applications across government. For example, the Finnish government proactively sends pre-filled tax proposals to citizens by post. A taxpayer has roughly one month in which to respond. The computerized tax system requires a high degree of integration of the back offices of various agencies, including 136 tax offices, 5 ministries and central agencies, 20 banks and other financial institutions, 20 social insurance agencies and pension foundations, about 100,000 stable employers (and an equal number of occasional employers), 10 trade unions, and 150 foundations, universities and research institutes.[20]

The European Union has developed a European Interoperability Framework for pan-European e-government services that deals with organizational, semantic and technical interoperability.[21] The German government has adopted a Standards and Architecture for e-Government Applications (SAGA) document for influencing the adoption of interoperability standards by vendors and government technical staff. The UK has developed a sophisticated e-government Interoperability Framework (e-GIF), which sets out the technical policies and standards to ensure interoperability of systems that deliver e-services. Compliance with e-GIF is mandated widely across the U.K. public sector. The United States has introduced a Federal Enterprise Architecture that includes both a data and a technical reference model for ensuring interoperability of applications developed by different parts of the federal government.

A number of approaches have been adopted for ensuring compliance with interoperability frameworks. In some cases as mentioned earlier, financing of e-government applications is centralized and, consequently, the ICT agency oversees adherence to common standards. In a somewhat different approach the E-Government Unit of the UK, has established an e-GIF Accreditation Authority.

The Authority is operated by the National Computing Centre and its subsidiary, the Institute of IT Training, under contract to the E-Government Unit. The e-GIF Accreditation Authority takes up accreditation of both public and private sector organizations, and also undertakes certification of skills.[22] There is a view that this approach has not been as effective and there is a need to place the E-Government Unit under the Chancellor of the Exchequer to ensure that every project is compliant with e-GIF.[23]

Prioritizing e-government applications

Given the financial constraints faced by developing countries it is important that resources spent on e-government are spent in the most judicious manner. This requires an objective methodology for prioritizing e-government applications across different ministries and departments.

IT investments in the private sector are justified using quantitative methods, such as the payback period, net present value, internal rate of return and economic value-added. It is difficult, however, to use these methods in government. The outcomes and benefits of government projects are not merely financial—they often produce positive externalities, such as improved education, technology adoption and higher employment, which also should be measured. While the private sector can envision employee layoffs as a result of deploying ICT applications, such an approach would be all but unthinkable for most governments. The price of e-government services is also difficult to determine through market mechanisms, as there is no real competition for such services.

A number of governments have developed evaluation systems to address these concerns. The Australian Government Information Management Office, for example, has developed a demand and value assessment methodology for assisting agencies to develop transparent and auditable assessments of proposed online government programs. Demand assessment starts with the end-user, determining the nature of citizens' needs and how they can best be served. It moves on to quantifying demand and defining a clear strategy to respond to this demand. Value assessment typically centers on costs and benefits, including intangible benefits and the implications for governance.

The Gartner Group defines the public value of IT as "measures that demonstrate how IT-related changes and investments contribute over time to improved constituent service level, operational efficiency and political return."[24] These returns include elements such as greater citizen participation, bridging the digital divide, economic impact, greater government accountability and more effective policymaking.[25]

The United States uses a Performance Reference Model (PRM) as part of its Federal Enterprise Architecture. The PRM mandates strict measurement criteria, including at least one indicator from four measurement areas: mission and business results, customer results, processes and activities, and technology.

Most methodologies for prioritizing e-government projects have been designed for use in developed countries yet should be adaptable to the needs of developing countries. An objective methodology for prioritizing e-government projects can help focus governments in these countries on the results and outcomes of public investments in such projects.

Provision of shared services and infrastructure

Developing countries can save scarce resources by taking a "whole of government" approach to shared services and infrastructure. The advantages of this approach lie in the aggregated economies of scale and the ability to negotiate from a stronger position. Cost economies in shared services can be significant in high volume transaction areas such as finance, accounting and HR. A good example of shared services in government is the Queensland Shared Services Initiative in Australia[26] which adopts a "whole of government" approach to services that include Finance, Procurement, Human Resources, Document and Records Management, and Property and Facilities Management.

Sharing of infrastructure assets including networks, data centers and e-services gateways can also minimize public investments in ICT. A common e-services Gateway for example, can provide cryptography services for authentication and authorization. The Gateway can also provide payment services that can avoid the complexity of implementing individual payment mechanisms by each government department.

New approaches are emerging that leverage government requirements for ICT infrastructure to achieve larger e-society objectives, while minimizing government costs. The state government of Andhra Pradesh provides an illustrative example of this approach. Andhra Pradesh is one of the larger states in India, with a population of 80 million and an area bigger than the United

Kingdom. In the late 1990s, the state adopted Vision 2020, which identified information technology as an engine of growth and a means of improving governance. One of the first projects of the state government was to establish a statewide area network that connected state headquarters with key government offices in 23 districts. UTL, a private-sector company, was entrusted with the project on a BOOT (Build Own Operate Transfer) model.

At the end of the project period, the state government decided to leverage its own need for bandwidth to facilitate a state-of–the-art network that would provide high speed connectivity across the state, including for its 21,000 villages. The all-IP network would offer a bandwidth of 10 Gbps between state headquarters and the districts, 1 Gbps between the districts and 1,127 mandals at the next administrative level, and at least 100 Mbps to each of the 21,000 villages in the state. The shift to an all-IP network was expected to dramatically reduce costs for broadband services.

In order to catalyze the network, the state government offered to become an anchor client of the network for a fixed annual fee. It also took an equity stake in the network and offered free rights of way to the company that built the fiber optic network.[27] The bidding process was conducted in a way that minimized the government's contribution to equity, reduced the cost of bandwidth and maximized coverage and rollout speed. At the end of the bidding, it was established that the network would cost US$90 million, of which government would contribute US$5.7 million in equity and pay a fixed annual fee of US$2.8 million for bandwidth for its 40,000 offices. The cost of bandwidth for citizens would be as low as US$7 per quarter for downloading 100 megabits of data.

The outcome of the bidding process brought together companies with complementary strengths.[28] Interestingly, when BSNL, a government-controlled telecommunications company with the most extensive fiber optic network in the region, was first approached about the project, it quoted an annual cost of US$2.3 billion for such a network.[29]

Public-private partnerships

Many developed countries are making substantial investments on e-government applications. In the United States, for example, government spending on IT in fiscal year 2004 was estimated at US$59.1 billion[30]. According to IDC, by 2008 Europe will spend US$4.2 billion each year on e-government projects.[31] The UK will, for example, increase IT spending on e-government from US$828 million in 2004 to almost US$1.2 billion by 2008. Germany's expenditure on e-government will grow from US$985 million to more than US$1.4 billion over the same period.[32] And Hong Kong has spent an average of US$589 million on e-government for the last three years.[33]

Developing countries lack sufficient resources to adequately fund e-government initiatives and also lack in-house expertise and project management skills. These countries should therefore actively explore possibilities for working in synergy with the private sector when implementing e-government projects. Public-private partnerships can leverage limited government funds to achieve far greater impact, apart from improving the viability and reducing the risks of such initiatives. Of course, governments must carefully negotiate the terms of public-private partnerships to avoid special privileges accruing to the private sector, while at the same time providing private partners with adequate incentives.

The boundaries between the public and private sectors are blurring, allowing for numerous partnership possibilities. For example, the service of providing a certificate of residence in Austria involves partnerships with the private sector, including Austria's largest mobile phone provider (Mobilkom), for user authentication.[34] In Denmark, a citizen's portal was developed and is operated by a private company that is fully owned by the central organization of Danish municipalities.[35] In India, the government portal of the state of Andhra Pradesh was created as a joint venture between Tata Consulting Services (TCS) and the state government.[36]

In the United States, the State of Arizona has successfully partnered with IBM (with Ezgov, KPMG Consulting and Qwest as sub-contractors) to create a state portal. IBM met part of the upfront cost and provided support for infrastructure and application development. In return, the company receives subscription fees, convenience fees and transaction fees from e-government services provided through the portal.[37] Hong Kong used a public-private-partnership for its Electronic Service Delivery (ESD) Scheme. The private-sector operator is responsible for developing, financing, operating and maintaining the ESD system, while the government is required to pay transaction fees to the operator after transactions cross a certain threshold level. The private-sector operator is also permitted to use the ESD information infrastructure to generate revenues from advertising and private sector e-commerce. The model minimizes the business risk for government and provides clear incentives for the private sector operator to offer enhanced quality services, as well as to promote their wider use.[38]

Applications in e-procurement offer many examples of public-private partnerships. The Chilean model of Chile Compra, for example, is operated by a consortium that includes Sonda, Microsoft and Hewlett Packard[39]. Mexico was an early adopter of online procurement in 1996, with CompraNet[40]. It is now looking at revamping the system, based on a business model that allows the private sector operator to charge user fees in return for its investment.

Public-private partnerships can be facilitated by adopting a "whole of government" framework for such partnerships. The US 'E-Government Act of 2002' for instance provides for "share-in-savings" initiatives and even an employee exchange program with the private sector. The government of Québec has created a new state entity that specializes in public-private partnerships: the Agence des partenariats public-privé du Québec.[41] Created in May 2005, the Agency advises the government on public-private partnerships and offers its expertise to public bodies to conduct PPP feasibility studies, select partners and negotiate, conclude and manage partnership contracts.

Monitoring and evaluation

A monitoring and evaluation (M&E) framework must be a integral part of the design and implementation of any e-strategy (see chapter 3), not an *ex-post facto* "add-on" merely to analyze the success or failure of an e-government program. Elements of a monitoring and evaluation framework can often be incorporated into the design of an e-government application. For example, the number and type of transactions taking place on a government portal can be captured in real time, together with feedback from users on the quality of online services. Another approach is to create a third party to oversee quality standards. China, for example, has experimented with third-party supervision of e-government projects.[42]

Table 5.1 (following page) illustrates a monitoring and evaluation framework for e-services. Since e-services relate to different government departments and agencies, the framework adopts a pan-government view. While it is important to have sectoral/departmental mechanisms for monitoring and evaluation in place, it is also important to have a more macro level perspective when it comes to dealing with the e-government agenda.

The framework also underscores the importance of institutional arrangements for making the CIO's office effective so that it becomes easier to acquire and act on information relating to different government entities in a timely and effective manner.

Open source software

This paper has taken the position that a "whole of government" approach is important while dealing with e-government. However, it is equally important not to go over-board with such an approach and over centralize decision making. We would like to illustrate this point using the example of open source software.

Open source software (OSS) refers to software programs whose source code is made available for use or modification by users or other developers. The distribution of open source software must comply with certain criteria that guarantee its transparency and non-proprietary exploitation.[43] Open source software is perceived to offer significant potential cost savings, greater flexibility and the prospect of a more rapid scaling up of applications.

Significantly, a number of commercial OSS providers have emerged, including Red Hat, SuSE, MySQL, Sleepycat and Sophos. At the other end of the spectrum, companies like Microsoft have

Table 5.1 Illustrative monitoring and evaluation framework for delivery of e-government services

Pyramid Layer	Objective	Indicator	Responsibility for Gathering and Analyzing M&E data
Policy goals	Create an efficient, responsive and transparent government	■ Perception of overall administrative burden ■ Perception of government effectiveness	Office of Government and Ministry of Local Government
Strategic priorities	Offer cost-effective online government transactional service anywhere anytime	■ Perception of government online services ■ % government agencies with transactional sites ■ % government agencies online (by agency)	E-government CIO's Office
Key initiatives	■ Create online versions of offline services (to cut costs and redeploy resources more efficiently) ■ Raise public awareness through online and offline channels. *Examples: ID cards, certifications (death, birth, marriage, divorce), land ownership titles, registrations (automobiles, change of ownership), public procurement (tenders), tax and fine collection*	■ Number of online services ■ % of possible services that are online (by agency) ■ % of total customers transacting online (per service) ■ Usage growth rate (per service) ■ Time to complete transaction (per service)	E-government CIO's Office
Actions	■ Establish guidelines for selecting online services ■ Establish mechanism for interagency coordination and system integration ■ Assess technology and organizational needs ■ Develop online transactional platforms, integrating with interactive and informational platforms ■ Address the concerns of government workers whose roles will change ■ Provide necessary feedback and possible training ■ Build confidence in security and privacy ■ Develop publicity campaign to promote new e-government ■ Solicit feedback on usability and usefulness of online government services ■ Benchmark processing times for individual services and transactions criteria	■ Guidelines for selection established by month A ■ Relevant services identified by month B ■ Interagency mechanisms and procedures established by month C ■ System functional requirements completed by month D ■ Mid term implementation review conducted by month E ■ Staff and user training complete by month F ■ Public satisfaction survey results ■ Disburse X% of grant funds to eligible institutions by month C ■ Staff X% of institutions by month D ■ Effectiveness of demand-side subsidies in encouraging take-up of broadband services	Project team or Central M&E unit

launched a Shared Source Initiative to enable sharing of proprietary source code with customers, partners and governments.

OSS is being increasingly used by governments of developing nations. Chile, for example, has been deploying open source extensively in schools with the Edulinux system.[44] The Extremadura region of Spain has been promoting Linex, a local software bundle consisting of an operating system, desktop software and other applications.[45] The French government agency ATICA (Information and Communication Technologies Agency) recommends OSS for at least some applications being developed for government.[46] The European Commission has included a preference for OSS as part of its e-Europe policy[47], although this preference has proven controversial. (The EU's public procurement directives require technology neutrality in purchasing decisions).[48]

Venezuela however, presents an example of a highly centralized approach to the use of OSS by mandating its use in public administration since December 2004.[49] Venezuela's approach of prescribing OSS by government fiat in our view is perhaps not the best one. Developing countries need to carefully balance the benefits of OSS (openness, flexibility and source code availability) with its challenges (OSS skills and support) by creating an environment that levels the playing field between commercial and open source software.

OSS will have greater chances of acceptance as a grass-roots movement, than as the implementation of a grand scheme. Take the case of an initiative started in France by the Association of Developers and Users of Open Source Software in Administrations and Local Communities (ADULLACT). Founded in 2002, ADULLACT currently encompasses more than 80 local authorities in France, 20 associations and more than 50

service companies. In less than three years ADULLACT has rallied a number of local authorities to its goal of encouraging the adoption and development of open source software by local authorities. The server running its development environment is available free at www.adullact.net. The number of projects developed by the ADULLACT community now exceeds 160.

"ADULLACT was an initiative taken by a group of local authorities, not a requirement superimposed by national policy. This has been a key factor in further aggregation and growth."[50] A flexible and pragmatic approach needs to be adopted while going about e-government so as not to quell innovation and enterprise.

The U.K. policy on the use of open source software within government provides a possible model for developing nations. According to the policy, the "U.K. Government will consider OSS solutions alongside proprietary ones in IT procurements. Contracts will be awarded on a value for money basis."[51] Similarly, Australia's strategy for e-government service encourages "trials of open source software within the framework of fit-for-purpose and value-for-money,"[52] while recognizing that OSS offers opportunities for innovation, cost savings, greater sharing of IT systems and improved interoperability. This is a far more sensible approach as compared to a "whole of government" requirement mandating OSS adoption.

Launching e-Government

Evolutionary approach

Developing countries often grapple with where to begin with e-government. One approach has been to look at e-government as an evolutionary process: governments can begin their journeys with simple applications and move to more complex applications through a series of phases. One of the most widely used frameworks for understanding e-government evolution is the four-phase model developed by the Gartner Group (a research and consulting firm specializing in ICT): presence, interaction, transaction and transformation.[53] Each successive phase involves increasing cost and complexity.

At the risk of simplifying the Gartner model, while the presence phase involves providing information through web sites, the interaction phase allows for the downloading and submission of forms.[54] The transaction phase graduates to services like electronic payments and the transformation phase is "characterized by redefining the delivery of government services by providing a single point of contact to constituents that makes government organization totally transparent to citizens."[55]

The benchmarking survey of online public services in the European Union classifies online public services into the four stages of information, one-way interaction (downloadable forms), two-way interaction and transaction (full electronic case handling).[56] The survey found that in the case of the European Union, only 40 percent of the public services were fully transactional online.[57] The United Nations *Global E-Government Readiness Report 2004* uses a five-stage typology of emerging presence, enhanced presence, interactive presence, transactional presence and networked presence.[58]

These models of the phases of e-government assume a linear progression towards more sophisticated services. Technological development, "disruptive" technologies and the possibilities of forging partnerships to leapfrog certain phases can, however, complicate the calculus of such a progression.

Entry point examples

Evolutionary models of e-government do not adequately capture the complexities of the real world. Priorities, conditions and constraints differ between countries, making it simplistic to reduce e-government to a uni-dimensional process. As the examples below demonstrate, e-government entry points vary considerably across countries and do not strictly follow the evolutionary path discussed above. It is possible for developing countries to leapfrog into higher stages of e-government without going through the evolution defined by such models.

Often, a good e-government entry point is a department that is widely perceived to be corrupt and inefficient. Corruption thrives on the monopoly enjoyed by government functionaries to dispense certain services and influence, delay or stall decision-making processes.[59] E-government can minimize contact between citizens and government functionaries and introduce speed and transparency into decision making, effectively reducing, if not eliminating, corruption. Unfortunately, evidence suggests that corruption can continue to thrive despite computerization (see box 5.1).

The examples below drawn from different countries illustrate e-government entry points in increasing order of sophistication and complexity.

Mexico. Mexico used the Internet to achieve better citizen participation in its planning process, undertaking a major public consultation exercise for the drafting of the country's 2001–2006 National Development Plan. A formal mechanism was put in place to ascertain citizen's opinions, proposals and expectations on 110 national issues. The Web page set up for this purpose extended the possibilities of participation, spurred the registration of opinions and permitted the

Box 5.1 Computerization and corruption

The Government of Andhra Pradesh launched its CARD (Computer-aided Administration of the Registration Department) initiative in 1998. Prior to computerization, employees of the department were known to drive citizens to private 'Document Writers' by continuous requests for additional information to seemingly address 'errors' in documents. The 'Document Writers' wrote property sale and related agreements on official stamp paper, secured the registration of documents for their clients and collected bribes on behalf of the staff of the Sub-Registrar's office. Citizens were kept in the dark about the correct registration and stamp duties to be paid by them and had to depend on the 'Document Writers' for this information. Following computerization it was found that while the time to register a document came down from eight to three days, there was no impact on information transparency, staff behavior and the payment of bribes to secure document registration.

Source: Jonathan Caseley, "Public Sector Reform and Corruption: CARD Façade in Andhra Pradesh", Economic and Political Weekly, 2004, Vol.39, Issue 11, pages 1151-1156.

submission of 43,000 proposals from Mexicans living abroad.[60]

Argentina. Argentina used the Web to introduce greater transparency in the devolution of public funds. The 1999 Fiscal Responsibility Law of Argentina requires that citizens have access to information on the administration of public funds. The Argentinean government accordingly set up the CRISTAL website in February 2000 (http://www.cristal.gov.ar) for this purpose. Information is provided not only on the funds allocated to different programs, but on how these funds are administered. The site had initial problems stemming from inadequate information, but was re-launched and attracted greater usage. The site is subject to external audit by Fora Transparencio, a body of 15 non-governmental organizations.

Karnataka (India). Karnataka is one of the southern states of India, known best by its capital city of Bangalore. The government of Karnataka's first major success in e-government was the Bhoomi project, which computerized 20 million records of land ownership pertaining to 6.7 million farmers. The project made it much easier for farmers to obtain copies of the Record of Rights, Tenancy and Crops (RTC), enabling them to sell and inherit land and take advantage of agricultural credit. Savings in bribes previously paid to village accountants to issue RTCs was estimated at over US$18.3 million annually,[61] while government investment in the project was only US$4.2 million.

Ghana. GCNet is an electronic trade documentation system that processes approvals for imports and exports. Led by the Ministry of Trade and Industry, GCNet was formed in November 2000 and is designed along the lines of Singapore's TradeNet, only less sophisticated.

GCNet is a joint venture company with equity of US$5.3 million in which Société Général de Surveillance S.A., a private company, holds the majority (60 percent) of shares. Other shareholders include the Customs Excise and Preventive Services (20 percent), the Ghana Shippers Council (10 percent) and two local banks (each with 5 percent).[62] GCNet has succeeded in improving the efficiency of trade in Ghana. For example, the average clearance times at the KIA airport have dropped from 3 days to 4 hours, and the time required to review customs documentation, from 24 hours to 10 minutes.

Catalonia (Spain). In 2002, the government of Catalonia established ".Cat," a public company owned by the government and a consortium of 800 local authorities. All government interactions with citizens are conducted through the .Cat portal (http://www.cat365.net), which serves as the one point of contact between citizens and the government. Cat uses customer relationship management (CRM) software and benchmarks the quality of services delivered to citizens.

South Korea. In 1997, the South Korean government began reforming its public procurement system, which was widely regarded as corrupt, complicated, lacking accountability and non-transparent. The results of the e-procurement system that was introduced have been extremely encouraging. On an investment of US$80 million (since 2002), the government generated savings estimated at US$2.8 billion in 2004. The system also allows cross-agency comparisons of procurement, making the process more transparent and accountable.[63]

As can be seen from the above examples drawn from both developed and developing countries it is not necessary to follow a long and circuitous path to reach the phase of transactional services. With proper planning and appropriate models it should be possible for developing countries to leapfrog to higher levels in the evolutionary chain. In the case of Ghana for example, while many government departments have yet to establish an effective web presence, the department of Customs Excise and Preventive Services was already at the transactional stage with GCNet.

m-Government

The market penetration of mobile phones is growing rapidly in developing countries and far exceeds PC penetration. In such a scenario, there is a distinct opportunity for developing countries to use mobile platforms to deliver government services ("m-government"). These services can increase the productivity and effectiveness of public sector personnel, improve the delivery of government information and services, increase channels for public interaction and lower costs.

The government of Hong Kong, for example, is sponsoring the domestic Wireless Technology Industry Association to create new m-government initiatives. Among such applications in Hong Kong are those that allow citizens to book appointments to obtain or replace a smart ID card and search available timeslots to file marriage notices. Other m-government services currently available in Hong Kong include weather and air pollution information, news, government press releases and the use of mobile technology by field staff of government departments (e.g., drainage, housing and postal field staff).[64]

Malta offers m-government services that include acknowledgement and status of customer complaints; notice of court deferrals, license renewal, exam results and direct credit payments from the Department of Social Security.[65] In Norway and Sweden, people use SMS text messaging to confirm whether their tax returns are accurate.[66] The London Metropolitan Police sends out security alerts on mobile phones.[67] In a survey conducted in Ireland, respondents in the 15-to-24-year old group favored text messaging as way to interact with government.

Some 48 percent of respondents noted that they would be interested in receiving text messages and reminders regarding such issues as national car tests, driving tests and hospital appointments.[68]

The Philippines provides a good example of how mobile phones can be used in innovative ways. Mobile users in the Philippines use SMS text messaging extensively—more than 200 million SMS text messages are sent daily in the country. Globe Telecom's G-Cash application uses SMS text messaging to enable micro monetary transactions between families, friends and local merchants. The service allows users, including those without bank accounts or credit cards, to send money phone-to-phone, buy goods and services, pay for business permits and receive micro-financing and international remittances. Bangko Sentral ng Pilipinas (BSP) recently endorsed G-Cash for use by banks and automated teller machines. BSP has also ensured that G-Cash complies with security and regulatory requirements, including those related to anti-money laundering laws. The Philippines Bureau of Internal Revenue (BIR) is currently using the application for business registration and renewal payments. The Rural Banks of Philippines are in the process of piloting G-Cash for loan micro-payments.[69]

Developing countries should look carefully at the G-Cash model because it allows the poor to overcome the lack of bank accounts, credit cards and bank branches in rural areas. It also enables the government to avoid investments in conventional infrastructure to deliver e-government services to a large number of citizens.

The rapid proliferation of mobile phones presents an opportunity to developing countries to deliver information and services to citizens and businesses in new and innovative ways. The full potential of this medium remains largely unutilized as of now. Developing country governments would do well to consider mobile service delivery as a cost-effective platform while designing e-government applications and solutions.

Conclusion

E-government offers both challenges and benefits to low-income countries. This chapter has outlined some of the cross-cutting issues for developing successful e-government applications and provided many examples from both developed and developing nations. Although complex, e-government applications can potentially increase government efficiency, reduce corruption and provide better-quality services to citizens. Public-private partnerships and creative use of existing technologies, such as mobile phones, can make e-government applications increasingly viable in many developing nations.

Developing country governments should proceed on the path of e-government with caution, but proceed they must. In the words of Manuel Castells, the eminent sociologist, "One might say, "Why don't you leave me alone? I want no part of your Internet, of your technological civilization, of your network society! I just want to live my life!" Well, if this is your position, I have bad news for you. If you do not care about the networks, the networks will care about you, anyway. For as long as you want to live in society, at this time and in this place, you will have to deal with the network society. Because we live in the Internet Galaxy."[70]

Notes

[1] E-government has been defined in a variety of ways. The United Nations *Global E-Government Readiness Report 2004* defines it as "the use of information and communication technology (ICT) and its application by the government for the provision of information and basic public services to the people." [United Nations, *Global E-Government Readiness Report 2004: Towards Access for Opportunity* (New York: United Nations, 2004), 15]. According to the European Commission, e-government is defined as "the use of information and communication technologies in public administrations – combined with organisational change and new skills – to improve public services and democratic processes and to strengthen support to public policies." (Europe's Information Society Thematic Portal, http://europa.eu.int/information_society/soccul/egov/index_en.htm; accessed July 28, 2005). Gartner Group defines e-government as "the transformation of public sector internal and external relationships through net enabled operations and information and communications technology to optimize government service delivery, constituency participation and internal government operations." (Andrea Di Maio and John Kost, "Hype Cycle Shows E-Government Overcoming Disillusionment," Gartner Research, Stamford, Connecticut, March 17, 2004).

[2] The Economist, "Behind the Digital Divide," *Technology Quarterly*, 12 March 2005, 22.

[3] An initiative was categorized as a total failure if it was never implemented or was implemented, but immediately abandoned. Partial failure was characterized by non-attainment of major goals and/or significant undesirable outcomes. An initiative was considered successful if most stakeholder groups attained their major goals and did not experience significant undesirable outcomes (See Richard Heeks, "Success and Failure Rates of eGovernment in Developing/Transitional Countries: Overview" IDPM, University of Manchester, Manchester, UK, 2003, http://www.egov4dev.org/sfoverview.htm; accessed July 28, 2005).

[4] Lester Haines, "MPs Condemn e-Uni Disaster – Again," *The Register,* March 4, 2005, http://www.theregister.co.uk/2005/03/04/e_uni_committee_report/print.html; accessed July 28, 2005.

[5] Select Committee on Work and Pensions, "Assessment of CSA's IT and telephony System", The United Kingdom Parliament, 2004, http://www.publications.parliament.uk/pa/cm200304/cmselect/cm; accessed August 1, 2005.

[6] Electricnews.net, "Ireland Faces •50m E-voting Write-off," *The Register,* February 4, 2005, http://www.theregister.co.uk/2005/02/04/ireland_evoting_bill;accessedJuly28,2005.ThomasC.Gre; accessed July 28, 2005.

[7] Thomas C. Greene, "FBI Blew $170 m on Doomed IT Upgrade," *The Register,* January 14, 2005, http://www.theregister.co.uk/2005/01/14/fbi_flushes_trilogy_money/print.html; accessed July 28, 2005.

[8] Claudio Orego Larrain, "Chile's E-procurement System: Transparency, Efficiency and PPP" presentation available at http://www.transparency.org/integrity_pact/dnld/orrego_e-procurement.pdf; accessed July 28, 2005.

[9] R.P.Sisodia, Director e-Seva, email to author, May 2, 2005.

[10] Kenneth Bennoit, "Appendix 2J: Experience of Electronic Voting Overseas", The Policy Institute, Trinity College Dublin, http://www.cev.ie/htm/report/first_report/pdf/Appendix%202J.pdf; accessed July 28, 2005; 6.

[11] European Commission, "The Role of E-Government for Europe's Future," SEC (2003) 1038, EC, Brussels, September 26, 2003, 4.

[12] John Kost, Richard G.Harris, John P.Roberts, "New Appointment in Victoria, Australia, Is Seen as a Vote of Confidence for CIOs", Gartner Research, Stamford, Connecticut, May 5, 2005.

[13] See AGIMO, "Agency Overview," in *Annual Report 2003–2004*, Australian Government Information Management Office, Parkes, Australia, 2004, http://www.agimo.gov.au/publications/2004/10/annrep03-04/part_2_-_agency_overview; accessed July 28, 2005.

[14] International Council for Information Technology in Government Administration (ICA), "The Office of the e-Envoy Transitions to the e-Government Unit," ICA Information No. 82: General Issues, ICA, Surrey, UK http://www.ica-it.org/docs/issue82/ICA_Issue_82_2004_05.pdf; accessed July 28, 2005.

[15] Public Sector Technology & Management, "Migrating Citizens to e-Government Channels in Hong Kong," PTSM.net, Singapore, February 3, 2005, http://www.pstm.net/article/ index.php?articleid=511; accessed July 28, 2005.

[16] US Congress, "E-Government Act of 2002", 3602 (a).

[17] See www.core.gov; accessed July 31, 2005.

[18] Stephen J.Dorgan and John J.Dowdy, "When IT lifts productivity", The McKinsey Quarterly, 2004 number 4. See also The McKinsey Quarterly Chart Focus Newsletter, "Does IT improve performance?", June 2005, http://www.mckinseyquarterly.com/newsletters/chartfocus/2005_06.htm; accessed July 31, 2005.

[19] European Commission, "The Role of E-Government for Europe's Future", [SEC (2003) 1038], http://europa.eu.int/eur-lex/lex/LexUriServ/LexUriServ.do?uri=CELEX:52003DC0567:EN:HTML; accessed July 30,2005.

[20] Jeremy Millard and Jonas Iversen Svava, "Reorganization of Government Back Offices for Better Electronic Public Services: European Good Practices (Back-office Reorganization)," Final Report to the European Commission, Danish Technological Institute, Taastrup, Denmark, January 2004, 74.

[21] EC, European Interoperability Framework for Pan-European e-Government Services, ver.1 (Belgium: European Communities, 2004), http://europa.eu.int/idabc/servlets/Doc?id=19528; accessed August 1, 2005.

[22] See http://www.egifaccreditation.org/introduction.html; accessed July 29, 2005.

[23] Philip J.Allega, "'Do It Yourself' Is Not Sufficient for British Government and Enterprise Architecture Projects", Gartner Research, Stamford, Connecticut, June 8, 2005.

[24] Andrea Di Maio, "How to Measure the Public Value of IT," Gartner Research, Stamford, Connecticut, July 8, 2003.

[25] John Kost and Andrea Di Maio, "Creating a Business Case for a Government IT Project," Gartner Research, Stamford, Connecticut, January 6, 2003.

[26] Queensland Government, http://www.qld.gov.au/sharedservices/about_ssi/index.html; accessed July 31, 2005.

[27] According to Article 10.1 of the Contract for development, implementation, operation and maintenance of AP Broadband Network between AP Aksh Broadband Limited and Aksh Broadband Limited and Andhra Pradesh Technology Services Limited on behalf of Information Technology and Communications Department, Government of Andhra Pradesh signed April 21, 2005, "The GoAP agrees to provide free RoW by way of GOs, including free ROW on AP Transmission Corporation (APTransco) electricity poles of 11 KVA and other low tension distribution poles".

[28] The consortium that won the bid consisted of Aksh Optifibre Ltd. (a fiber optic manufacturer), Railtel Corporation (a government company owned by the Railways), In Cable Net (a cable television provider with a subscriber base of about 400,000), Spectranet (an ISP), Tata Indicom (an existing telecommunications player), and Nuzveedu Seeds Ltd. (a cash-rich company with personnel on the ground). See http://www.aponline.gov.in/Quick%20Links/events/APTS/PressNote_03Jan05.htm; accessed July 28, 2005.

[29] General Manager (BD) BSNL Hyderabad, letter to Director Communications IT&C Department, Government of Andhra Pradesh, April 16, 2004 (Lr. No.TA/10-40/2004/TP).

[30] Input/Output, "Federal Government Requests $59.8 billion for FY2005 IT Spending", Reston, February 2004, http://www.newsletterscience.com/ejkrause/pdf/00000034.pdf; accessed July 28, 2005.

[31] Cited in Lucy Sheriff, "E-gov to Cost Europe •4bn+," The Register, February 4, 2005, http://www.theregister.co.uk/2005/02/04/idc_euro_gov_spend/print.html; accessed July 28, 2005.

[32] IDC Press release, "IT Spending on eGovernment Continues to Grow in Western Europe, Says IDC", October 12, 2004, http://www.idc.com/getdoc.jsp?containerId=pr2004_10_05_171108; accessed July 28, 2005.

[33] Public Sector Technology & Management, "Migrating Citizens to e-Government Channels in Hong Kong," PTSM.net, Singapore, February 3, 2005, http://www.pstm.net/article/ index.php?articleid=511; accessed July 28, 2005.

[34] Jeremy Millard et al., "Reorganisation of government back-offices for better electronic public services – European good practices", January 2004, Volume 3, Annex 6, http://europa.eu.int/information_society/activities/egovernment_research/doc/back_office_reorganisation_volume3.pdf; accessed July 28, 2005.

[35] Jeremy Millard et al., "Reorganisation of government back-offices for better electronic public services – European good practices", January 2004, Volume 3, Annex 6 vii, http://www.elo.nl/elo/Images/Case08-Denmark_tcm70-54624.pdf; accessed July 28, 2005.

[36] Government of Andhra Pradesh, Information Technology and Communications Department, GOMs.39 dated September 12, 2002 available at http://www.apvatonline.com/ctportalnew/gosnotifications/GO3912092002.htm; accessed July 28, 2005.

[37] Maria T.Gresham and Jeremy Andrulis, "Using hybrid funding strategies to support the State of Arizona", IBM Institute for Business Value, New York, 2002, 4, http://www-1.ibm.com/services/us/imc/pdf/g510-1678-01-wheres-the-money-hybrid-funding.pdf; accessed July 28, 2005.

[38] Robin Gill, "Cooperation between the Public and Private Sectors to Improve Service Delivery: The Hong Kong Experience", presentation available at http://www.info.gov.hk/digital21/e-gov/eng/press/doc/20031118.pdf; accessed July 28, 2005.

[39] Claudio Orego Larrain, "Chile's E-procurement System: Transparency, Efficiency and PPP" presentation available at http://www.transparency.org/integrity_pact/dnld/orrego_e-procurement.pdf; accessed July 28, 2005.

[40] See http://www.compranet.gob.mx/; accessed July 28, 2005.

[41] National Assembly of Canada, *An Act respecting the Agence des parternariats public-privé du Québec*, Bill 61 (2004, chapter 32), Thirty-seventh Legislature (Québec: Québec Official Publisher, 2004). http://www2.publicationsduquebec.gouv.qc.ca/dynamicSearch/telecharge.php?type=5&file=2004C32A.PDF; accessed July 28, 2005.

[42] Companies like QingHua Wang Bo (an IT service provider linked to QingHua University), Ken SiJie (a computer system research institute) and China Software Testing Center have all been involved as third-party supervisors of Chinese government projects.

[43] The criteria for OSS include (i) freedom to redistribute; (ii) inclusion of source code; (iii) freedom to create derived works; (iv) integrity of the author's source code, i.e., an amended work must be distinguished from the original version; (v) no discrimination against persons or groups; (vi) no discrimination against fields of endeavor; (vii) distribution of a license that is technology-neutral, not specific to a product and does not add further restrictions (such as non-disclosure agreements or restrictions on other software). See European Union, "Free and Open Source Software Directory of Key Terms," Europe's Information Society Thematic Portal, Brussels, http://europa.eu.int/information_society/ activities/opensource/doc/pdf/key_terms.pdf; accessed July 28, 2005.

[44] See http://www.edulinux.cl/english/index_p2.php?id_contenido=730&id_seccion=1473&id_portal=1; accessed July 28, 2005.

[45] Open Source Observatory, Interchange of Data between Administrations, "Case Study: Extremadura LinEx" November 2003, http://europa.eu.int/idabc/servlets/Doc?id=1641; accessed July 28, 2005.

[46] ATICA, "Guide to choosing and using free software licences for government and public sector entities", December 2002, http://www.adae.gouv.fr/upload/documents/free_software_guide.pdf; accessed July 28, 2005.

[47] European Commission, "eEurope 2005: An information society for all", COM(2002) 263 final, Brussels, May 28, 2002, http://europa.eu.int/information_society/eeurope/2002/news_library/documents/eeurope2005/eeurope2005_en.pdf; accessed July 28, 2005; 11.

[48] "The technical specifications drawn up by public purchasers need to allow public procurement to be opened up to competition. To this end, it must be possible to submit tenders which reflect the diversity of technical solutions. Accordingly, it must be possible to draw up the technical specifications in terms of functional performance and requirements and, where reference is made to the European standard, or in the absence thereof, to the national standard, tenders based on equivalent arrangements must be considered by contracting authorities.", European Union, "Directive 2004/18/EC of the European Parliament and of the Council on the Coordination of Procedures for the award of Public Works Contracts, Public Supply Contracts and Public Service Contracts", Strasbourg, March 31, 2004, 18.

[49] Computer Business Review Online, "Venezuelan government opts for open source approach", January 5, 2005, http://www.cbronline.com/article_news.asp?guid=B4AD0DAB-0611-4F6C-8C9F-8846A38A6525; accessed July 28, 2005.

[50] Andrea Di Maio, "Local Governments in France Move to Open-Source Applications", Gartner Research, Stamford, Connecticut, July 8, 2005.

[51] E-Government Unit, *Open Source Software: Use within UK Government,* ver. 2, Cabinet Office, Office of Government Commerce, London, October 28, 2004. http://www.govtalk.gov.uk/ documents/oss_policy_version2.pdf; accessed July 28, 2005.

[52] See AGIMO, "Efficient Application of Technology: Organizing for e-Government," in "Better Services, Better Government," AGIMO, Parkes, Australia, 2002, http://www.agimo.gov.au/ publications/2002/11/bsbg/application_of_technology; accessed July 28, 2005.

[53] Christopher H. Baum and Andrea Di Maio, "Gartner's Four Phases of E-Government Model, Gartner Research, Stamford, Connecticut, November 21, 2000. Gartner has subsequently proposed a new way to measure the progress of e-government in order to capture its complexities. The new measure takes into account the need for horizontal and vertical integration across public and private sector organizations and defines four levels of

e-government: presentation, data exchange, transaction and sharing. The first level, "presentation," refers to providing access to services, applications or data through the same user interface (e.g., website or portal), with applications and data remaining distinct. The next level, "data exchange," refers to the stage where common data standards and architecture enable exchange of data between applications without changing semantics. The third level, "transaction," integrates data and process flows across vertical and horizontal divides. Finally, at the "sharing level," application components, data and process elements are shared across organizational boundaries. (Andrea Di Miao, "It's Time for a New Way to Measure Progress of E-Government," Gartner Research, Stamford, Connecticut, 14 October 2004).

[54] An interesting example of this initial phase is the Lebanese government portal, www.informs.gov.lb. Launched in 2002, the portal is devoted to making forms available from across the central government, the country's five regional governments and over 760 municipalities. The portal also provides advice and instructions for completing and submitting each form to the relevant government agency.

[55] Christopher H. Baum and Andrea Di Miao, "Gartner's Four Phases of E-Government Model", Gartner Research, Stamford, Connecticut, 21 November 2000.

[56] Capgemini, *Online Availability of Public Services: How is Europe Progressing? Web-based Survey on Electronic Public Services, Report of the Fifth Measurement, October 2004* (Brussels: Directorate General for Information and Media, European Commission, 3 March 2005), 7.

[57] Capgemini, *Online Availability of Public Services*, 45.

[58] United Nations, *Global E-Government Readiness Report 2004: Towards Access for Opportunity* (New York: United Nations 2004), 17.

[59] Government corruption is a major problem in many countries. According to data collected by the World Bank, 97.8 percent of firms surveyed in Bangladesh reported that they paid bribes as part of doing business. World Bank, *World Development Report 2005, Investment Climate Surveys* (New York: World Bank and Oxford University Press, 2005), 246.

[60] Douglas Holmes, email to author, March 3, 2005 attaching a paper on "eGov in Latin America".

[61] Albert Lobo and Suresh Balakrishnan, *Report Card on Service of Bhoomi Kiosks: An Assessment of Benefits to Users of the Computerized Land Records System in Karnataka* (Bangalore: Public Affairs Centre, November 2002), http://unpan1.un.org/intradoc/groups/public/documents/APCITY/UNPAN015135.pdf; accessed July 28, 2005.

[62] Luc De Wulf and Jose B.Sokol, *Customs Modernization Initiatives: Case Studies* (Washington: World Bank and Oxford University Press, 2004), 19-32. http://www.worldbank.org/transport/learning/learning%20week/trade_facil_2005/Case%20Studies/World%20Bank%20(2004f)%20Customs%20Modernization%20Initiatives%20Case%20Studies.pdf; accessed August 1, 2005.

[63] The World Bank, "Korea's Move to E-Procurement," *PREM Notes*, no. 90 (July 2004), Poverty Reduction and Economic Management Network, World Bank, Washington, DC. See also http://www.pps.go.kr/neweng/; accessed August 1, 2005.

[64] See http://sc.info.gov.hk/gb/www.info.gov.hk/digital21/e-gov/eng/init/mgov.htm; accessed July 30, 2005.

[65] See http://www.gov.mt/egovernment.asp?p=106&l=1; accessed July 30, 2005.

[66] Swedish Tax Agency, "Taxes in Sweden 2004: An English Summary of Tax Statistical Yearbook of Sweden", 2004, Section 3.1.5, http://www.skatteverket.se/broschyrer/104/10405.pdf; accessed July 30, 2005. For Norway see also Emmanuel C.Lallana, "eGovernment for Development: mGovernment Applications and Purposes Page", 2004, http://www.egov4dev.org/mgovapplic.htm; accessed July 30, 2005.

[67] Lallana, "mGovernment Applications and Purposes".

[68] Matthew Clark, "Irish people want m-government: survey", electricnews.net, December 10, 2004, http://new.enn.ie/news.html?code=9569739; accessed July 30, 2005.

[69] Robin Simpson and Eleana Liew, "Globe Telecom's G-Cash a Mobile Commerce Success Story", Gartner Research, Stamford, Connecticut, March 1, 2005.

[70] M. Castells, *The Internet Galaxy: Reflections on the Internet, Business, and Society* (New York: Oxford University Press, 2001), 282.16.

Chapter 6

Beyond Secondary Education

The promise of ICT for higher education and lifelong learning

by Ron Perkinson

The use of ICTs to improve the access and affordability of higher education[1] is perhaps the greatest unrealized promise of e-development. Most developing countries have to some degree adopted the use of ICTs in their schools and institutions of higher education. Although significant digital, social and learning divides still exist between developed nations and many of the world's poorest countries, a number of developing countries (e.g., China, India, South Africa and Malaysia) have been able to close such gaps over the last five years. This process has, however, been slow and uneven.

This chapter evaluates the changing global market for higher education and training, together with the challenges that developing countries face in this sphere. Today, the majority of global e-learning applications are found mainly in the developed world. By comparison, developing countries have made only small beginnings in the field. Yet it is in the latter countries that e-learning holds the greatest chance of bridg-

ing the access, cost and quality gaps in higher education, a global enterprise that is struggling to reach the one-quarter of 18-to-25 year-olds currently enrolled in higher education. This is especially true given the priority that developing nations have placed on achieving the Millennium Development Goals in primary and secondary education. This priority, together with falling levels of public funding for higher education, is forcing higher education institutions in developing countries to find alternative ways of funding future development.

The first section of this chapter highlights the changes facing the global higher education market and examines the steady growth of online students (and their changing profiles) in what is still a small number of countries. The second section explores some of the key future challenges of the e-learning agenda. It highlights the challenges posed by inadequate access and affordability and reflects on the need for champions who can address these key obstacles in developing countries.

The third section looks at the economics of technology-based teaching, noting that legacy mass technologies are likely to remain more appropriate and cost-effective in certain developing nations for the foreseeable future. The section also examines the economies of technology-based teaching and how the parallel universe of e-training (particularly corporate training) may provide greater validation of the increased cost-efficiency of e-education.

The fourth section examines the path that many higher education institutions in both developed and developing countries are traversing towards Web-based learning. The analysis argues that different mixes of e-learning, based on both intranet and distance-learning technologies, can be expected to serve as stepping stones towards more cost-efficient, Web-based delivery. Cost-effective solutions will depend on available infrastructure and resources, prevailing and future student profiles, together with applicable economic and affordability drivers.

The fifth section examines promising developments and success factors in the delivery of affordable e-learning programs, in spite of prevailing physical, geographic and economic constraints. The section reviews programs that have made significant gains in advancing the e-learning agenda, including cross-border delivery of education services among developing countries.

The sixth and final section addresses the future of e-learning and e-training and offers six key recommendations. These recommendations are essential for enabling developing countries to optimize the potential gains from e-learning and to break down the barriers of remote locations, affordability and appropriateness of ICT use in education, training and lifelong learning.

Part I. The changing global market for higher education

Background: Global higher education

Total estimated student enrollment in global higher education in the year 2000 was around 90 million. By 2003, more than 100 million students were enrolled in higher education worldwide, with China alone accounting for approximately 4 million of the increase. Even if only the most populous nations of China and India are considered, there is clearly growing demand for places in higher education institutions. In China in 2004, more than 30 percent of higher education students were in their first year of study, with a total of 26 million senior secondary school students about to enter the higher education system. This number translates into roughly 15 million Chinese students who hope to enroll in tertiary education programs over the next four years.[2]

In India, it is not unheard of for some higher education programs to receive 6,000 applicants per place.[3] With over 60 percent of India's population falling in the 0-to-25-year age group,[4] the nation faces daunting demand for both secondary and higher education. A comparison is useful for understanding the gravity of the challenge facing India. The United Kingdom has more than 330 universities[5] for a population of around 60 million people. If the same university-to-population ratio were applied to India, the country would require more than 5,500 additional universities to put it on an equal footing with the United Kingdom.

Since the early 1990s, both public and private higher education institutions in most countries have struggled to keep up with growing enrollment demand. Particularly in developing countries, governments have been forced to balance education system needs against fiscal realities. As a result, they have begun to seek alternative ways to fund the development of higher education through more innovative models that can more readily satisfy the changing demands of market-led economies and knowledge societies.

Forces of change

Higher education systems in both developed and developing countries are being forced to navigate their way through "a perfect storm" of seven converging forces of change:

- the increasing importance of knowledge as the major driver of economic development, which has increased the importance of education, training and lifelong learning;

- an increasing world population, with a large cohort of potential higher education students;

- the impact of globalization on both higher education and local markets, which has created a global market for higher education and training;

- the impact of increasing competition, both within and outside borders, in a globalized economy and the consequent emergence of new, borderless providers of tertiary education;

- the continuing impact of internationalization on higher education, including international student enrollment and faculty and student exchanges. Internationalization has also increased the number of institutional relationships and alliances, with many affiliations leading to commercial initiatives by both public and private-sector players. It has also contributed to greater transferability of qualifications (both within nations and across borders);

- the continuing ICT revolution and use of the Internet, which are impacting the way education is organized and delivered at all levels of the education system; and

- the global decline in public financing, especially for higher education.

Changing student profiles. The changing landscape of global higher education is reflected in changed student profiles in most countries. According to the U.S. Department of Education, over 5.9 million, or 39 percent, of all students enrolled in higher education programs in the USA in 2004 were over the age of 24. This number is projected to reach 6.6 million in 2007 and 6.9 million in 2012. In OECD member countries, the proportion of adults with tertiary education qualifications has almost doubled over the past 25 years, rising from 22 percent in 1980 to around 41 percent today. In Canada, around 30 percent of undergraduate students are over the age of 25; in Australia, New Zealand, Denmark, Norway and Sweden, over 20 percent of first-year university students were over the age of 27 in 2000.[6]

The lifelong learning agenda is also taking hold in developing countries. Although little statistical data is available, many developing countries with more flexible age participation policies are also attracting new kinds of learners to higher education programs. Their students are becoming more diversified, older and a growing percentage pursue their studies on a part-time basis. Countries such as Chile, China and Malaysia are beginning to place increasing importance on accommodating these new learners, as they recognize the potential contribution that a more highly skilled workforce can make to economic development.

Decline in public financing. In most countries, even where education is supposedly free, new or supplementary charges are being introduced that shift an additional share of costs to students and their parents. Some of these charges have been quite substantial. For example, contributions from non-state sources recently increased from 2 to 23 percent of educational spending in Hungary. In Canada, average undergraduate tuition fees increased by 135 percent between 1991 and 2001.[7] Austria introduced tuition fees of roughly US$750 per year in 2001.[8] In Great Britain, Parliament recently approved a plan to allow university tuition fees for British students to rise up to US$5,450 a year as of September 2006.[9]

In China, public universities currently derive more than 40 percent of their income from non-state sources; household spending on education in the country is estimated at 10 percent and is expected to climb to 14 percent by 2010. And in Cambodia, one of the world's least developed countries, it is estimated that less than 40 percent of total higher education funding comes from the state.[10]

Use of new technologies. Many countries have been forced to adopt the use of mass education models to cater to changes in local markets, demographics, employer demands and student profiles. Such models are intended to advance higher education and training through non-state financing. An additional motivation has been to increase access and opportunity for a new generation of students who have grown up with information technologies and enjoy using computers, mobile phones and the Internet.

Today, sound online programs appeal to students who prefer to learn independently *and* with peers. For some, the use of ITCs and the Internet facilitates greater student engagement and participation than do traditional one-way lectures. Improved online pedagogies are providing greater opportunities for active learning by project groups, with the benefit of more regular personalized feedback and formative assessment.

Many young adults have also changed their outlook on how and where they would like to learn and upgrade their skills in a changing world of work. Over the last decade, the adoption of e-learning technologies in classrooms at all levels of education, as well as in corporate training programs, has been increasing. It should be noted, however, that these increases are modest compared to the projections for Web-based learning that were made only five years ago. However, formal education systems across the globe are showing increasing interest in e-learning not simply as a medium for adding value to teaching and learning, but also to serve "anytime, anywhere" initiatives in ways that were not previously possible.

E-learning. Electronic learning can be defined as instructional content or learning experiences delivered or enabled by electronic technology. The term covers a wide range of applications and processes, such as Web-based learning, computer-based learning, virtual classrooms and digital collaboration. It can be used to describe the delivery of content via the Internet, intranets or extranets (i.e., LANs or WANs), audio- and videotape, satellite broadcast, interactive TV, CD-ROM and other electronic means.

Compared to conventional mass media technologies, e-learning is more appropriate for knowledge-based applications, whereas the former have become the preferred medium for skills training (although such programs certainly involve some knowledge transfer). Conventional mass technologies also tend to be used where up-to-date Web-based applications are not available.

International expansion of e-learning

In China, close to one million students are estimated to be studying online today.[11] In the United States in 2003, there were 1.9 million online higher education students. This figure increased to 2.6 million students (a 24 percent increase) in 2004, meaning that 16 percent of all higher education students in the United States were studying online. Approximately 40 percent of this group were fully online students, an 18 percent increase over the prior year.[12] Very conservative estimates project that the online e-learning subsector will become a global, US$150 billion plus industry by 2025.[13]

With some justification, contemporary providers of international e-learning programs believe that the international market for online education will continue to grow substantially in most countries. Some specialists believe that working adults will increasingly opt for either a quality U.S. or alternative foreign program and qualification without living in the USA or another foreign country. The emerging trend for working adults is to access online courses without leaving their jobs and incurring the high travel and living costs, as well as stringent visa requirements, of studying abroad.

For example, in 2003, the University of Phoenix Online had students located in approximately 91 countries. In addition, many U.S. and residents of other OECD countries who live and work in developing countries benefit from the opportunity to continue their education while living abroad. In fact, international providers of online tertiary education have been conducting market research in selected countries where potential demand exists for their programs. As more students from developing countries seek either a foreign qualification or choose an e-learning model, successful models in the developed world are likely to determine the models adopted in developing countries.

Part II. Future challenges of e-learning

Four barriers challenge the e-learning agenda: access, affordability, appropriateness of ICT use in e-learning and the need for "champions" at both the political and educational provider level. The mix and degree to which these barriers impact development differ depending on each country's social, economic, political and technological situation.

Access

Access alone does not determine successful implementation of e-learning and online learning. The sample of developing countries shown in table 6.1 shows that the advancement of e-learning is definitely assisted by improved ac-

Table 6.1 Information infrastructure vs. e-learning & online learning development, 2003

	Mainlines per 100	Mobiles per 100	Internet Hosts (millions)	E-Learning Development 1 = Low 10 = High
China	20.9	21.5	0.16	3
India	4.6	2.5	0.08	2
Indonesia	3.9	8.7	0.06	1
Mexico	16.0	29.5	1.30	5
South Korea	53.8	70.1	3.80	5
Malaysia	18.2	44.2	0.10	2
Philippines	4.1	27.0	0.02	1
Singapore	45.0	85.2	0.48	5
Turkey	26.8	39.4	0.35	2

cess to information and communications infrastructure, but not in isolation from other key determinants of successful implementation. Turkey, for example, has a higher number of (telecommunications) main lines per 100 inhabitants, but is still a relatively low adopter of e-learning when compared to Mexico, India or China. Mexico and China also have lower mobile telephone market penetration rates per 100 population than Turkey, yet have adopted e-learning across their formal tertiary systems to a greater degree.[14]

Clearly, access to ICT infrastructure at affordable rates is important for advancing the e-agenda. It should be noted that the choice of technology is not the main driver of e-learning. However, improved access to affordable ICTs will determine the extent of their use, as well as how quickly new modes of ICT-assisted delivery will be deployed. Access remains a major challenge for governments and telecommunications companies, which must work together to find better ways of investing in a country's human capital by providing enhanced access to Internet-based resources. Such resources will ensure greater affordability of ICTs and the more flexible education and training programs that they can deliver.

Affordability

Affordability is another important challenge that has yet to be successfully addressed in many developing countries. In African countries, for example, economic barriers, technology constraints and government policy are key barriers to more scaleable and viable business models for e-learning. In many such countries, the affordability of infrastructure is an obstacle to the introduction new technologies. The average annual per capita income in Sub-Saharan Africa, for example, is US$490 per year—lower than the average annual cost of 20 hours of dial-up Internet service per month (approximately US$720).

Given existing conditions, the high cost of Internet services will predetermine higher delivery costs of distance education providers, which they will need to pass on if they are to remain in business. Coupled with low per capita incomes, the challenges of affordable access to ICTs in schools and institutions of higher learning is one of the most important priorities that governments of least-developed countries and their telecommunications service providers will face in the immediate future.

Where Web-based learning and mixed delivery models (i.e., models that combine face-to-face learning with e-learning) are working, real costs and benefits remain difficult to evaluate. Outside of the United States, no systematic data is available on e-learning costs, a key issue that most governments must face in the near term. The need for governments and higher education and training providers to identify sustainable, cost-efficient delivery models for e-learning investments is another crucial element of advancing the e-agenda. The few virtual universities that exist do not appear to be replacing conventional campuses, nor does the use of online materials appear to be supplanting faculty.[15] Certain new models that blend face-to-face and online delivery can reduce costs and increase both access and affordability, but no data yet indicates that an increase in online delivery results in significant cost savings that could substantially reduce tuition fees.

One case where cost reductions have indeed been realized is that of Tec Milenio in Mexico. Tecnologico de Monterrey founded Tec Milenio in 2002 to reach the growing market of lower-middle income working students. Tec Milenio's Universidad Virtual uses Tecnologico de Monterrey professors to deliver online courses from its parent campus to modestly equipped satellite campuses; teaching practitioners support the delivery of the courses at these campuses. The online provider delivers its programs at about one-third of their original cost, making access more affordable for lower-income students. After two years of operation, Tec Milenio had around 8,400 students enrolled in its programs, which are targeted mainly at young working adults who seek to return to tertiary studies to upgrade skills and qualifications, as well as low-income students interested in getting a better education.[16]

The Open University in the UK is also gradually moving away from traditional distance-learning courses that use books, video cassettes and CD-ROMs towards online courses, and has reported that its per-student cost is one-third the average cost of a similar on-campus program. In this case, fixed capital costs were lower and student feedback prompted the university to deploy staff in support of e-learning processes rather than "traditional" university courses.[17]

Appropriateness of ICT use

Appropriateness of ICT use and its impact on quality have become important determinants for the success of e-learning models. In many settings, e-learning appropriately adds value to existing courses or gives such courses a new thrust by adding new materials, such as information from the Internet or multimedia materials. New forms of e-learning can also improve the *quality* of tertiary education and the *effectiveness* of learning by:

- increasing the flexibility of the student learning experience;

- enhancing access to information resources for more students; and

- potentially driving innovative ways of learning, as well as providing the basis for more cost-effective delivery models for both teachers and learners.

E-learning also provides a means for students to take courses from several institutions at once, as well as to combine learning environments (e.g., combining campus-based with fully online courses). E-learning thus offers great potential for improving student choice of curricula and thus, the overall student learning experience, regardless of pedagogical changes.

Champions of change

Champions of change are needed to advance the use of e-learning in program and training delivery. When faculty and institutional leadership are prepared to advocate new approaches and adopt e-learning in their programs, the methodology will have much greater impact. Two examples where effective leadership has led to the adoption of successful e-learning models are Tecnologico de Monterrey in Mexico (Universidad Virtual) and Istanbul Bilgi University (which has an online e-MBA program). In the case of Universidad Virtual, advocates of online learning championed not only a change in the means of delivery, but also sought to reach new types of higher education students, including women, community groups, workers in small and medium enterprises and other constituents in more geographically remote settings.

Government champions

Government champions of e-learning, especially in countries with low age-group participation[18] in higher education, can also be an important catalyst for change. In Turkey, for example, the Higher Education Council (Yuksek Ogrenim Kurumu, or YOK) approved the introduction of Istanbul Bilgi University's first full online MBA program in 2000 at a time when many e-learning start-ups around the world were struggling to achieve their educational and financial objectives. The decision of YOK to support Bilgi University's e-MBA start-up subsequently

Box 6.1 Universidad virtual: An innovative model for reaching widely disbursed communities

Universidad Virtual, which offers e-training initiatives through a network of Community Learning Centers (Centros Comunitarios de Aprendizaje, or CLC), is an example of how innovative use of online delivery, blended with face-to-face learning, can increase affordable access to higher education, continuing education and SME training. The program provides constituents in dispersed communities new educational opportunities that allow them to improve their skills and quality of life while contributing to the development of their communities.

Universidad Virtual's network of 1,048 CLCs are located in both Mexico (942 CLCs) and across the United States (106 CLCs). To date, they have delivered blended online courses to over 70,000 students and adults. Course offerings include 23 computer courses for people of all ages, one of the most popular of which is the "Basic Abilities Course." The Universidad Virtual also offers 14 undergraduate and 10 postgraduate degrees. Its continuing education programs offer 64 online courses, a total of 1,696 instructional hours, for such diverse students as teachers, public officials, civil groups, health workers and family education workers. These programs also include courses especially designed for Hispanics living in the United States, which aim to help them cope faster and better with American culture.

Special online courses are also offered to entrepreneurs and small and medium enterprises (SMEs) on such topics as "How to Start a Business," business administration skills and business planning. E-training courses are also offered to municipal managers on participative and open government, public finance, and introduction to e-government. In addition, the CLCs can offer short, e-training courses online to health and first-aid workers on such topics as women's health, healthcare and exercise, AIDS, managing diabetes, hypertension and respiratory infections. Online programs are also offered to NGOs on a range of topics, including organizational development, project administration, finance, management, marketing and the creation of funds, sustainable development, planning, and strategies for environmental conservation.

Source: Correspondence and conversations of the author with Tecnologico de Monterrey, 2005.

proved a good decision, setting an example of what can be achieved with positive support from government, both for countries in the Central European region as well as other developing countries. The Bilgi University program also offers a strong online learning model.[19]

Online education and training in the United States

Online learning, in both the formal and informal sense, has become a mainstream activity in most universities and many large multinational firms in the United States. Most students enroll at university and begin employment with the expectation of using the Internet both in their everyday lives and to support their daily work activities by accessing specific resources or acquiring work-related knowledge.

Between 2000 and 2002, training in U.S. companies delivered in a classroom dropped by almost 10 percent, while training delivered via learning technologies, especially e-learning, increased 12 percent. Today, many large U.S. corporations are using Web-based knowledge management and proprietary learning programs, putting greater demands on institutions of higher education to produce graduates who can easily use new learning technologies (e-learning and e-training) in the workplace.[20]

Outside of the United States, the development and application of e-learning and e-training has been much slower. In some countries, particularly in Africa and parts of Asia, e-learning and the use of the Internet are still too expensive and thus less viable mediums of delivery than other forms of mass delivery (e.g., TV, radio and correspondence courses) that continue to be used, based on satisfactory success over time.

Need for innovative solutions

For poorer countries in Africa and other parts of the world, the advantages that ICTs and the Internet could bring to women and groups in remote regions and poor societies has yet to be realized. In 1998, women in Africa represented around 35 percent of higher education enrollments, but only 23 percent of university students.[21] Given these low enrollment figures, there is great potential for African women to increase their participation in higher education through innovative distance-education delivery models, should the problem of costly infrastructure be resolved.

The use of ICTs to enhance distance delivery also holds the promise of giving African women access to a wider range of education and training programs through more interactive forms of e-delivery. Women in Muslim communities and women studying from home are, for example, on the rise in many countries. In South Africa, roughly 70 percent of students at Vista University and 50 percent of students at UNISA (Open University of South Africa) are women. In Namibia, 77 percent of distance-education stu-

dents are women, highlighting the potential importance using e-delivery models to reach this market.[22]

The expectation that e-delivery will eventually enhance these opportunities and make higher education programs more accessible, affordable and appropriate, enhancing employability and productivity in both urban and remote geographic locations, has yet to materialize. Governments and donors must think more innovatively about how to improve access to low-cost telecommunications and ISP services. Affordable infrastructure can then foster e-learning opportunities to reach wider and disbursed constituencies with special needs.

Part III. Emerging economics of technology-based teaching

There is no evidence to date that e-learning provides cost savings to the public sector in either developed or developing countries. This may partly be due to the fact that the majority of e-learning initiatives of significant size are mostly private, for-profit enterprises. There are also very few existing, reliable studies that accurately compare the costs of delivery across institutions. Course design and development costs, teaching salaries, communications costs, access to computers and faculty support are just some of the variables that can impact learning environments.

The University of British Columbia in Vancouver tracked the costs of development and delivery of Web-based and print-based distance-learning programs over a five-year period, using a ratio of one instructor per thirty students (see figure 6.1). As the figure demonstrates, compared to the assumed costs of face-to-face or Web-supplemented face-to-face teaching, mixed mode and fully online teaching were more cost-effective forms of delivery, once approximately 200 students had completed each course (40 per course offering). The University of British Columbia study also highlighted the pitfalls of supplementing face-to-face teaching with Web-based materials, which adds resources but does not lead to corresponding cost reductions elsewhere.[23]

The findings of the British Columbia study mirrored the experience of the e-MBA program of Istanbul Bilgi University. Launched in 2005, the program passed the threshold of 300 students after three years of operation, delivering positive educational outcomes and financial returns. These results do not, however, mean that the same experience will automatically apply to other e-learning ventures, given wide variations in salaries and development costs between countries.

Growing economic advantage of e-learning

E-learning does not necessarily offer an inherent economic advantage over other forms of delivery, particularly mass delivery (i.e., via television or radio). Given positive market conditions, supported by quality, cost-effective access and affordable educational programs, however, there is a great chance that unmet demand for higher education will increase consumption of online programs in developing countries. As previously mentioned, e-learning may be more appropriate for knowledge-based applications, whereas mass media technologies are arguably more suitable for skills training or countries where two-way, interactive Web-based applications are not available. In this context, yields on the use of mass media technologies will initially be higher.

As e-learning and instructional technologies improve and facilitate stronger interest and student engagement in learning, this can lead to higher yields in both student numbers and edu-

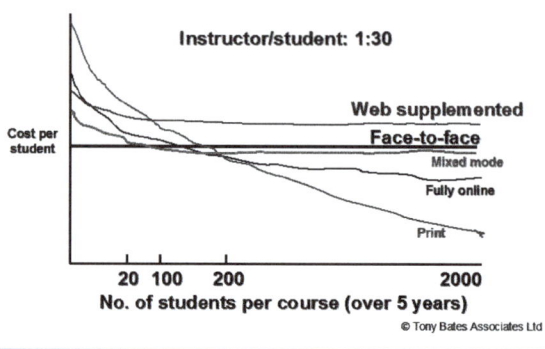

Figure 6.1 Economics of technology-based teaching

Source: Tony Bates Associates, Ltd., UK, 2005. Reprinted with permission.

cational outcomes. More sustainable e-learning business models are needed, however, that are scaleable in terms of both student volume and geographic reach.

Only five years ago, the perspective offered in figure 6.2 rightfully challenged that virtual universities, e-learning and Internet delivery would not be as effective as other forms of mass delivery. In some of the world's poorest countries, this argument holds firm today. However, significant advances in ICT infrastructure in many developing countries over the last four years, particularly in China, India and Mexico, have led to significant adoption of different forms of e-learning.

Figure 6.2 describes the ideal case as one with low costs and high yields; the least attractive case is located in the lower right segment of graph. In 2001, correspondence courses represented the best mix of cost and yield. This form of distance learning has been used for more than 100 years and still has a place in poor countries. The inclusion of Web-based distance delivery on the chart in 2005, however, indicates its potential as a competitive alternative.

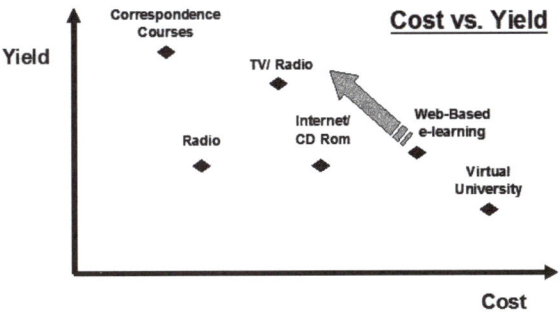

Figure 6.2 Cost vs. yield of different distance-learning delivery methods

Source: Ruth and Shi, "Is Anyone Measuring Cost-Benefits?" George Mason University, Fairfax, Virginia, 2001. (Arrow added in 2005.)

The African continent presently has approximately one-fifth of one percent of the world's Internet host sites.[24] Experience shows, however, that the use of simple technologies gradually leads to higher usage rates and ultimately, to the gradual leveraging of existing capacity with newer capabilities. The current progression of technologies used to deliver distance learning begins with correspondence courses and progresses to radio and TV courses, and ultimately, different forms of Web-based, Internet or e-learning courses.

A relevant example of this progression can be seen in China, which has leveraged the benefits of mass education. China has experienced two generations of technology-assisted distance education: one based on television and the other, on the Internet. China Radio and TV currently serves 1.5 million students.[25] Whereas only 200,000 students were studying via the Internet in 2000, this number is estimated to have reached close to 1 million in 2005.[26]

Growth in e-learning delivery across the world appears inevitable, as access, affordability and the development of newer and better models emerge. However, given that the promise of improved access and affordability to adequate communications infrastructure and up-to-date education technologies in some of the world's poorest countries has yet to be realized, it may be another generation before low-income countries can take advantage of these technologies on a mass scale.

Corporate e-training reduces costs

In a recent study of 30 universities in the United States that have introduced e-learning, preliminary results showed that all institutions had reduced their costs by about 40 percent on average (the range was 20 to 84 percent). The project projected that the estimated savings of the universities involved would be close to US$3.6 million each year.[27]

For many years, salaries have represented the major cost component of corporate training, followed by the cost of training venues and conferences. The advent of technology-assisted learning and e-learning is now allowing companies to optimize the use of salaried instructional staff through the more cost-effective distribution of e-learning. U.S. employers have also turned to e-learning to improve employee training, especially its delivery. Employers have come to realize that the flexibility, convenience and cost-effectiveness of e-learning not only improve training delivery, but also aid business development and profitability.

Although e-learning can require a substantial up-front investment, the results of implementations by large users are encouraging. When classroom training is replaced with e-learning solutions, corporations have claimed that their costs dropped as much as 50 to 70 percent. In some cases, the per-learner cost over a five-year period is estimated to drop as much as 85 percent. For example, Hewlett-Packard estimates that it saved US$5.5 million on training 700 engineers by switching to an e-learning system.[28]

As a result of implementing an e-learning system, Novell reduced its per-learner costs from US$1,800 to between US$700 to US$900; Buckman Labs reduced its total training costs from US$2.4 million to around US$400,000; and IBM within a one-year period saved US$200 million on its management development program, while providing five times as much training at one-third of the cost.[29]

Ford Motor Company saved US$17 million between 1999 and 2002 by introducing e-learning systems for company education and training. The Ford Learning Network (FLN), launched in 1999, is based on the concept of just-in-time knowledge and learning for employees. FLN integrates all training, management, online testing and learning resources into a single user interface that includes access to a library of more than 400,000 content titles, including 1,500 online courses, 1,900 e-books, 800 instructor-led classroom courses, an array of internal Web sites, and hundreds of journals, periodicals and other resources.[30]

Parallel partnerships

A number of organizations have forged partnerships with universities to deliver learning to their personnel. The U.S. military, for example, must train 2.4 million men and women in four services (army, navy, air force and marines), plus roughly one million civilian employees and a large number of military dependents. The military's educational strategies, needs and equipment are continually evolving at a rapid pace, with extremely sophisticated technology playing a greater and greater role in its educational services.

In response to a recruiting crisis, in 2001 the U.S. Army created a unique e-learning program called "eArmyU" for military personnel. The program presently enables soldiers to take classes and earn associate's, bachelor's, and master's degree from 32 universities and colleges around the United States. The program offers some 150 degree programs with more than 3,000 courses.

Courses are asynchronous, enabling soldiers to do classwork whenever their schedule permits. An offline learning application allows students to download all course materials from the course management system, work offline and then submit assignments online whenever they can access the Internet. Online tutoring and academic support, a virtual library, and an online help desk, bookstore and career services are also provided. Two years after its launch, some 31,181 soldiers had enrolled in the program. The most popular degree programs are in general studies, criminal justice, computer sciences, business and management.[31]

E-learning as a customer service

In the corporate sector and governments of advanced industrial societies, informal use of e-learning is becoming a part of everyday operations. For some years, both governments and private firms in these countries have provided training to their customers and service providers through e-learning systems. Global information technology companies like IBM, Microsoft, Cisco and Oracle, for example, provide product-related instruction and courses to customers or partners via e-learning systems. The exact growth of this type of e-learning is difficult to track, but irrespective of the data source, growth in this sector is compelling.

Part IV. The gradual continuum towards web-based learning

The continuum

Educational institutions across the world are positioned at different points on the road map between campus- or classroom-based learning and Web-based learning. E-learning, moreover, can use any of the delivery modes of the classroom, blended classroom/online delivery or pure online delivery.

On-campus classroom delivery can include bringing Internet sites of relevance and interest from around the world into the classroom. Students can also access topics or course materials and use the Web in ways that enhance, but do not replace, traditional teaching methodologies.

Blended classroom/online delivery can partially replace face-to-face teaching with online learning. Students might, for example, access topic or course materials online, or manage certain aspects of their learning and interact with others (synchronously and/or asynchronously). Throughout the phase of blended delivery, teachers introduce changes in pedagogical strategies to support the changing requirements of online students.

Pure online delivery is located at the more advanced end of the continuum, where students access either intranet-based or Internet-based learning objects (distributed learning systems), downloading topic or course materials and contacting tutors and each other entirely over the Web. The design of new pedagogical models and a shift toward greater peer-to-peer models of learning becomes important during this phase.

Figure 6.3 Use of e-learning

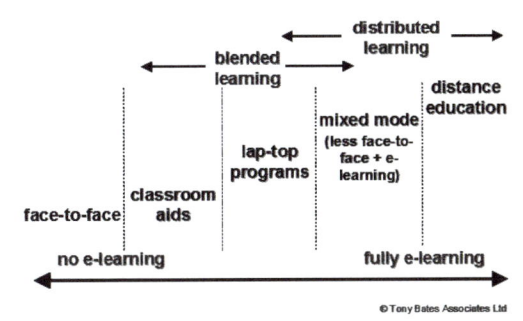

Source: Tony Bates Associates, Ltd., UK, 2005. Reprinted with permission.

One of the biggest challenges of many universities is convincing faculty to accept the changes required by online delivery. Typically, the introduction of pedagogical innovations and methodologies is challenging when e-learning becomes a partial substitute for traditional face-to-face teaching. To effect changes in the way professors organize their teaching activities and use new technologies, consultation with and buy-in on the part of faculty is needed.

Higher preference for blended models

The most popular e-learning programs today are in the fields of business, administration, finance and IT. It appears that blended learning will remain the most popular mode of delivery for these programs for some time to come. Depending on course objectives, blended learning can also help improve delivery by adding an online component, while preserving instructor-led learning for concepts not easily delivered outside of a classroom (e.g., clinical-based medical surgery). Although blended learning is the most popular form of e-learning delivery today, greater experimentation with pure online delivery is likely to occur in the future.

Open education resources

Although countries and institutions that are developing open educational resources (OER)[32] are still on a steep learning curve, such resources have the potential to expand educational access, affordability and quality. Digitization and the potential for instant, low-cost global communication have opened tremendous new opportunities for the dissemination and use of learning materials. This trend has spurred an increased number of OER initiatives that are available for free on the Internet, including (i) open courseware; (ii) open software tools (e.g., learning management systems); (iii) open material for faculty and staff capacity building; (iv) repositories of learning objects; and (v) free educational e-learning courses.

Nevertheless, expectations of the commercial possibilities of e-learning, especially at the tertiary level, are increasing the trend toward accessible OER. Virtually all cross-border e-learning today is commercial, with the majority of providers private, for-profit enterprises.[33] It is thus likely that non-state investors and providers will lead the way in e-learning and pioneer new and more affordable delivery models in both formal and non-formal education and training systems. How open source software and systems, along with open source courseware, will develop in tertiary education remains to be determined. Issues that need further study include:

- how copyright practices and rules for e-learning material will develop in tertiary education institutions;

- the true costs of customizing software or courseware to fit local contexts;

- the extent to which learning object models will prove successful and be used by teaching staff;

- the demand for free e-learning material versus "fee-paid" material; and

- the role of private companies in promoting e-learning investments.

Impact on the learning experience

The use of ICTs and e-learning potentially offer increased possibilities to positively impact teaching and learning in a world where the number of technically savvy students with a preference for using new technologies for "anywhere, anytime" learning will continue to grow. This newer breed of learner is better adapted to distance learning based on ICTs that promote learner-centered, self-paced learning. Without doubt, face-to-face exchange remains important in most forms of educational delivery. However, the use of new technologies increases the capacity for newer and better ways of knowledge-sharing and teamwork.

Growing evidence shows that accessing online courses and online applications can enhance student learning and interest. The aforementioned study of 30 U.S. universities concluded that online instruction improved student attitudes towards learning, attendance, modes of instruction and completion rates. (More than 50,000 students nationwide were involved in the study.)[34]

New technologies can also be effective in teaching specific subjects. The Policy and Leadership Studies Group at the National Institute of Education (NIE) in Singapore, for example, has designed a computer simulation to teach education managers and leaders how to structure an organization. The computer simulation, "Organization Structures," was designed to create an active learning environment. Students go through online processes of planning, implementing, gathering feedback and refection, and are then able to see the results of their organizational strate-

---

Box 6.2   E-learning impact and its drivers

According to Larsen and Vincent-Lancrin, the positive impacts of e-learning are driven by:

- *Facilitated access to international faculty and peers*, e.g., with the possibility of online lectures or joint classes with remote students;

- *Flexible access to materials and other resources*, allowing students to revise a particular aspect of a course, while providing part-time students more flexibility and remote students easier access to library materials;

- *Enhancement of face-to-face sessions,* as the availability of archived lectures online frees faculty to focus on difficult topics (the debate on pedagogy sparked by the introduction of e-learning also influences these sessions); and

- *Improved communication* between faculty and students and increased peer learning.

Source: Larsen and Stephan, "The Impact of ICT on Tertiary Education: Advances and Promises," OECD, Paris, 2005, 8.

---

gies. Although this simulation is still undergoing revision and development, it highlights the kind of engaged learning that is now occurring in e-learning, illustrating how such learning is changing traditional face-to-face delivery.

Electronic communications are also being increasingly used in problem-based learning. Teaching teams at the Law Department of Temasek Polytechnic in Singapore have, for example, introduced online inquiry and online discussion forums into paralegal training. The course design requires students to collaborate in teams to conduct a series of inquiries and client interviews. Using online forums, students post factual questions and probe their clients, who are online twice per week.

The "positive impact" of e-learning on the overall learning experience is itself a significant achievement, although it has not radically transformed teaching and learning processes. While institutions that have adopted e-learning generally have a positive view of its possible impact on quality, little convincing evidence exists concerning the superior or inferior quality of fully online learning compared to other modes of tertiary education.

Simulated e-learning through digital games

In certain settings, e-learning is also being conducted via digital games. The U.S. military, for example, uses games to train soldiers, sailors, pilots and tank drivers to master expensive, sensitive equipment. The military does not need to simulate a tank or airplane, but to train people's minds so that when they get into a real tank on a battlefield, they do the right thing. Many action games thus teach essential skills like teamwork, communication, as well as concepts of command and control. Most of the games used in military training are developed by the military in partnership with commercial game software vendors.

Weakening differentiation of online degrees and qualifications

Differentiation between online qualifications and conventional campus-based degrees is starting to wane and is expected to disappear over time.

Even in China, where qualification certificates denote the form of delivery, this practice is diminishing as e-learning delivery becomes mainstreamed. Employer perceptions of and resistance to online qualifications have all but disappeared in the developed world. No clearer example of this trend can be given than the University of Phoenix Online (UPOL) in the USA. UPOL students are based in 91 countries, including many developing countries; more than 50 percent of their tuition fees are subsidized by employers (who clearly like what is taught and do not object to the mode of delivery.) [35]

Part V. Emerging issues and success factors in e-learning

Technology solutions

When designing a successful e-learning implementation, whether campus-based or for distance education, the functional needs of pedagogy and learning should determine the technology selected. Acquisition of new technologies should thus follow rational planning that has specified the functionality required to support pedagogical strategies. This approach will not only ease the burden of unnecessary capital expenditures, but will also result in better and more efficient use of new technologies as they become available.

Satellite communications, for example, are opening distance education and training programs to more remote areas of China. Shanghai Aerospace Computer System Engineering Co., Ltd. (SAC) currently offers a satellite-based distance medical education and training service called the China Modern Distance Education Project (CMDE). The aim of the project is to upgrade the qualifications of nurses, working healthcare professionals and doctors throughout the country. Health and medical courses are delivered by the Shanghai Second Medical University, which

is the university of record for the project and the provider of all qualifications. [36]

SAC plans to establish around 300 distance-learning centers (DLCs) in existing hospital or medical school locations across China, plus an additional 90 continuing medical education (CME) learning centers for doctors between 2005 and 2007. The DLCs and CMEs will be supported by 30 strategically sited technical support centers across the country, with satellite communications used to provide links to programs in regions where landline telecommunications services are either difficult or more expensive to access. [37]

The siting of DLCs inside existing hospital locations allows nurses, health workers and doctors to study after hours at their place of work, taking courses provided by one of the country's leading medical universities. The strategic location of participating hospitals also makes access to continuing education easier for general practitioners, who in some cases would have to travel hundreds of miles every month to fulfill continuing medical training obligations. In this example, satellite technologies and rich media content have proven more cost-effective than the more conventional, browser-based content delivered by China's Education Research Network (CERNET). [38]

Istanbul Bilgi University (Bilgi) in Turkey is another example of how decentralized campuses can provide online programs and resources for students, SME workers and individuals in geographically remote locations. The university's online e-MBA program was launched in 2001 and provides instruction in both Turkish and English. Following its initial success, Bilgi in 2005 began to plan a network of remote distance-learning centers (DLCs) across Turkey. Given that over 50 percent of Turkey's population is under

---

Box 6.3 Nine success factors of a bankable e-learning project

1) Positive regulatory environment for private investment.

2) Attractive market conditions: unmet demand and supply, plus scalability (many e-learning models need high enrollments to offset high initial development costs).

3) Saleable services (unmet demand and affordability are converted into consumption).

4) Predictable revenues.

5) A proven and trusted education business model that balances fair financial returns against the enhancement of teaching and learning provided by electronic delivery.

6) Quality and relevance of learning content, including credentials, qualifications, assessment strategies and quality management systems.

7) Strong financial condition of the provider, including positive cash flows that will produce near-term profitability and/or surpluses.

8) Strong governance and management, with a proven successful track record.

9) Clear strategic vision and strong internal control systems.

Source: R. Perkinson, "Summary of Education Investment Workshop," International Finance Corporation, Washington DC, February 2003.

---

30 years of age, there is considerable unmet demand for places in higher education institutions among young people, both employed and unemployed. Bilgi intends to reach this cohort by linking decentralized centers with online courses. Online capability will also allow less-advantaged groups in semi-urban areas to access seminars and special workshops involving leading academics and business leaders.

Courses blend online and instructor-led delivery and will target mid-life executives, managers and lifelong learners from a wide cross-section of Turkish society. These students would otherwise find it difficult to access similar programs due to their geographic locations. As the numbers of students increase, the DLCs will eventually make the cost of short courses more competitive for the emerging Turkish middle class.[39]

Success factors

Most distance e-learning initiatives delivered by both public and private higher education institutions are commercially driven. Many are private and for profit. Public providers conveniently use the word "surplus" as an alternative to the more conventional terms "profit" or "net income" taught in their business schools. Whether public or private, the International Finance Corporation identifies nine success factors of successful commercial e-learning models in both developed and developing countries (see box 6.3).

The factors listed in box 6.3 determine the risks and barriers to entry, particularly with respect to investments in e-learning ventures. Governments can play a critical role in fostering non-state investment in these ventures. Investors look for positive regulatory environments for investment, avoiding smothering regulations that create commercial uncertainty. An example of a policy that can jeopardize commercial objectives is the capping of tuition fees, which can increase the risk to marginal returns, as well as unfairly restrict a provider from reinvesting surpluses to improve quality. Capping tuition fees can also result in financial returns that are insufficient to service debt or provide fair returns to shareholders.

Regulations that limit equity and ownership will also turn local and foreign investors away. Uneven playing fields, where public-sector institutions receive more favorable treatment, added to inconsistent and inefficient approval processes that disadvantage private investors, are additional reasons that cause investors to shy away from investing in educational ventures. In many developing countries, these barriers also apply to national investment in e-learning initiatives, leaving cross-border delivery the sole option for interested students.

A growing global phenomenon

Despite the financial distress of many e-learning ventures in the late 1990s, online initiatives are on the rise. Although investors today are more cautious when evaluating new investments in online learning, signs nevertheless indicate that these ventures will grow significantly in the future, especially in developing countries. It is in such countries where optimized use of new technologies can lower the barriers of access and affordability.

China, for example, is perhaps the world's largest potential online education market. The country has one of the world's lowest percentages of university graduates per capita. As a result, over 100 million people aged between 18 and 25 do not have a university education. China also has a potential continuing education market 10 times

the size of that of the United States. As a result, the Chinese government is openly supporting the advancement of online solutions to improve access to higher education throughout the country.

The use of ICTs and e-learning has a good chance of reaching an increasing number of non-traditional higher education students by:

- expanding participation at both the tertiary university and non-university level

- increasing the flexibility of participation and modes of delivery

- increasing service to people living in remote areas

- reaching foreign students who might wish to pursue foreign programs while remaining resident in their own country

Developing countries with unmet demand for higher education programs in topics such as business, IT and finance are finding that foreign e-education providers are stepping in to fill the gap. A number of large, scaleable e-learning programs are creating attention around the world, a few of which are based in developing nations.

Laureate Education Inc., USA. Laureate Education offers online undergraduate and graduate degree programs for working professionals, as well as degree programs at international campuses. Laureate's online tertiary units consist of Canter & Associates, Walden University, National Technological University (NTU), and Laureate Online Education, B.V. Collectively, these units offer degree programs in education, psychology, health and human services, management, engineering and information technology, primarily to students outside the United States.

Laureate's online higher education institutions are assisting the group's campus-based institutions to launch distance-learning initiatives, including joint and coordinated degree programs.[40]

Canter & Associates (Canter) is the largest teacher-education and professional development organization in the United States. Canter has established partnerships with accredited universities and colleges to produce materials for graduate-level courses and degree programs. Since 1976, it has enrolled more than 1 million teachers in partner master's degree programs and graduate courses. Over 200,000 kindergarten to 12th-grade educators have participated in professional development courses through Canter's research-based distance-learning format, which links educators with respected educational experts and leaders via the use of printed materials, video and the Internet.

Walden University is based in the United States and provides online distance programs to students from more than 30 countries, specializing in master's and doctoral degree programs. Courses are offered through four schools: Education, Management, Psychology and Health and Human Services. Walden is accredited by the Higher Learning Commission and a member of the North Central Association (NCA), a regional accrediting association recognized by the U.S. Department of Education.

National Technological University (NTU) was the first regionally accredited virtual university in the United States. Established in 1984 with the backing of industry leaders such as IBM, Lockheed Martin, Boeing, Hewlett-Packard and Motorola, NTU offers master's degree programs and graduate-level certificate programs, as well as non-credit professional development courses. Courses are delivered via videotape, CD-ROM and online through partnerships with leading schools of engineering across the United States.

These partnerships give NTU students access to the nation's best professors and the most up-to-date advances in their fields of study.

Laureate Online Education, B.V., is a new worldwide e-learning partnership between Laureate and the University of Liverpool in the UK that specializes in the delivery of online graduate programs to working professionals in over 95 developed and developing countries around the world. Online students typically have between 8 and 15 years of work experience.

The Apollo Group/ University of Phoenix Online. The adult education market in the USA is a significant and growing component of the post-secondary education market, estimated by the U.S. Department of Education to be a US$280 billion industry.[41] As mentioned earlier, over 5.9 million, or 39 percent of all students enrolled in higher education programs are over the age of 24.[42] Many working adults seek accredited degree programs that can accommodate the fixed schedules and time commitments of their professional and personal obligations. The University of Phoenix serves this market both in the United States and worldwide through the University of Phoenix Online (UPOL), the largest private, for-profit online educational provider in the U.S. tertiary sector today. The university's enrollment rates reflect the rapidly growing market for its services: 18,000 students were enrolled in 2000, 79,000 in 2003 and over 109,000 in 2004.

Tecnologico de Monterrey, Mexico. In 2004, Tecnológico de Monterrey in Mexico had 101,000 students on all of its campuses, of which over 80,000 were taking one or more of their courses online through Universidad Virtual, the online division of the university. Tecnologico de Monterrey is a good example of a "wired" university by world standards. It has a digital library that houses more than one million online articles and a Business Information Center that offers 110 databases, an exhibition hall, projection rooms and "connected" study cubicles for student use.

As noted earlier, Tecnologico de Monterrey also has a division named Tec Milenio University, which uses Tecnologico de Monterrey professors to design courses from the parent campus, which are then delivered to modestly equipped campuses at about one-third of their original cost. In 2003, Tec Milenio had six campuses that employed 491 faculty and 6,440 students. In 2004, student enrollments rose to 8,611.

Another innovative Tecnologico de Monterrey project is Prep@NET, which uses undergraduate students to teach and mentor secondary students online. Prep@NET currently offers preparatory school programs to students in grades 10, 11 and 12 . The programs are financed by three state governments of Mexico. Computers and Internet access for the students are provided through collaboration between the state governments, local companies and vendors—an example of how governments and telecommunications providers can work together to advance innovative education delivery models.

Manipal Universal Learning (ManipalU), India. ManipalU provides distance learning and e-training initiatives through the Manipal Academy of Higher Education (MAHE) and the Sikkim Manipal University of Health, Medical and Technological Sciences (SMU). The program offers 52 programs to 40,000 students through 500 learning centers in India and serves nearly 2,000 international students in more than ten countries in the South Asia, Africa and the Far East. Its MBA and health sector courses are designed for working professionals. Programs are offered

in such fields as information technology; management sciences; fashion design; hotel, travel and hospitality management; journalism and mass communications; insurance and actuarial services; health programs; ecology and environmental science; biotechnolgy and bioinformatics.[43]

The university uses a mix of new technologies to overcome the typical constraints that its students face, such as finances, family, geography and careers. Virtual classrooms use both interactive satellite technology and open classroom teaching. To improve its reach and benefit from economies of scale, the program has invested significantly in very small aperture terminals (VSAT) to reach remote locations where the Internet and other conventional delivery mediums are not readily available. Students can directly access the university's distributed learning system, which contains self-instruction materials, standard lectures by key faculty, tutoring and student support via special Learning Centre faculty, plus other online learning materials and self-assessment modules.[44]

ManipalU's delivery mediums accommodate interactive learning methodologies, including synchronous and chat modes, email, voice-based interactivity and white board presentations. As student numbers have grown, economies of scale have allowed the university to keep its tuition fees competitive, depending on the location. Certain learning communities have found it cost effective to invest in minimal infrastructure (e.g., the purchase of a small dish antenna and related hardware) to make their communications with the university more affordable and of higher quality.[45]

PRCEDU, China. PRCEDU is one of the larger online university operations and education service providers in China. Not an accredited university in its own right, it partners with such uni-

Figure 6.4 Tecnologico de Monterrey course design and delivery

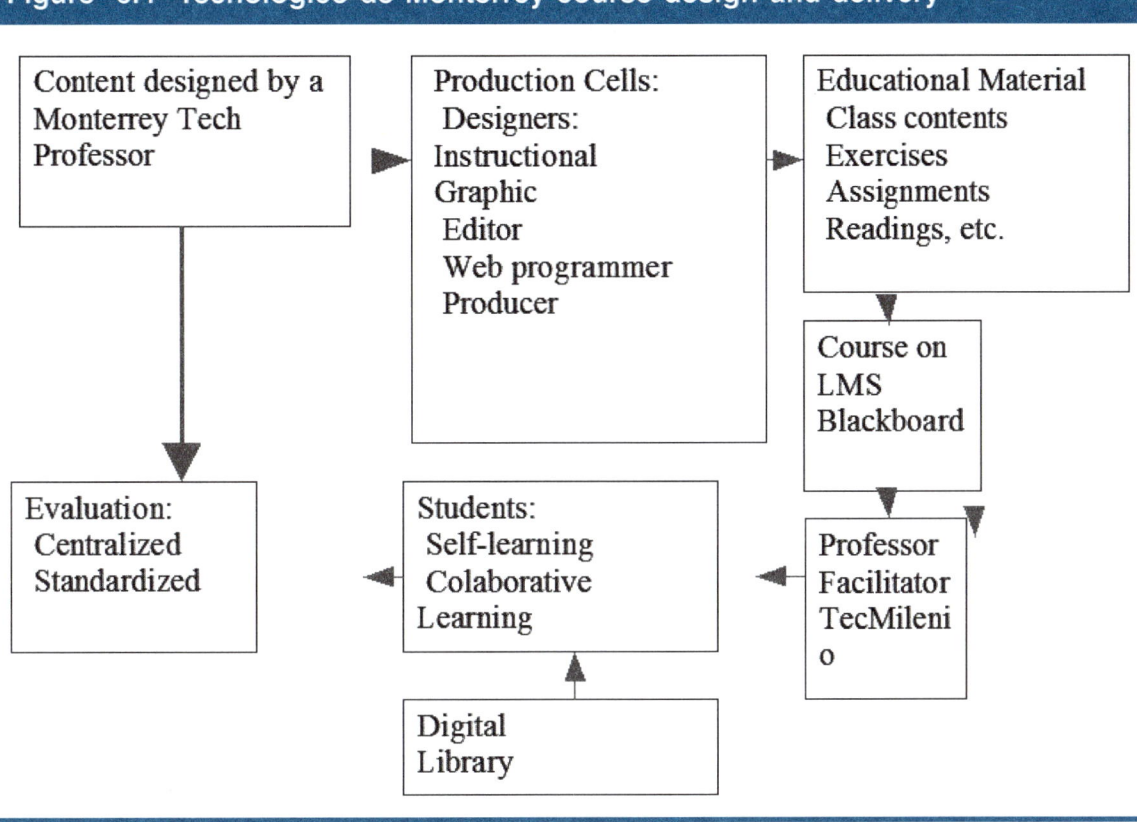

Source: Correspondence and conversations of the author with Tecnologico de Monterrey, Mexico, 2005.

versities to offer online degrees throughout China. In 2004, the PRCEDU platform had enrolled over 100,000 students in partner universities.[46]

Reaching the disadvantaged

Individuals and SMEs in socially disadvantaged settings are beginning to benefit from online and blended learning. New Zealand's South Auckland area, for example, is made up of pockets of poor socioeconomic groups originating from the Pacific Islands. In 2004, Technocatz Web Training Ltd., an online training provider, enrolled over 5,000 Pacific Island adults in basic IT training courses. Technocatz delivers its courses online to different community locations, where the delivery of basic IT courses is supported by local practitioners.

In less than 12 months, the courses created new employment opportunities for people who had previously found it very difficult to secure employment in administrative and clerical positions. By tracking their students, the company has determined that the earnings of people who had completed Technocatz training were 15 to 25 percent higher than their previous earnings. Some successful certificate students are now setting up their own online training centers for training other Pacific Island groups, using the online courses provided by Technocatz. Online scalability has allowed the company to reduce charges for its IT courses to below US$150 per person, making it accessible to even very poor groups.[47]

Technocatz also delivers courses online to farms in remote settings. These courses, which would otherwise be difficult to access, are partly subsidized by Fonterra, a large milk ingredients corporation that does business with the farming communities. The courses provide basic IT training to assist farmers and their wives to manage their holdings more effectively by recording financial information, managing live stock and inventory and gaining access to market prices for stock and produce. The programs have particularly benefited more remote farmers, both large and small, including an important group of New Zealand's indigenous Maori farming population.[48]

Conclusion: The changing landscape ahead

A recent survey in the United Kingdom found that professionals working in both the public and private sector rated the improved access and flexibility of online learning ahead of cost savings.[49] Cost savings did score very high in their evaluations, but the survey findings suggest that arguments regarding the return on investment in e-learning need to become more sophisticated. Overall, the added value of e-learning was seen to be of great importance.

Over the last decade, the e-learning industry has faced high set-up costs, inadequate technical infrastructure in many regions, low consumer confidence, cultural resistance, as well as concerns about the quality and relevance of online programs. Despite these difficulties, e-learning is still on the rise, creating its own momentum. Providers are also using better methodologies for both mass delivery and greater personalization of program delivery. There has also been a noticeable increase in the importance and adoption of online learner support modules, which provide both mentoring and technical help.[50]

E-learning markets are still predominantly local or country-based and face many language and cultural barriers. Simultaneously, learners are increasingly adapting to e-learning, particularly mid-life working executives, who benefit from the greater flexibility and convenience of studying "anytime anywhere," as opposed to attending traditional campus-based programs. In the private sector, e-learning is helping firms avoid the impractical costs of developing, upgrading and transferring knowledge via traditional training delivery methods.

Increased connectivity and bandwidth is making the delivery of quality training via Internet or satellite more practical in an increasing number of developed, and some developing, countries. In emerging economies, however, it can be a challenge to have job-related tutorials and training courses delivered in a cost-effective manner, especially when students and locations are scattered. At the same time, a shortage of instructors and travel difficulties in these countries make traditional training methods very costly.

Outlook for the future

In 2003, 82 percent of all public universities in the United States offered online courses.[51] Many technology courses in the country now feature Web-accessible e-learning (e.g., training in technology) as a standard part of course delivery. Lack of comprehensive data from other countries—especially developing countries—makes it difficult to document these trends in other parts of the world. Existing surveys, however, indicate that e-learning delivery will increase in the future. This finding is reinforced by the first international survey on online learning conducted in 2002 by the Observatory on Borderless Higher Education (OBHE) of the United Kingdom. The survey revealed that, among the 42 U.K. institutions that participated in the worldwide survey,

Box 6.4 Recommendations for advancing the e-learning agenda

1) Governments and telecommunications companies must work to reduce the cost of access to information and communications technologies, as this cost plays a critical part in determining the extent and uptake of e-learning, as well as how quickly new modes of ICT-assisted delivery are implemented.

2) Both governments and telecommunications companies must work together more cohesively to find better ways to invest in the human capital of individual countries by providing improved Internet-based communications and resources at all levels of education.

3) Governments and telecommunications providers need to think more innovatively about how to provide low-cost telecommunications and ISP services to optimize e-learning opportunities for disbursed constituencies with special needs.

4) Governments must play a critical role in fostering non-state investment in e-learning ventures. Investors will look for positive regulatory environments and avoid smothering regulations that create commercial uncertainty.

5) In the near term, governments much address the lack of systematic data on the costs of e-learning.

6) Allow the functional needs of pedagogical and learning strategies to determine the technology of e-learning programs, whether such programs are campus-based or fully online.

62 percent had developed or were developing an online learning strategy. Most had already done so as far back as 2000.[52]

The second OBHE survey in 2004 indicated that 79 percent of the 122 universities surveyed from Commonwealth countries either had an institution-wide "online learning" strategy (46 percent) or were developing one (33 percent). Only 9 percent of the institutions surveyed had no e-learning strategy in place or under development in 2004.[53] These findings indicate significant adoption and/or willingness to adopt some form of e-learning on the part the higher education sector. In general, however, the adoption of e-learning by universities is still at a relatively early phase worldwide.

The most effective reasons for adopting e-learning will continue to be driven by the needs of teaching and learning, not new and available tech-

nologies. Recent OBHE surveys show that on-campus enhancement of teaching and learning, plus improved flexibility of delivery, were the primary rationales for developing institutional e-learning strategies. Only 10 percent of the institutions considered the enhancement of distance learning more important than enhancement of on-campus learning.[54]

The international movement towards knowledge societies, combined with the need for lifelong learning systems and their growing importance for economic development, will all continue to force change on education systems and corporate training worldwide. It is especially important that higher education expand to include new systems that accommodate new kinds of learners, many of whom require flexible learning options not bound by time or location. Globalization and internationalization will also continue to impact higher education systems and their use of ICTs, with e-learning environments playing an important role in helping higher education institutions optimize the benefits of globalization.

In addition, the considerable growth in educational, instructional and research networks will have a potentially far greater positive impact on developing countries than e-learning programs alone. "Internet2," for example, is a generic term for the next-generation National Research and Education Networks (NRENs) of the world's universities and research centers. A limited-access research and development vehicle for experimenting with new collaborative and instructional technology, it appears that Internet2 will be able to provide better and more appropriate network capabilities to support research and educational activities of universities worldwide.[55]

In 2005, all high-income and many middle-income countries are participating in second-generation NREN projects.[56] Regional (REN) projects are also proliferating, including "Géant" in Europe, "Red Clara" in Latin America and "APAN" in the Asia-Pacific region. Internet2 also holds the promise of linking universities in developing countries with regional networks around the world. Not only can these networks provide new opportunities for collaboration and advancement of instructional technology and e-learning, they can encourage greater global collaboration, knowledge creation and transfer in countries currently without good e-development networks.

ICTs and the Internet will continue to influence the ways in which higher education has traditionally been delivered. In the future, new technologies will lead to new modes of delivery that will advance quality-based mass education to groups and regions that have not yet been reached by more conventional delivery models.

Notes

[1] As used in this chapter, the term "higher education" is used to denote different levels of post-secondary education, sometimes referred to as "tertiary university" and "tertiary non-university" education. Higher education in this context therefore also applies to the parallel world of training, including vocational, "certified" industry, corporate and information technology training.

[2] Websites of the Chinese Education and Research Network, http://www.edu.cn/HomePage/english/ statistics/education/index.shtml (accessed January and July 2005) and the China Ministry of Education, http://www.moe.edu.cn/english/basic_b.htm (accessed January and July 2005). The data listed on these sites only goes through 2002; the numbers cited above are estimates based on IFC staff research in 2004–2005.

[3] Personal knowledge of the author.

[4] NationMaster, "Encyclopedia: Demographics of India," Sydney, Australia, 2003–2005, http://www.nationmaster.com/encyclopedia/Demographics-of-India (accessed July 2005).

[5] See Universities and Colleges Admission Service (ucas.com), Cheltenham, UK, n.d., http://www.ucas. ac.uk/instit/index.html (accessed July 2005).

[6] OECD, Education at a Glance (Paris: OECD, 2003).

[7] Statistics Canada, "University Tuition Fees," The Daily, August 21, 2002, http://www.statcan.ca/Daily/ English/020821/d020821b.htm (accessed May 2003 and July 2005).

[8] Austria Ministry for Education, Science and Culture, "Information on Tuition Fees at Universities," January 2004, http://www.bmbwk.gv.at/fremdsprachig/en/univ/ English_-_Universities_I7478.xml#H2 (accessed May 2003 and July 2005).

[9] A. Labi, "British Tuition Increase Passes Final Hurdle," The Chronicle o Higher Education 50, no. 45 (July 16, 2004); OECD, "OECD Economic Survey of the United Kingdom: Graduate Contributions For Higher Education," OECD Economic Survey of the United Kingdom (Paris: OECD, 2004), http://www.oecd.org/dataoecd/50/25/24834806.pdf (accessed July 2005).

[10] R. Perkinson, "IFC Appraisal," IFC, Washington, DC, 2001; estimate based on statistical data provided by the Ministry of Education, Youth and Sport, Phnom Penh, Cambodia.

[11] Author estimate based on conversations with universities and accumulated market appraisal data regarding a range of university distance providers.

[12] Sloan Consortium, Entering the Mainstream: The Quality and Extent of Online Education in the United States, 2003 and 2004, Sloan Center, Olin and Babson Colleges, Franklin W. Olin College of Engineering, Needham, Massachusetts, http://www.sloan-c.org/resources/survey.asp (accessed July 2005).

[13] Michael T. Moe, "The Book of Knowledge: Investing in the Growing Education and Training Industry," Merrill Lynch & Co., Inc., New York, 2000.

[14] International Telecommunications Union database, ITU, Geneva, 2005. Observations are based on the author's current role in evaluating many tertiary, distance- and e-learning projects internationally.

[15] Author's observation, based on numerous international project evaluations.

[16] Correspondence and conversations of the author with Tecnologico de Monterrey, 2005; printed here with its permission.

[17] Kurt Larsen and Stephan Vincent-Lancrin, "The Impact of ICT on Tertiary Education: Advances and Promises," OCED, Paris, 2005.

[18] The term "age-group participation" refers to the participation of 18-to-24 year-olds in higher education.

[19] Unpublished data of the author, based on an IFC project, 2005.

[20] X. Cao, "Workplace Learning and E-Learning Adoption: Experience of the Private Sector in the United States." World Bank Institute, Washington, DC, 2004. Unpublished.

[21] William Saint, Tertiary Distance Education and Technology in Sub-Saharan Africa, Document 20992, Education & Technology Technical Notes Series 5, no. 1, World Bank, Washington, 2000, 97.

[22] Saint, Tertiary Distance Education, 2000, 7.

[23] A.W. Bates, Technology, E-Learning and Distance Education (London: Routledge, 2005).

[24] Stephan Ruth and Min Shi, "Distance Learning in Developing Countries: Is Anyone Measuring Cost Benefits?" George Mason University, Virginia, USA, 2001.

[25] Ruth and Shi, "Distance Learning in Developing Countries," 2001.

[26] Author's estimate of 2004, based on conversations with Chinese universities and accumulated market appraisal data involving a range of university distance providers.

[27] Carol A. Twigg, "Improving Learning and Reducing Costs: New Models For Online Learning," The Observatory on Borderless Education, London, UK, 2003.

[28] B. Hall, Benchmark Study of Best Practices, e-Learning, a Forbes special advertising section, 2000 http://www.forbes.com/specialsections/elearning/e-05.htm#b (accessed January and July 2005).

[29] W. Horton, Designing Web-based Training: How to Teach Anyone Anything Anywhere Anytime (Hoboken, New Jersey: John Wiley & Sons, Inc., 2000).

[30] Correspondence and conversations of the author with Latitude Consulting Group, Inc., and Novations Learning Technologies, Lansing, Michigan, 2005. Printed here with their permission.

[31] Danna Voth, "The Army Boots up for e-Learning," Learning and Training Innovations, Advanstar Communications, Lansing, Michigan, 2003, http://www.sfu.ca/~dchen/Cmns453/html/reading1.htm (accessed January and July 2005).

[32] The term open education resources (OER) typically refers to educational resources that are free and open to all, such as those based on open source software and courseware, including non-copyrighted digital resources. See, for example, the MERLOT (Multimedia Educational Resource for Learning and Teaching Online) repository of OER at http://www.merlot.org/Home (accessed July 2005).

[33] Author's observation, based on evaluations of many tertiary, distance- and e-learning projects internationally.

[34] Twigg, "Improving Learning and Reducing Costs," 2003.

[35] Apollo Group, Inc., Annual Reports (Phoenix, Arizona: 2003 and 2004), http://www.apollogrp.edu/Investor/AnnualReports.aspx (accessed January and July 2005); Charles Schwab Corporation, Company Research Report, Charles Schwab Corporation, San Francisco, CA, September 15, 2004.

[36] Correspondence and conversations of the author with SAC in 2004; printed here with its permission.

[37] Ibid.

[38] Funded by Chinese government, CERNET is a national communications backbone that connects universities and colleges across China. It was started in 1994 to improve networking across the sector and to accommodate the future demands of China's strategies for distance education connectivity and growth. See China Education and Re-

search Network, "CERNET Evolution," Beijing, China, August 15, 2001, http://www.edu.cn/20010815/188550.shtml (accessed July 2005).

[39] Correspondence and conversations of the author with Istanbul Bilgi University, May 2005, which approved this text.

[40] Correspondence and conversations of the author with Laureate Education, Inc., Baltimore, Maryland, 2005; printed here with its permission. The main source of information for this section is Laureate's corporate website, http://www.laureate-inc.com/univOnline.php (accessed January and July 2005).

[41] Apollo Group, Annual Report, 2003.

[42] "College Enrollment by Age of Students, 2002," The Chronicle of Higher Education, 2004.

[43] Correspondence and conversations of author with MAHE, 2005; printed here with its permission.

[44] Ibid.

[45] Ibid.

[46] Correspondence and conversations of author with PRCEDU, Beijing, China, 2005; printed here with its permission.

[47] Data provided by Technocatz, Auckland, New Zealand, 2005; printed here with its permission.

[48] Correspondence and conversations of author with Technocatz, Auckland, New Zealand, 2005; printed here with its permission.

[49] Epic Group Plc, "Epic Survey 2003: The Future of E-Learning," White Paper, Epic Group, Plc, Brighton, UK, 2003, http://www.epic.co.uk/content/resources/white_papers/survey2003_htm (accessed January 2005). Printed here with the permission of Epic Group.

[50] Author's observation, based on numerous reviews of international projects.

[51] Sloan Consortium, Entering the Mainstream, 2004.

[52] OBHE, "Online Learning in Commonwealth Universities" (surveys), OBHE, London, United Kingdom, 2002 and 2004, http://www.obhe.ac.uk/products/briefings (accessed May 2005).

[53] Ibid.

[54] Ibid.

[55] M. Foley, unpublished paper, World Bank Institute, Washington, DC, 2005.

[56] Ibid.

Chapter 7

The Role of International Cooperation in e-Development

by Bruno Lanvin and Isabel Neto

To a large extent, dealing with the e-agenda is generally seen as a domestic matter, whether one addresses e-strategy (chapter 3), e-leadership (chapter 4) or even the enabling environment for ICT development (chapter 2). Yet telecommunications and other information-intensive services are the first candidates for internationalization, since they rely on the most mobile global factor of all, namely, information. The process that led to the World Summit on the Information Society (WSIS) is itself recognition of the international dimension of information-related issues.

The international community now faces a number of challenges and expectations with respect to e-development. On one hand, it is expected to support national efforts to build information societies and bridge the digital divide. Efforts to build infrastructure, connect less densely populated areas and offer innovative ways for local communities and businesses to create value from better connectivity are the core mandate of bilateral donors and multilateral development agencies in this sphere. Such efforts are not only financial (i.e., official development assistance), but more importantly, policy-related (i.e., sharing best practices and assisting nations to create effective regulatory institutions).

On the other hand, the international community at large has a responsibility to respond to challenges that are broader than those faced by individual nations, such as the technical, economic and policy rules that will constitute universally accepted rules of the game. This category of activity includes norms and standards (the ITU), trade agreements (the WTO), but also to some extent, Internet governance (the WGIG). It also includes international financial support for regional infrastructure and other types of cross-border cooperation.

The international community also has a role in developing analytical and policy tools that allow developing nations to better conceptualize the role of ICT in development. It also has a role in stimulating long-term investment in relevant areas.

Collecting available data and statistics, as well as formulating internationally agreed development goals (such as the MDGs or the WSIS goals) is one part of this task. Another is to facilitate collaborative efforts. Effective global collaboration in cyber-security will, for example, require establishing new relationships and new connecting paths for information between private and public-sector entities.

Last but not least, the international community must provide forums where all of these issues can be discussed openly and professionally. The G-8 Digital Opportunity Task (DOT) Force, the U.N. ICT Task Force and WSIS all fall under this category.

It would nevertheless be a tragic mistake to limit the definition of international community to the public international community (i.e., bilateral and multilateral donors). The private sector and civil society at large are increasingly being called to the fore to help local communities, national economies and international entities face the challenges of the emerging global information economy. The WSIS has been breaking new ground by involving civil society organizations in intergovernmental debates. This practice is in line with the efforts of a number of international bodies (e.g., G-8 DOT Force, the U.N. ICT Task Force and entities incubated by the World Bank, such as the Development Gateway) to do the same. The involvement of the private sector and civil society organizations in public international proceedings is contributing to the mutual cross-fertilization of stakeholders involved and to new forms of cooperation among them (e.g., private-public partnerships). Similar efforts and innovations are expected in coming years.

The purpose of this chapter is not to provide a state-of-the-art matrix of who is doing what and where in e-development.[1] Nor does it aim to prescribe, judge or rank ongoing international efforts to bridge the digital divide. Its goal is to offer a global view of recent efforts to achieve internationally agreed development goals through better use of ICTs, as well as to facilitate better worldwide distribution of the benefits of ICTs. The paper thus endeavors to answer two major questions: What major trends are observable in international cooperation for e-development? What new roles and *modus operandi* could the international community adopt to maximize the positive effects of ICT on global development?

Section 1. Trends in e-development and international cooperation

This section looks at both the supply and demand sides of international e-development efforts. When considering possible roles and responsibilities of the international community, financing is a natural first topic (the supply side). Are international aid and investment flows helping to finance the connectivity needs of poorer regions? Do they focus on areas and sectors likely to provide a quick economic return? Do they concentrate on infrastructure (e.g., mobile telephony, broadband capacity), services (e.g., ICT in education), or multisectoral approaches (e.g., e-government)? How do public and private funding combine and/or substitute for one another in such efforts? Is e-development a priority in development assistance or is the appeal of ICT for development fading in the face of other concerns such as terrorism, HIV/AIDS, and access to drinkable water?

It is important not to reduce the issue of international cooperation to the supply side. Defining demand for e-development is equally important.

What are the demand trends in developing countries and economies in transition? What do these countries identify as the main roadblocks to efficient, competitive and fair information economies? What kind of support do they expect from the international community?

The rise in private financing for the ICT sector

In recent years ICT infrastructure investments and financing in the developing world have reflected decreasing levels of official development assistance (ODA) and increasing levels of private sector-funding (see chapter 1), with ODA shifting towards specific ICT applications. ODA flows for infrastructure in general (whether energy, transport, ICTs, irrigation, water supply, sanitation or the infrastructure components of rural and urban development) have been declining since 1996. The decrease in ODA commitments was especially sharp in the ICT sector: plunging from US$1.2 billion in 1990 to US$194 million in 2002.[2]

Figure 7.1 illustrates the magnitude of OECD bilateral donor commitments to the ICT infrastructure, both in total volume and as a share of these countries' total allocable ODA. The numbers speak for themselves: the share of aid for ICT infrastructure dropped from 4.5 to 0.6 percent of total bilateral ODA in the period 1990–2002. This trend resulted from the wave of privatizations of national telecommunications providers that occurred in the 1990s, plus the perceived profitability of the ICT sector, which prompted bilateral and multilateral donors to strengthen the role of private investment in infrastructure development.[3]

It is now generally accepted that the private sector and foreign direct investment (FDI) in particular have been the primary sources of ICT development and finance over the past two de-

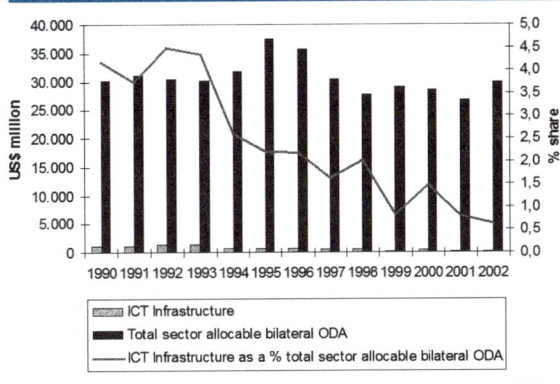

Figure 7.1 Total DAC donor bilateral ODA committments to ICT infrastructure

Legend:
- ICT Infrastructure
- Total sector allocable bilateral ODA
- ICT Infrastructure as a % total sector allocable bilateral ODA

Notes: DAC: OECD Development Assistance Committee; ODA: Official Development Assistance.
Source: OECD Development Assistance Committee (DAC)/OECD, *Financing ICTs for Development,* 2005.

cades. Several decades ago, the ICT sector was in the hands of state-owned enterprises. Following a wave of PTT privatizations and the introduction of competition, especially in mobile telephony, a number of private telecommunications operators has emerged. These private operators have helped increase teledensity significantly. In Africa, for example, there are now more mobile phones than fixed and teledensity (both fixed and mobile) has increased fivefold since 1995.[4] In addition, the private sector has made significant investments in the sector. Over the last decade, the combination of PTT privatization, mobile network licensing and other private ICT investment opportunities have drawn over US$250 billion of private investment into ICT infrastructure in developing economies.[5]

The ICT sector worldwide, even in some of the least-developed countries, has proven highly profitable in many areas. Financial resources are thus naturally drawn to the sector, given the opportunity for a favorable return on investment (particularly in the case of mobile telephony). However, a significant amount of recent investments were tied to privatizations and the payment of license fees, not necessarily to the construction of new facilities (i.e., they correspond in some instances to one-time infusions, not long–term, sustained flows). In addition, FDI in ICT infrastructure has declined markedly in recent years following the euphoric boom years of the 1990s.[6]

Given the dramatic shift of telecommunications infrastructure from public to private ownership, both multilateral and bilateral donors and the governments of developing countries have substantially reduced their role in funding capital ICT investments. Indeed, even though there is clearly still a role for public financing of ICT (e.g., with respect to ICT-for-development projects), other priorities, such as health, water, food, and emergency relief are competing for public funds.

Most donors have abandoned support for ICT infrastructure, leaving the job to the private sector. The World Bank in particular believes that investment in ICT infrastructure should continue to come predominantly from the private sector. Consequently, it generally advises governments against investing scarce public funds in infrastructure, except for situations where public investments can be a catalyst for private investment, the market alone will not meet access objectives (e.g., rural access) or ICT infrastructure is considered a public good.

At the same time that investment in the ICT sector has shifted from public to private sources, a stronger international commitment to reduce poverty has changed the focus of international donors from infrastructure and technology *per se* to ICT applications that can promote development. Many donors have thus "mainstreamed" ICTs in their development assistance programs, using ICT in different projects (e.g., health or education) as a tool of development. As a con-

sequence, the ICT component of these projects is sometimes difficult to quantify or even identify. This trend, discussed in more detail in the following section, also explains to some degree why investment flows into the ICT sector are decreasing—part of the decrease can be explained by the fact that this investment is attributed to specific social and economic sectors, instead of as an ICT expenditure or investment. Indeed, it is extremely difficult to track ICT-for-development investment figures.

The challenges of mainstreaming ICT as a tool for development

Since the mid-1990s, bilateral and multilateral development agencies have been supporting ICT-for-development (ICT4D) though a variety of pilot activities. This funding gave rise to a multiplicity of projects, often of small financial value, scattered across all sectors and regions. The rationale behind this approach was clearly heuristic: at a time when no previous experience or theory existed about how to use information technologies for development, donors believed it useful to "let a hundred flowers bloom" and then compare results. In the first years of the twenty-first century, this initial approach ran into two distinct challenges:

- The constellation of small pilot projects generated a myriad of anecdotal evidence that showed how imaginative uses of ICTs could enhance the delivery of education, health, gender balance, better governance and other significant development goals. However, such anecdotal evidence provided little concrete information about the macroeconomic impact of ICTs on developing countries or the scalability and sustainability of such projects.

- Following the burst of the ICT "bubble" around 2000, development circles lost interest in ICT, as development professionals came to view ICT as gadgetry, when compared to lasting development issues such as endemic diseases or new challenges such as international terrorism.

Given these challenges, the effort to mainstream ICT into "traditional" development projects was problematic. As the private sector took increasing interest and responsibility in financing information infrastructure and developing telecommunications and information services worldwide, the international donor community appeared to struggle with its own role in bridging the digital divide. Was the time ripe for moving beyond pilots and anecdotal results? Should donors be involved in scaling up successful projects, or should sustainability be a pre-requisite before additional resources were devoted to ICT4D projects? Were good practices emerging from the multiplicity of small projects financed in the 1990s? Was ICT a major tool for development or merely a technical dimension of development efforts in sectors such as health and education?

To address these complex issues, the international community has relied on a number of forums, the mandate of which cut across sectors. These forums have included international bodies such as the G-8 DOT Force (created in 2000), the U.N. ICT Task Force (also launched in 2000), as well as the WSIS process (which gathered momentum in approximately the same year). The thinking of donors in this area was also stimulated by (i) ongoing efforts to coordinate aid flows and increase the efficiency of development assistance in general,[7] and (ii) the new momentum in favor of internationally agreed development targets such as the Millennium Development Goals (MDGs). Major public donors subsequently devoted specific attention to mainstreaming ICT in development programs. For example, the OECD Development Assistance Committee

(DAC) commissioned a major survey of how bilateral and multilateral donors had mainstreamed ICT in their activities (see box 7.1).

The OECD/DAC also produced a detailed matrix of "who is doing what" in ICT for development.[8] The matrix confirmed that most donors had overcome the trauma of the "ICT crash," realized that ICT was a major ingredient of development and were mainstreaming it in their development work.

Recently, public donors have adopted a different view of what mainstreaming means. For example, the OECD/DAC matrix of 2003 (see Box 7.1) showed a different picture than the 2001 version (see Box 7.2). The same 2003 exercise underlined the difficulty in identifying and quantifying the ICT component of various projects, suggesting that most donors had mainstreamed ICT in their development programs. However, the exercise also clearly recognized that the total volume of funding for ICT had not increased between 2001 and 2003 and remained "well short of US$1 billion."

Beyond "either/or"

The old debate of the 1990s about choosing between ICT and other development imperatives (e.g., the argument that investment in ICT draws precious resources away from more urgent development needs) has now shifted. The old idea of trade-offs has given way to a new idea of complementarity. It is now clear that these new technologies are not an end in themselves. Nor will a one-size-fits-all approach work—developing countries vary too greatly in geography, culture and level of economic attainment. ICT cannot eliminate the need for political stability, physical infrastructure, human capacity or basic health care, nor can it offer a panacea for all development problems.

Box 7.1 Survey of donor ICT for development activities

The Development Assistance Committee of the OECD conducted a survey in 2003 on how bilateral and multilateral donors have mainstreamed information and communication technologies (ICT) in their development assistance programs to more effectively achieve development goals, particularly the Millennium Development Goals (MDGs). The survey covered twenty-three DAC members and twenty-five multilateral agencies. Its main findings were:

- The vast majority of donors recognize the potential of ICT as a catalyst for socioeconomic development, but not all of them are at the same stage of using ICT to meet development objectives. While some are planning to develop new ICT strategies, others have already used ICT for years and have drawn lessons from their past experience;

- In all cases, donors are using ICT in service of broader strategic objectives in a number of development sectors (health, education, e-commerce, e-government, etc.). Their focus is on meeting objectives, not on technology *per se*;

- Achieving the MDGs, particularly poverty reduction, underpins most donor ICT strategies. These strategies aim to create an inclusive information society with special attention to underserved regions, including least-developed countries (LDCs) and vulnerable populations; and

- Most donors have built ICT4D strategies on partnerships that involve a number of actors from other bilateral and multilateral agencies, ministries (communication, education, etc.), civil society, the private sector, universities and research institutions in both developed and developing countries.

Source: OECD/DAC, "Survey of Donor ICT for Development Activities and the Lessons Learnt," OECD, Paris, 2003.

Evidence is growing, however, that ICT is a potentially powerful tool in an overall development strategy, when used in the right way. This new approach requires innovative and close partnership between governments, business and civil society.[9] ICT is, in fact, a general-purpose technology (GPT) characterized by "(1) wide scope for improvement and elaboration; (2) applicability across a broad range of uses and in a wide variety of products and processes; and (3) strong complementarities with existing or potential new technologies. GPTs play the role of 'enabling technologies,' opening up new opportunities, rather than offering complete solutions."[10]

ICT is a powerful tool to pursue development objectives at the national level

The new ICT approach of major donors is mirrored in national development strategies that view ICT as a major instrument to kick-start certain development efforts (e.g., reforming government through e-government activities) or accelerate others (e.g., using ICT to facilitate trade).

Over the last few years, however, one of the most striking changes that has affected demand in developing countries and countries in transition is a shift from "i-demands" (ICT-focused and ICT-specific needs) to "e-demands" (requests related to the e-development agenda, such as e-government, e-commerce, e-health and e-education). Even more recently, there has been a shift from "e-demands" to "k-demands" (knowledge-related needs, particularly in the area of service-based competition, innovation and vocational training).

The international donor community finds such demands (whether e- or k-based) more difficult to address because these demands do not cut simply across sectors, but also across donor and beneficiary audiences. When a national government includes ICT development as a priority in its national strategy, the international community has relatively little difficulty translating this priority into direct (e.g., connectivity, IT equipment)

and indirect needs (e.g., strengthening the regulatory and competition environment, building viable economic models for universal service and interconnection).

When the same government begins to formulate priorities as "developing e-commerce," or "promoting e-government" and to aggregate these priorities under the umbrella of "e-strategies," the translation challenge becomes significantly more complex for the donor community. Suddenly, donors have to consider and discuss the appropriateness of such objectives, touching on new issues of e-readiness, the sequencing of e-strategies and the sustainability of application-based projects (as opposed to projects based on generic technologies such as telephony). The

---

Box 7.2 Changes in the OECD/DAC matrix, 2001 to 2003

- By 2003, most donors had developed a strategy not only to use ICT within existing and new programs, but within their own agencies to improve the delivery of development programs.

- Long-term experience in the field with ICT-for-development pilot projects is shaping strategies, as are in-depth studies. The needs of developing countries, particularly the priorities identified in the Millennium Declaration, guide these strategies.

- Donors consider ICTs in the broad sense, encompassing both older technologies (radio, television) and newer technologies (Internet, mobile phones); some donors emphasize the need to combine the two in order to realize maximize benefits.

- In most cases, donors view ICTs as tools to meet development objectives, not as a separate sector. Some donors underline the need to create an enabling environment as a prerequisite for effective use of ICTs as tools of development. These donors view investment in telecommunications infrastructure and the creation of the necessary technological, legal, regulatory and human framework as a priority.

- Guiding principles for the use of ICT emphasize respect for national ownership and demand-driven support and assisting developing country governments to formulate their own ICT development strategies. When developing countries decide to harness ICT for development, some donors recommend that their respective ICT strategies be incorporated into Poverty Reduction Strategy Papers (PRSPs).

Source: OECD/DAC, "Survey of Donor ICT for Development Activities," 2003.

fundamental ingredients of success (e.g., conducive regulatory and institutional framework and economic regimes that ensure the viability of the ICT sector) have not lost their value, but they are now one step further from the current needs of potential aid recipients, which are expressed at a higher level.

The advent of knowledge societies has further complicated the picture for donors: in an increasing number of countries, ICT is seen as a tool to pursue an e-agenda, itself only one set of priorities for achieving broader concerns, such as international competitiveness or fair and dynamic information societies. Paradoxically, by reaching a higher level of complexity, the international community may soon have an unprecedented opportunity to solve the difficult dilemma of e-development.

Section 2. What next? Possible new roles for the international community

The previous section has identified some of the trends, demands and expectations of the international community in the area of ICT for development. It also highlighted some of the changes that have begun to be implemented and/or acknowledged in this sphere, such as increasing the role of the private sector and shifting from an ICT-based to a development-based agenda.

This section attempts to suggest some of the ways in which the international community (public donors, international organizations, the private sector and civil society at large) could play a more active and decisive role in building a truly global information society that support development.

Two possible avenues will be explored in detail: (i) the need to learn from experience by measuring how ICT concretely benefits development, and (ii) the urgent necessity for international players to revisit and revise their roles.

Monitoring, evaluation and stocktaking: Learning from experience

Chapter 3 addressed the need for monitoring and evaluation frameworks for ICT-based development initiatives. The international community (donors in particular) has recently become more aware of the importance of such frameworks, as well as the necessity to identify best practices and share knowledge about how ICT can contribute to specific development objectives. Without going into technical details, this section will review some of the trends in this domain and how they affect the roles of international organizations.

Measuring the benefits of ICT and the success or failures of specific projects is particularly urgent because current data is limited. ICT projects are difficult to track and there is insufficient rigorous data to serve as a basis for policy decisions. Certain organizations are tracking different aspects of ICT. The ITU's *World Telecommunications Development Report* (WTDR),[11] for example, focuses on telecommunications. *The Global Information Technology Report* (GITR) edited by the World Economic Forum also tracks ICT, but from a strong private-sector perspective.[12] A recent report produced by the WSIS Task Force on Financing Mechanisms[13] provides helpful information on tracking ICT investments; the publication is the result of a substantial effort to gather information from different sources.

The multidisciplinary nature of ICT and the fact that it is a relatively new area makes it especially difficult to track. Given the aforementioned shift from providing technology to fostering development through sectoral applications, ICT project components have become neither separately identifiable nor quantifiable. Even the task of trying to track investments in ICT can be challenging. Investments in the sector include infrastructure projects, support to the IT industry and funding of ICT applications. Where ICT is only one component of a larger project, as opposed to a standalone project, it can be difficult to track and monitor donor commitments, which potentially leads to incomplete or inconsistent reporting.

As mentioned in Chapter 1, there is also little rigorous, comparable evidence or project evaluation that documents the benefits of ICT to development. International cooperation organizations need to measure how ICT benefits development in order to (i) justify their investments, specifically, the use of public funds, (ii) use these measurements as a strategy and activity planning input and (iii) promote sustainable models that work. In this respect, international organizations may be in a privileged position to enable stock taking and the dissemination of shared experience.

The sheer volume and diversity of initiatives in the ICT field reflect that international development organizations recognize the potential power of ICT to promote development. In some cases, significant resources have already been earmarked for ICT. Yet for ICTs to become a more effective tool of sustained growth and poverty reduction, it is urgent that donors move beyond experimentation to a more rigorous, coordinated, results-oriented approach.

Donors need to determine how they are going to use available resources: both in terms of funding

and practical implementation. Best- and worst-practice knowledge is crucial in this context. Best-practice examples should focus not simply on projects that have succeeded, but the critical success factors, including business analysis and strategic planning for ICT-based solutions; capacity development inputs, activities and outputs that can be measured; and risk management. Similarly, worst practices should analyze the causes of failure and identify the obstacles that prevented good projects from achieving sustainability, scalability, and on-time completion within budget.

Additional data and analysis can assist e-development actors to design comprehensive frameworks for evaluating how ICT assists the development process, providing rationales for sectoral decision makers to promote ICT in their respective areas. An example of such framework is the "multiplier vs. subtracter" approach developed by Lanvin and Qiang and briefly described in box 7.3.[14] In this model, the ICT sector is used as a lens to re-think development strategies and a tool to help all sectors reach development objectives. This approach explicitly recognizes the role of ICT as a cross-sectoral force.

Measuring and evaluating ICT projects will identify which models work and can achieve sustainability and, ultimately, scalability. International organizations are in a privileged position to conduct such stock taking, compile best practices and disseminate information, as well as provide forums for research and reflection. Examples of such initiatives are *info*Dev (www.infodev.org) and the Development Gateway (www.developmentgateway.org). Certain international cooperation organizations have already started working in this area, or have at least identified it as key priority. A forthcoming World Bank publication, for example, will look at

Box 7.3 The "multiplier vs. subtracter" approach: A framework for ICT

The "multiplier vs. subtracter" approach provides:

1) A conceptual frame of reference that decision and policy makers can use to (1) see the big picture, (2) identify causalities between actions and anticipated effects and (3) choose the preferred political path, relative emphases and sequencing of their own activities and those of their public and private partners. Such a framework provides examples, references and methodologies for estimating the effects of higher investment in ICT on various social and economic objectives (including the MDGs).

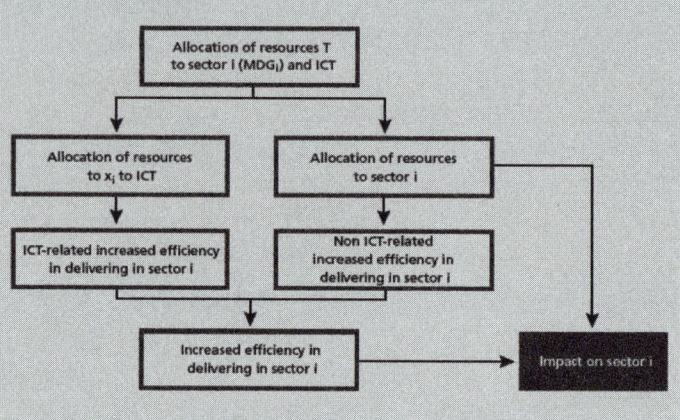

2) A set of "scorecards" that policymakers, local stakeholders and international contributors can use to (1) measure the efforts made at different levels of decision making, (2) evaluate their impact along the chain of causalities described above and (3) mobilize energies and support where any "missing link" or imbalance is identified that could imperil the pursuit of established development objectives.

3) Feedback mechanisms (particularly at the local level) for the public and private sector to promote ICT as a tool for development and growth.

Source: Lanvin and Qiang, "Poverty 'E-readication,'" 2003.

trends in the information society and provide an ICT index.[15] The UNDP has identified both research and analysis of effective strategies and the use of ICT to enhance achievement of MDGs as key areas of work for its ICT portfolio. Last but not least, recently defined UNCTAD priorities include research and analysis on ICT for economic development, measurement of e-business and related indicators, and assessments of the digital divide.

New roles for international cooperation

Although the international community—including public donors, international agencies and the private sector—will continue to play a major role in financing local, regional and global efforts to bridge the digital divide and build vibrant, competitive and fair information societies, this community will increasingly be called to accept new responsibilities and roles. Specific areas of international cooperation with immediate relevance are described in the paragraphs below.

Provide globally accepted frameworks for analysis, measurement, monitoring and evaluation. Globally comparable indicators are needed that can describe the relative strengths and weaknesses of individual economies vis-à-vis information-intensive competition. Indicators that measure e-readiness or knowledge pillars may, for example, progressively become core elements of investment climate analyses and national development plans.[16] National statistical offices will seek international guidance to provide reliable and international comparable data about the state and availability of ICT infrastructure and services in their respective economies.[17] Last but not least, monitoring and evaluation of efforts will become more central to the decision making of donors, investors and beneficiaries of ICT4D initiatives and programs.

Facilitate new sources of financing for ICT4D. Because an international viewpoint is often a pre-requisite for collecting and identifying best practices and successful experiences, international players will continue to have the core responsibility for testing, studying and disseminating new business models for financing ICT for development. This role is particularly important in domains such as universal service, in which public entities and the private sector can join forces in a mutually beneficial way. International public donors also have an increasingly important role to play in ushering private funds into ICT financing in emerging economies,[18] with special attention given to risk mitigation and sub-sovereign lending.[19]

Ensure that developing nations have a voice in the development of new governance frameworks. A growing number of ICT-related issues are likely to become cross-border issues in coming years. Internet governance, for example, is a harbinger of broader issues of global governance. In this context, the international community must ensure that developing countries have a voice in discussing and adopting governance frameworks that may endure for some time to come.

Facilitate mechanisms for e-security. Given the cross-border nature of cyber-crime, networks for exchanging know-how and expertise relating to new legal frameworks will be required to investigate, prosecute and deter cyber-crime and e-security threats. Telecommunications regulators or ministers with ICT portfolios will increasingly be required to anticipate the impact of next-generation networks on economic and social sectors that are dependent on telecommunications and Internet services. These bodies are now facing complex new challenges, including certain challenges of convergence (e.g., SMS integration with e-mail and Voice-over-IP). In many countries, regulatory bodies will need to establish an overall e-security framework in which security concerns relating to basic telecommunications, the global grid and the Internet are part of a complex, international set of institutional arrangements.[20]

Lead experimentation and disseminate best practices. Information technologies continue to change at a rapid pace. It is likely that breakthrough innovations which combine ICTs and other domains (e.g., biology, genetics, agriculture) will occur with increasing frequency in the near future. The international community's role here must be to encourage and support pilot projects that illustrate how such innovations contribute to specific development objectives. It must do so in a true spirit of technological neutrality (i.e., giving priority to development goals over technology adoption). The international community may also be able to provide guidance to the scientific community, stimulating greater efforts to include development concerns into fundamental scientific research. Exploring the applicability of specific technical solutions to poorer countries may yield positive and important lessons for governments and the private sector.[21]

Provide forums for the exchange of views. Last but not least, information societies are being built without textbooks. Technologies are changing too rapidly, and new successful practices are blossoming too fast, for a stable list of standard procedures to be established. The building of information societies also raises a number of social, ethical and political issues that cannot be addressed in the absence of society-wide debates. A major responsibility of the international community in the years to come will be to provide neutral ground for such debates at the global level. Hopefully, these forums will become "circles of confidence" where new partnerships can be built between stakeholders at local and international levels. Stimulating such partnerships should be a priority objective of international cooperation.[22]

Conclusion: Taking advantage of new momentum

The trends emerging today will accelerate in coming years—compounded or mitigated by trends that have not yet been identified. One of the main tendencies of ICT for development is not going to fade away quickly: the shift towards turning ICTs into instruments of development.

During the 1980s and early 1990s, governments sought greater connectivity as an end in itself, and were focusing on the conditions that would allow them to get there, including attracting foreign investment and improving their regulatory frameworks (an "i-driven" agenda). As of the mid-1990s, an "e-everything" era began in which the e-agenda (e-commerce in particular) drove ICT4D. National governments formulated ICT needs along the lines of e-agendas, geared towards improving specific sectors (e.g., education, health, governance), which became the heart of the ICT4D rationale. In the last few years,

however, a more integrated vision of development has begun to combine these two perspectives: an increasing number of developing countries are realizing that their current and future role in the global information economy depend on their ability to mobilize and use knowledge.

Competitiveness and the ability to create value in innovative ways are increasingly seen as interdependent. The e-agenda thus becomes a core set of objectives and priorities within a larger knowledge agenda ("k-agenda") and ceases to be an end in itself. Although the original i-agenda of the 1980s and early 1990s has not lost its importance, is now increasingly seen (by both donors and developing countries) as an intermediate set of priorities and infrastructure conditions that allow countries to pursue higher-level objectives. Meanwhile, the environmental conditions of rule of law, good governance, and conducive regulatory and competition frameworks remain as important as ever.

For the international community, the progression in how ICT deployment has been perceived (moving from an "i" to "e" to "k" agenda) has been the source of additional challenges. The better circumscribed an issue is, the easier it is to elaborate suitable institutional and conceptual frameworks. This was the case when the international community dealt with expanding and harmonizing telegraph networks across national borders. However, when seemingly unrelated issues (e.g., interconnection regimes, trade negotiations, freedom of expression, intellectual property, education, knowledge and governance issues, to name but a few) start converging under the single heading of "information societies," the existing international approach to these issues, including forums, institutions and mechanisms, needs to be revisited.

Given this background, the MDG+5 Summit of September 2005 and the second phase of the WSIS in November 2005 should be seen as an unprecedented window of opportunity that will not repeat itself in the near future. The former has the ability to make ICT a priority of the development agenda, whereas the latter can make development the main objective of ICT-related international debates. The ambition of the international community should be to seize this moment to reconfigure the ICT-for-development debate, both the development and ICT sides. By accepting the new roles described above, governments, international organizations, business and civil society at large are in a position not only to turn the information revolution into an instrument of global prosperity, but also to shape the ways in which they interact with each other in the face of other global challenges.

Notes

[1] Such an exercise would necessarily have a short life expectancy and is more properly handled by online observatories such as those developed by the OECD (e.g., the Development Assistance Committee, or DAC), the Development Gateway or the stock-taking work of the WSIS.

[2] Organisation for Economic Cooperation and Development, Development Assistance Committee, Financing ICTs for Development: Efforts of DAC Members; Review of Recent Trends of ODA and its Contribution, Report to the U.N. Task Force on Finance Mechanisms for ICT for Development (Paris: OECD, 2005).

[3] The downward trend in ODA was also related to financial crises in Asia, Latin America and Russia in the mid- to late 1990s.

[4] World Bank, GICT (Global Information and Communication Technologies Department), "Financing Information and Communication Infrastructure Needs in the Developing World: Public and Private Roles," Draft, GICT, World Bank, Washington, DC, 2005.

[5] Calculated on the basis of data from the World Bank Private Participation in Infrastructure (PPI) database. Data from 1992–2002 for all regions. For more info on PPI, see http://ppi.worldbank.org.

[6] See UNCTAD (United Nations Conference on Trade and Development), E-Commerce and Development Report 2004 (New York and Geneva: UNCTAD, 2004).

[7] On February 24–25, 2003, a path-breaking meeting took place in Rome. Senior officials of over 20 multilateral and bilateral development organizations and about 50 countries spent two days discussing how they could improve the effectiveness of their work—how they could better fight poverty—by working more closely together. The main message, expressed through the Rome Declaration on Harmonization, is clear: donor aid, however well-intentioned, has come to levy a high toll on recipients in terms of transaction costs. Donors can alleviate this problem by doing more to coordinate their efforts, harmonize (and thus reduce) their multiple requirements, and assist partner countries to take charge of their own development process. At the Forum, donors and partners presented their plans for carrying this work forward. ("High-level Forum on Harmonization," http://www1.worldbank.org/harmonization/romehlf, last accessed 19 July 2005). On the same topic, see also the Development Gateway Special Report "Aid Harmonization:What Will It Take to Meet the MDGs?" http://topics.developmentgateway.org/special/ aidharmonization (last accessed 19 July 2005). More recently, a follow-up high-level forum took place in Paris (February 28–2 March 2005) on "Joint Progress Toward Enhanced Aid Effectiveness: Harmonization, Alignment, Results," under the leadership of the World Bank, the OECD, regional development banks and the French government.

[8] The original matrix was produced by the OECD Development Center. See OECD/DAC, Donor ICT Strategies Matrix (Paris: OECD, 2003), http://www1.oecd.org/dac/ictcd/ docs/matrixdocs/FullMatrix.pdf (last accessed 19 July 2005).

[9] B. Lanvin and C. Qiang, "Poverty 'e-Readication:' Using ICT to the Meet MDG; Direct and Indirect Roles of e-Maturity," in The Global Information Technology Report 2003-2004 (New York and Oxford: Oxford University Press, 2003).

[10] Nagy K. Hanna, Why National Strategies are Needed for ICT-enabled Development, ISG Staff Working Papers, no. 3 (June) (Washington, DC: Information Solutions Group Informatics Advisory Services, World Bank, 2003), 11, http://www.apdip.net/documents/policy/misc/ policy_strategy1.pdf (last accessed 19 July 2005).

[11] See ITU, World Development Report (Geneva: ITU, 2002 and 2003).

[12] A forthcoming World Bank publication. World Information and Communication for Development Report 2006: Trends and Policies for the Information Society," will include a broader set of indicators.

[13] WSIS, "The Report of the Task Force on Financial Mechanisms for ICT for Development: A Review of Trends and an Analysis of Gaps and Promising Practices," WSIS, ITU, Geneva, 2004, http://www.itu.int/ wsis/documents/ doc_multi.asp?lang=en&id=1372|1376|1425|1377 (last accessed 19 July 2005).

[14] Lanvin and Qiang, "Poverty 'e-Readication,'" 2003.

[15] World Bank, World Information and Communication for Development (Washington, DC: forthcoming). With respect to knowledge pillars, the World Bank's Knowledge Assessment Methodology provides a set of policy-oriented tools to assess and compare countries' performance in education, innovation, information infrastructure and overall performance. See "Knowledge Assessment Methodology (KAM) Home Page," website of the World Bank Group, Washington, DC, http://info.worldbank.org/etools/ kam2005 (last accessed 19 July 2005).

[16] With respect to e-readiness, Bridges.org regularly updates its "E-readiness Assessment: Who is Doing What and Where" survey. See http://www.bridges.org/ereadiness/ where.html (last accessed 19 July 2005). Other tools for evaluating e-readiness that have gained international recognition include the Network Readiness Index of the World Economic Forum and INSEAD, which currently ranks 104 countries. See "The Networked Readiness Index Rankings," in S. Dutta, B. Lanvin and F. Paua, eds., Global Technology Information Report, 2004–2005 (New York: Palgrave MacMillan, 2005),http://www.weforum.org/pdf/ Global_Competitiveness_Reports/ReportsGITR_2004 _2005Networked_Readiness_Index_Rankings.pdf (last accessed 19 July 2005).

[17] Recent efforts in this domain include the constitution of the "Partnership on Measuring ICT for Development." Members of the initiative include the ITU, the OECD, UNCTAD, the UNESCO Institute for Statistics, the U.N. Regional Commissions (UNECLAC, UNESCWA, UNESCAP, UNECA), the U.N. ICT Task Force, the World Bank, and EUROSTAT. The Partnership aims to accommodate and further develop various ongoing initiatives regarding the availability and measurement of ICT indicators at the regional and international level. See "Partnership for Measuring International Development," website of the UNCTAD E-commerce Branch, UNCTAD, Geneva, n.d., http://measuringict.unctad.org/QuickPlace/ measuringict/ in.nsf/h_Toc/281E7067B40AD764C1256EE80048DACC/ ?OpenDocument (last accessed 19 July 2005).

[18] Within the World Bank Group, for example, the International Finance Corporation (IFC) is the primary provider of financing to the private sector. In order not to crowd out private investment, many of the multilateral development banks, or MDBs (e.g., AFDB, EIB, EBRD, IADB, and IFC) stipulate that their investments must be only part of total investment in a given project. In addition to directly supporting the private sector, MDBs also play a key role in bringing additional resources from the private sector to development projects. The EBRD, AFDB, IADB and IFC all provide this type of resource mobilization service. Syndicated loans, for example, have a significant catalytic impact: each dollar of IFC investment in a sector attracts on average approximately US$9 of outside funding.

[19] The World Bank Charter permits the Bank to lend only to national governments or under a sovereign guaranty. Historically, most regional multilateral development banks have also been sovereign lenders, although all MDBs now have important and growing private-sector programs. With the emergence of local and small-scale initiatives, such as local WiFi initiatives and municipal e-government programs, new schemes to address the financing needs of local entities have become urgent. The IFC, for example, has established a Municipal Fund modeled on a private equity fund and has worked with bilateral donors to develop a sub-sovereign, partial-risk facility (GuarantCo).

[20] See G. Weimann, "Cyberterrorism: How Real is the Threat?", Special Report 119, U.S. Institute of Peace, Washington, DC, 2004, http://www.usip.org/reports (last accessed 19 July 2005); T. Glaessner, T. Kellerman, and V. McNevin, Electronic Safety and Soundness: Securing Finance in a New Age, World Bank Working Paper, no. 26 (Washington, DC: World Bank, 2004); G. Sadowsky et. al.,Information Technology Security Handbook (Washington, DC: infoDev, World Bank and Global Internet Policy Initiative, 2003).

[21] For example, alternative broadband networks (e.g., those based on power lines) offer a range of new possibilities for "unconnected" areas where electrical networks exist or are being developed. Wth the rapid adoption of WiFi and WiMax solutions at local levels, many traditional approaches to last-mile connectivity are being revisited. See, for example, "Digital Cities Convention" on the webiste of the Wireless Internet Institute, Boston Massachusetts, http:// www.w2idigitalcities convention.com (last accessed 19 July 2005).

[22] See, for example, "Informal Summary of the Open Consultations on the Global Alliance, 13 April 2005, Dublin" on the website of the U.N. ICT Task Force, New York, http://unicttaskforce.org/perl/documents. pl?id=1523 (last accessed 19 July 2005).

Regression Results for the Determinants of E-Development

by Isabel Neto, Charles Kenny, and Subramaniam Janakriam

This annex describes in greater detail cross-country regressions discussed in chapter 1 of this report.

The data set for this regression analysis consists of one-period observations for 123 countries. Details of the data and sources are laid out in table A1.1. The variables cover secure Internet servers per capita (our chosen measure of e-development); GDP per capita (a measure of general development); the number of fixed and mobile phones per capita (a measure of infrastructure availability); an index of economic rights (a broad measure of policy and institutional quality); a measure of the quality of the Internet, including e-commerce legislation (designed to capture sector-specific policies and institutions); and a measure of secondary schooling (to capture human capital).

It is important to note that the level of e-development using our chosen measure is strongly correlated with overall development, as measured by GDP per capita. Table A1.2

shows that 79 percent of the variation in the number of secure servers per capita among countries can be predicted by looking at GDP per capita alone (regression 1). This result is significant, as it suggests that the "digital divide" measured in terms of advanced Internet use is very much part of the broader "development divide." This finding should temper some of the more optimistic hopes of e-development as a tool for "leapfrogging" stages of development.

However, the results of the regression analysis suggest that the use of secure servers is not determined by GDP per capita alone. Both infrastructure rollout and the broad measure of policy and institutional development also strongly and significantly correlate with the number of secure servers in a country. The second regression suggests that, allowing for income, a 10-percent improvement in economic rights would be associated with a 30-percent increase in the number of secure servers, and that a 10-percent improvement in the number of fixed and

Table A1.1 Data description and sources

Name	Description and Source	Average	Std Deviation
Log Secure Internet Servers/Capita	Log of Secure Internet Servers per 109 people, 2001 (World Bank)	8.35	2.63
Log GDP/Capita	Log of GDP per capita in PPP, 2001 (World Bank)	8.58	1.19
Log Phones/Capita	Log of the sum of mobile and fixed phones per 1,000 people, 2001 (World Bank)	5.31	1.76
Economic Rights	Fraser Institute composite measure covering size of government, legal structure and security of property rights, access to sound money, freedom to trade, regulation of credit, labor and business, ranking 0 (not free) to 10 (free), 2001 (Fraser Institute, Economic Freedom of the World, Annual Report [Vancouver, Canada: Fraser Institute, 2001])	6.41	0.99
Rights * Phones	Sum of Economic Rights * Log Phones/Capita		
Internet Legislation	Global Information Technology Report measure of the quality of laws relating to information and communication technologies (ICT) (electronic commerce, digital signatures, consumer protection) 1 = nonexistent, 7 = well-developed and enforced, based on survey results, 2003 (S. Dutta, B. Lanvin and F. Paua, eds., The Global Information Technology Report [New York: Oxford University Press, 2003])	3.72	0.96
Gross Secondary Education	Secondary enrollment measured as a percentage of the secondary education age group, 2000 (World Bank)	79.85	31.56

mobile subscribers would be associated with a 9-percent increase in the number of secure Internet servers.

Again, the comparative strength of these two additional variables suggests that broader measures of development are the key to e-development. An e-strategy that attempted to increase Internet use without looking beyond the ICT sector would generate very limited returns, compared to one that crossed sectors. Regression 3 in table A1.2 suggests that the impact of combined improvements in both infrastructure and the general policy and institutional environment has a more significant relationship with secure server rollout than either factor alone, thus coordinated improvements will generate the largest returns.

The importance of a broad approach is re-enforced by the fact that, when the broader measure of policy and institutional quality is included in the regression (regression 4), measures of the quality of Internet-specific legislation show only a weak positive relation to the rollout of secure servers. Finally, general stocks of human capi-

Table A1-2 Regression results for secure servers

Dependent Variable: Log Secure Internet Servers/Capita

Independent Variables	1		2		3		4	
	Coeff	Prob	Coeff	Prob	Coeff	Prob	Coeff	Prob
C	-12.18	0.00	-7.64	0.00	2.59	0.61	-10.58	0.00
Log GDP/Capita	2.31	0.00	0.91	0.01	0.60	0.13	1.12	0.00
Log Phones/Capita			0.89	0.00	-0.36	0.57	0.84	0.00
Economic Rights			0.41	0.02	-1.03	0.15	0.48	0.00
Rights * Phones					0.24	0.04		
Internet Legislation							0.16	0.10
Gross Secondary Education							0.00	0.63
Adjusted R		0.79		0.81		0.82		0.91
N		100		100		100		71

tal as measured by secondary education rates do not appear to be a significant determinant of advanced Internet use to date.

Finally, it is worth emphasizing a few caveats. The regressions are simple least squares one-period analyses, which allow for no firm statements about causality and which have not been tested for robustness. Further, they include a composite variable (economic rights) of a type that has come in for criticism in the literature. Given these caveats, the results of these regression analyses should be treated with a suitable level of caution.

Selected List of National E-strategies

The following e-strategies (either national or sub-national) were reviewed as part of the background research for the World Bank toolkit, *Monitoring and Evaluation of E-strategies Results* (METER), discussed in Chapter 3.

Selected national e-strategies

Country (or region)	URL of the strategy
Albania	http://www.undp.org.al/?elib,428
Angola	http://www.uneca.org/aisi/nici/Angola/angola.htm
Azerbaijan	http://www.nicts.az:8101/
Bangladesh	www.bccbd.org/html/itpolicy.htm
Bhutan	http://www.dit.gov.bt/bips/documents/documents.htm
Bolivia	http://www.aladi.org/nsfaladi/ecomerc.nsf/0/E8147919B55D97A403256 BEA004D2EDA/$File/lineamientos.pdf?OpenElement
Chile	http://www.agendadigital.cl/agenda_digital/agendadigital.nsf/vw DocumentosWebLink/27363116E8E6631704256E5800549FE3 ?OpenDocument
China (Hong Kong)	http://www.info.gov.hk/digital21/eng/strategy2004/strategy_main.html
Colombia	http://www.agenda.gov.co
Czech Republic	http://www.micr.cz/scripts/detail.php?id=1288
Dominican Republic	http://www.edominicana.gov.do/interfaz/contenido.asp ?Ag=1&CategoriaNo=3

Country (or region)	URL of the strategy
Egypt	http://www.uneca.org/aisi/nici/Egypt/egypt.htm
Finland	http:://www.tietoyhteiskuntaohjelma.fi/esittely/en_GB/introduction
Ghana	http://www.uneca.org/aisi/nici/Ghana/ghana.htm
India (National)	http://www.gipi.org.in/ITPolicyInIndia.php
India (Andhra Pradesh)	http://www.gipi.org.in/state_policy/andhra.pdf
India (Delhi)	http://delhigovt.nic.in/icetpolicy.pdf
India (Haryana)	http://www.gipi.org.in/state_policy/haryana.pdf
India (Orissa)	http://www.gipi.org.in/ITPolicyInIndia.php
Indonesia	http://www.sdnbd.org/sdi/issues/IT-computer/policy/indonesia.pdf
Ireland	http://www.taoiseach.gov.ie/index.asp?locID=181&docID=1773
Jamaica	http://unpan1.un.org/intradoc/groups/public/documents/CARICAD/UNPAN009931.pdf
Japan	http://www.kantei.go.jp/foreign/policy/it/index_e.html
Jordan	http://www.reach.jo
Korea	http://www.ipc.go.kr/ipceng/public/public_view.jsp ?num=2007&fn=&req=&pgno=3
Mauritius	http://ncb.intnet.mu/ncb/downloads/Downloads/Reports%20and %20surveys/Others/finalntp.doc
Mozambique	http://www.markle.org/downloadable_assets/mz_final_ict_strategy.pdf
Namibia	http://www.uneca.org/aisi/nici/Documents/ICT%20Policy %20Document%20Ver%208.2.pdf
Nigeria	http://www.uneca.org/aisi/nici/Documents/IT%20policy%20for %20Nigeria.pdf
Norway	http://odin.dep.no/nhd/engelsk/publ/rapporter/bn.html
Poland	http://www.informatyzacja.gov.pl/_d/files/projects/epoland-the_strategy_on _the_development_of_the_information_society.pdf
Romania	http://unpan1.un.org/intradoc/groups/public/documents/UNTC/UNPAN016044.pdf
Russia	http://www.e-rus.ru/eng
Rwanda	http://www.uneca.org/aisi/nici/Documents/rwanpap2.htm

Country (or region)	URL of the strategy
Singapore	http://www.ida.gov.sg/idaweb/aboutida/infopage.jsp ?infopagecategory=&infopageid=I226&versionid=2
Slovenia	http://unpan1.un.org/intradoc/groups/public/documents/UNTC/ UNPAN015723.pdf
South Africa	http://www.tsicanada.com/documents/Strategy.pdf
Tanzania	http://www.tanzania.go.tz/pdf/ictpolicy.pdf
Thailand	http://www.nectec.or.th/intro/e_nationalpolicy.php
Trinidad & Tobago	http://www.gov.tt/nict/
Tunisia	Hard copy only
Ukraine	http://www.e-ukraine.com.ua
United Kingdom	http://e-government.cabinetoffice.gov.uk/assetRoot/04/00/60/69/04006069.pdf
Venezuela	http://www.mct.gov.ve
Vietnam	http://mpt.gov.vn/english/introduction/?thucdon=in

References

Chapter 1

Boyle, G. 2002. "Putting Context into ICTs in International Development: An Institutional Networking Project in Vietnam." *Journal of International Development* volume 14, issue 1,101–12.

Cap Gemini Consulting. N.d. "Does e-Government Pay Off?" European Public Administration Network. <http://www.eupan.org/index.asp?option=documents&section=details&id=19>. Accessed 15th July 2005.

Cecchini, S., and M. Raina. 2003. "Electronic Government and the Rural Poor: The Case of Gyandoot." *Information Technology in Developing Countries* 13, no. 2 (November):<http://www.iimahd.ernet.in/egov/ifip/nov2003/article2.htm>. Accessed 15th July 2005.

Chidamber, S.R. "An Analysis of Vietnam's ICT and Software Services Sector." *The European Journal on Information Systems in Developing Countries* 13, no. 9:1–11.

Chinn, M., and R. Fairlie. 2004. "The Determinants of the Global Digital Divide: a Cross-country Analysis of Computer and Internet Penetration." National Bureau of Economic Research (NBER) Working Paper 10686. NBER, Cambridge, MA, USA. (A copy of this paper can be purchased online for a small fee at http://www.nber.org/papers/w10686.pdf.)

Chowdhury, S., and S. Wolf. 2003. "Use of ICTs and the Economic Performance of SMEs in East Africa." Discussion Paper No. 2003/06. World Institute of Development Economics Research. United Nations University. Helsinki, Finland.

Clarke, G., and S. Wallsten. 2004. "Has the Internet Increased Trade? Evidence from Industrial and Developing Countries." Policy Research Working Paper, No. WPS 3215. Development Research Group, Competition and Policy Regulation, World Bank, Washington, DC.

Datamonitor. 2001 "The Growth of the Software Industry in Estonia." Datamonitor, <http://www.bsa.ee/download.php3?file_id=81>. Accessed 15th July 2005.

De Wulf , L. (2005), Customs Modernization Handbook, World Bank. <http://www.thattechnicalbookstore.com/b0821357514.htm>. Accessed 20 July 2005.

Dutta, S., B. Lanvin and F. Paua, eds. 2004. *Global Information Technology Report 2003–04*. Oxford University Press.

Forestier, E., J. Grace, and C. Kenny 2002. "Can Information and Communication Technologies be Pro-poor?" *Telecommunications Policy* 26, no. 11 (December):623–46.

Grace, J., and C. Kenny. 2003. "A Short Review of Information and Communication Technologies and Basic Education in LDCs—What is Useful, What is Sustainable?" *International Journal of Educational Development* volume 23, number 6, November 2003, pp 627–36.

Hansabank Group. 2003. "Annual Report 2003. Hansabank Group, Tallinn, Estonia. <http://www.hansagroup.com/aa2003/english/index.html>. Accessed 15th July 2005.

Heeks, R. 1996. "India's Software Industry". New Delhi: Sage Publications" 1996.

Heeks, R. 1999. "Information Technology, Government and Development." Report on the IT, Government and Development Workshop (26 November 1998). Manchester, England.

Hepp, P., E. Hinostroza, E. Laval, and L. Rehbein. 2004. "Technology in Schools: Education, ICT and the Knowledge Society." World Bank, Washington, DC. <http://www1.worldbank.org/education/pdf/ICT_report_oct04a.pdf>. Accessed 15th July 2005.

Hinostroza, E. 1993. "Teaching and Learning via the Network Enlaces—Linking the Educational System with an Easy-to-Use Computer Network." Coalition for Networked Information to Advance Scholarship and Intellectual Productivity, Washington, DC. <http://www.cni.org/projects/netteach/1993/prop29.html>. Accessed 15th July 2005.

IICD (International Institute for Communications and Development). 1998. "ICTs in Developing Countries: Booklet IV; Examples of Applications." IICD, The Hague, The Netherlands. <http://www.iicd.org/articles/IICDnews.import13>. Accessed 15th July 2005.

IIM (Indian Institute of Management). 2002. "Gyandoot: Rural Cybercafés on Intranet, Dhar, Madhya Pradesh, India; A Cost-Benefit Evaluation Study." IIM, Amedabad, India.

IIPA (International Intellectual Property Alliance). 2003. "2003 Special 301 Report: Estonia." IIPA, Washington, DC. <http://www.iipa.com/rbc/2003/2003SPEC301ESTONIA.pdf>. Accessed 15th July 2005.

ITU (International Telecommunications Union). 2004. "The Application of Information and Communication Technologies in Least-developed Countries for Sustained Economic Growth." ITU, Geneva, Switzerland.

James, T., and Miller, J. 2004. "Analysis of the South African Information Technology (IT) Sector." Trigrammic, South Africa, Pretoria. Processed.

Kenny, C. 2003. "The Internet and Economic Growth in Less-developed Countries: A Case of Managing Expectations?" *Oxford Development Studies* 31, no. 1 (March):99-113.

Kenny, C., and C. Qiang. 2003. "ICT and Broad-Based Development." in *ICT and Development*. Washington, DC: Global Information & Communications Department, World Bank.

Kirkman, G., E. Driggs González, M. Lopes, M.

Putnam, and A. Ragatz. 2002. "The Dominican Republic Readiness for the Networked World." Information Technologies Group, Center for International Development, Harvard University, Cambridge, Massachussetts.

Lal, K. 2002. "E-Business and Export Behaviour: Evidence from Indian Firms." Discussion Paper No. 2002/68. World Institute for Development Economics Research, United Nations University, Helsinki, Finland. <http://www.wider.unu.edu/publications/dps/dps2002/dp2002-68.pdf>. Accessed 15th July 2005.

Lanvin, B., and C. Qiang. 2003. "Poverty 'E-readication:' Using ICT to Meet MDG; Direct and Indirect Roles of E-Maturity." In *Global Information Technology Report 2003–04*. Ed. S. Dutta, B. Lanvin, and F. Paua. Oxford and New York: Oxford University Press.

NASSCOM (National Association of Software and Services Companies). 1996. *"The Software Industry in India, 1996: Strategic Review"*. New Delhi: NASSCOM.

Odrats, Ivar, ed. 2002. "IT in Public Administration of Estonia: Yearbook 2002." Trans. Kadri Podra. Estonian Information Center, Tallinn, Estonia. <http://www.ria.ee/english/2002>. Accessed 15th July 2005.

Oxley, J; and B. Yeung. 2001. "E-Commerce Readiness: Institutional Environment and International Competitiveness." *Journal Of International Business Studies*, 32, no. 4:705–23. (A copy of this article can be obtained for a fee from the Palgrave Macmillan Journals website, http://www.palgrave-journals.com/cgi-taf/DynaPage.taf?file=/jibs/journal/v32/n4/full/8490991a.html&filetype=pdf.)

Peace Corps Online. 2002 (September 15). Directory: Dominican Republic. <http://peacecorpsonline.org/messages/messages/467/2014175.html>. Accessed 15th July 2005

Pigato, M. 2001. "Information and Communication Technology, Poverty, and Development in Sub-Saharan Africa and South Asia." Africa Region Working Paper Series No. 20. World Bank, Washington, DC. <http://www.worldbank.org/afr/ wps/wp20.pdf>. Accessed 15th July 2005.

Piatkowski,M. (International Monetary Fund) World Bank Seminar, December7th, 2004, Washington D.C., The Potential of ICT for Development in Transition Economies – Technological Leapfrogging or a Growing Digital Divide.

Potashnik, M. 1996. "Computers In The Schools: Chile's Learning Network." LASHC Paper Series No. 4. Human and Social Development Group, Latin America and the Caribbean Region, World Bank, Washington, DC. <http://www-wds.worldbank.org/servlet/WDSContentServer/WDSP/IB/2000/02/23/000009265_3961214152211/Rendered/PDF/multi_page.pdf>. Accessed 15th July 2005.

Pruitt, S. 2005. "Russia looks to make IT its 'next natural resource." *ITworld.com*. IDG New Service, London Bureau, April 12th 2005. <http://www.infoworld.com/article/05/04/12/HNrussianit_1.html>, Accessed 15th July.

Qiang, C., A. Pitt, and S. Ayers. 2003. "Contribution of ICT to Growth." World Bank Working Paper, no. 26. GICT Department, World Bank, Washington, DC. A later version of this paper can be found at http://info.worldbank.org/ict/WSIS.

Qiang, C., G. Clarke, and N. Halewood. 2005. "The Role of ICT in Doing Business." In *ICT Trends Report*. Ed. C. Qiang. Washington DC: World Bank.

Röller, L-H, and L. Waverman. 2001. "Telecommunications Infrastructure and Economic Development: A Simultaneous Approach." *America Economic Review* 91, no. 4: 909–23.

Schware, R., and Deane, A.. 2003 "Deploying eGovernment Programs: The Strategic importance of 'I' before 'E.'" *Info, The Journal of Policy, Regulation and Strategy for Telecommunications* 5, no. 4:10–19. Emerald Group Publishing Limited, London, United Kingdom. (A copy of the article can be accessed from http://www1.worldbank.org/publicsector/egov/ReinventingGovWorkshop/Deployingegovt.pdf.)

Schware, R. 2003. "Information and communications technology agencies: functions, structures, and best operational practices." *Info*, Vol.5 No.3. <http://wbln0018.worldbank.org/ict/resources.nsf/0/73f31a6af7fc3e5e85256da400504b5f/$FILE/p3-7,%20Schware.pdf>. Accessed 27th July 2005.

Solow, R. 1987. "We'd better Watch Out." *New York Times Book Review*. July 12.

South Africa, Western Cape, Provincial Treasury. 2003. CITI- (The Cape IT Initiative) Western Cape Socio-Economic Review, Cape Town.

Sudan, R. 2002. "Towards SMART Government: The Andhra Pradesh Experience." IAS, Special Secretary to Chief Minister, Government of Andhra Pradesh. <http://unpan1.un.org/intradoc/groups/public/documents/APCITY/UNPAN005509.pdf>. Accessed 15th July 2005.

Thornton, Grant. 2004. "Second Annual International Business Owners Survey 2004," Grant Thornton.

Uchitelle, L. 2000. "Economic View: Productivity Finally Shows the Impact of Computers." *New York Times*. Section 3. March 12.

UNCTAD (2000), 'Building Confidence: E-commerce and Development' <http://r0.unctad.org/ecommerce/docs/edr00_en.htm>. Accessed 20 July 2005.

World Bank. 2003. "Reaching the Rural Poor - Annexes". Chapter : Rural information and knowledge system in Russia in Annex 4 - Successful Bank Operations in Agricultural and Rural Development. Washington DC.: World Bank.

World Bank. 2004. *Chile: New Economy Study*. Volume Two. Report No. 25666-CL. World Bank, Washington, DC.

World Bank. 2005. "Financing Information and Communication Infrastructure Needs in the Developing World: Public and Private Roles." GICT, World Bank, Washington, DC.

World Employment Report 2001; Developing countries in international division of labour in software and services industry: Lessons from Indian experience. <http://www.bib.ulb.ac.be/cdrom/wer_lawtie/back/ind_2.htm>. Accessed 20 July 2005.

Yusuf, S. 2004. Innovative East Asia: The Future of Growth. New York: Oxford University Press.

Chapter 2

Arab Advisor Group. 2005. "An Analysis of E-commerce Adoption in Jordan and the Gulf Region based on Reported Figures from Visa International." Amman, Jordan: Arab Advisor Group.

Analysys, Harris Wiltshire & Grannis LLP. 2004. *Telecommunications Trade Liberalization and the WTO*. Washington, DC: GICT Department, the World Bank. Processed.

Attenborough, N. et al. 2004. *Framework for evaluating the effectiveness of telecommunications regulators in Sub-Saharan Africa*. Washington, DC: GICT Department, the World Bank. Processed.

Report prepared by NERA for the GICT Department, World Bank April 2004.

Balancing Act,: GISP calls on Ghanaian Government to help reserve Internet shopping ban Balancing Act Balancing Act's News Update 247 of 3 March 2005. <http://www.balancingact-africa.com/news/back/balancing-act_247.html>. Accessed July 2005.

Babnet Tunisie. 2005. "Ordinateur familial: Rude et...douloureuse sera la concurrence." March 5, 2005. <http://www.babnet.net/cadredetail.asp?id=2549>. Accessed July 2005.

Bressie, K, M Kende, and H Williams. 2003. "Participation in the WTO Global Trading System inTelecommunication is a Motor for Domestic Sector Reform." GICT Department, World Bank, Washington, DC. Processed.

Christopher Caldwell. 2005. "The price of privacy is high." *Financial Times* April 16/17 2005, p. 7.

Cisco Systems and University of Texas. 2001. "Measuring the Internet Economy." University of Texas, Austin. <http://www.internetindicators.com/jan_2001.pdf>. Accessed July 2005.

Dunn, M., and I. Wigert. 2004. *International CIIP Handbook 2004: An Inventory and Analysis of Protection Policies in Fourteen Countries.* Edited by Andreas Wenger and Jan Metzger. Zurich: Swiss Federal Institute of Technology.

Ecorys Research and Consulting, *Best practice Options for Improving and Extending Access to Electronic Communications in Lithuania* a publication for GICT, 2005 p.41 available at http://www.worldbank.org/ict

Elmer, Laurel. 2002. "Vietnam's ICT Enabling Environment: Policy, Infrastructure and Appli-cations." U.S. Agency for International Development, Washington, DC.

EU (European Union). 1995. "Directive 1995/46/EC of 24 October 1995 on Personal Data Privacy Protection." *Official Journal of the European Communities.* Brussels.

———. 1999. "Directive 1999/93/EC of 13 December 1999 on Electronic Signatures." *Official Journal of the European Communities.* Brussels. <http://europa.eu.int/eur lex/pri/en/oj/dat/2000/l_013/l_01320000119en00120020.Pdf>. Accessed July 2005.

———. 2002. "Directive 2002/58/EC of 12 July 2002 on Privacy and Electronic Communications." *Official Journal of the European Communities.* Brussels. <http://europa.eu.int/eur-lex/pri/en/oj/dat/2002/l_201/l_20120020731en00370047.pdf>. Accessed July 2005.

———. Asia IT&C Program. 2004. "Promoting Internet Policy and Regulatory Reform in Vietnam: Assessment Report 2004." GIPI Vietnam, <http://www.internetpolicy.net/about/20040300vietnam.pdf#search='BCC%20Vietnam'>. Accessed July 2005.

Fiber Optics Weekly update, Andha Pradesh to be connected with fiber this year , <http://www.findarticles.com/p/articles/mi_m0NVN/is_1_25/ai_n8699107>. Accessed July 2005.

Geradin, D., and M. Kerf. 2003. *Controlling Market Power in Telecommunications: Striking the Right Balance Between Antitrust and Sector-Specific Rules and Institutions.* New York?: Oxford University Press.

Glaessner, T. Kellerman, and V. McNevin. 2004. "Electronic Safety and Soundness: Securing Finance in a New Age." World Bank Working Paper No. 26, World Bank, Washington, DC.

Goldstein, A., and D. O'Connor. 2002. "E-commerce for Development: Prospects and Policy Issues." Development Centre Studies, OECD Development Center, OECD, Paris. <http://e-jis.ncsi.iisc.ernet.in/bc/societal-issues/201/201>. Accessed July 2005.

ICANN (Internet Corporation for Assigned Names and Numbers). 2005. "Domain Name Dispute Resolution Policies." ICANN, Marina Del Rey, California, <http://www.icann.org/udrp/#udrp>. Accessed July 2005.

ITU (International Telecommunications Union). 2002. "The Role of Effective Regulation: Morocco Case Study." ITU, Geneva. <http://www.itu.int/itudoc/itu-d/publicat/ma_ca_st.html>. Accessed July 2005.

————. 2002. *World Telecommunications Development Report: Reinventing Telecoms.* Geneva: ITU.

————. 2003. *The Birth of Broadband.* Geneva: ITU.

Khanifsa A. *Ordi-densite.* <http://www.itmag-dz.com/article.php3?id_article=248&>. Accessed July 2005.

Mann, Catherine L., 2004 "Information Technology and E- Commerce in Tunisia: Domestic and International Challenges and the Role of the Financial System." <http://tunis.usembassy.gov/wwwftunisia_report.pdf>. Accessed July 2005.

OECD (Organization for Economic Cooperation and Development). 1980. "Guidelines on the Protection of Privacy and Transborder Flows of Personal Data (Privacy Guidelines)." OECD, Paris.

————. 1999. *The Economic and Social Impact of Electronic Commerce: Preliminary Findings and Research Agenda.* Paris: OECD.

————. 2003. "Broadband Driving Growth: Policy Responses." DSTI/CCP92003. Final. OECD, Paris.

————. 2003. "Privacy Online: Policy and Practical Guidance." OECD, Paris. <http://www.olis.oecd.org/olis/2002doc.nsf/LinkTo/dsti-iccp-reg(2002)3-final>. Accessed July 2005.

————. 2001 "Inventory of Consumer Protection Laws, Policies and Practices Applied to E-Commerce." OECD, Paris <http://www.olis.oecd.org/olis/2000doc.nsf/LinkTo/DSTI-CP(2000)5-FINAL>. Accessed July 2005.

Peter Smith and Hien Tu Thiu. 2004. "Summary of selected Municipal Backbone initiative." World Bank. Processed.

Qiang, C. and Guislain P.(2005). "Foreign Direct Investment in Telecommunications," in *World Information and Communication for Development Report 2006*, World Bank, Washington, DC.

Rostenne, J. 2004. "Togo: First VOIP Call Center in Africa." Balancing Act, no. 47. <http://www.balancingact-africa.com/news/back/balancing-act47.html>. Accessed July 2005.

Sadowsky, G., J.X. Dempsey, A. Greenberg, B.J. Mack and A. Schwartz. 2003. *Information Technology Security Handbook.* Washington, DC: *info*Dev, World Bank and Global Internet Policy Initiative. <http://www.infodev.org/files/834_file_IT_Security.pdf>. Accessed July 2005.

Satola, D., R. Sreenivasan and L. Pavlasova. 2004. "Benchmarking Regional e-Commerce in Asia and the Pacific and Assessment of Related Regional Initiatives." In "Harmonization of Legal and Regulatory Systems for E-Commerce in Asia and the Pacific: Current Challenges and Capacity Building Needs." United Nations, New York.

Singh, H., and K.W. Jun. 1995. "Some New Evidence on Determinants of Foreign Direct Investment in Developing Countries." Policy Research Working Paper, No. 1531. World Bank, Washington, DC.

UNCTAD (United Nations Conference on Trade and Develoment). 2004. *E-Commerce and Development Report 2004*. New York and Geneva: UNCTAD.

USOTEC (U.S. Office of Technology and Electronic Commerce). 2003. "Africa: Tariffs and Taxes on Computer Hardware and Software." USOTEC, International Trade Administration, U.S. Department of Commerce, Washington, DC, 2003. <http://web.ita.doc.gov/ITI/itiHome.nsf/9b2cb14bda00318585256cc40068ca69/3383d207e223fd3485256d83006f3aa6!OpenDocument>. Accessed April 2005.

Wellenius, Bjorn. 2002 "Closing the Gap in Access to Rural Communications: Chile 1995–2002." *info*Dev Working Paper. *info*Dev, World Bank, Washington, DC. <http://www-wds.worldbank.org/servlet/WDS_IBank_Servlet?pcont=details&eid=000094946_0203070403326>. Accessed July 2005.

Wellenius, B., C. Rosotto and A. Lewin. 2004. "Morocco: Developing Competition in Telecommunications." Working Paper. Global Information and Communications Technologies Department, World Bank, Washington, DC, 2004. <http://wbln0018.worldbank.org/ict/resources.nsf/InfoResources?OpenView>. Accessed July 2005.

Wayne A. Leighton, Broadband Deployment and the digital Divide, A primer. OECD Policy Analysis August 7, 2001.

WGIG (Working Group on Internet Governance). 2005. "Working Papers." WGIG, Geneva. <http://www.wgig.org/WGIG-Report.html>. Accessed July 2005.

WIPO (World International Property Organization). Arbitration and Mediation Center. N.d. Alternative dispute resolution procedures. <http://arbiter.wipo.int/center/index.html>. Accessed July 2005.

World Bank. N.d. "Chilean Tax System Online." Abstract. E*Government. GSPR net (Governance and Public Sector Reform Sites). World Bank, Washington, D.C. <http://www1.worldbank.org/publicsector/egov/chile_taxcs.htm>. Accesse July 2005.

———. 2003. "Competition in International Voice Communications." GICT World Bank, Washington, DC.

———. 2003. *Operations Evaluation Department Report*. Washington, DC: World Bank.

———. 2004. "Private Participation in Infrastructure" databaseWorld Bank, Washington, DC.

———. 2005. "Connecting Sub-Saharan Africa: A World Bank Group Strategy for ICT Sector Development. World Bank Working Paper, No. 51. GICT Department, World Bank, Washington, DC.

———. GICT. 2005. "Financing Information and Communication Infrastructure Needs in the Developing World: Public and Private Roles." Draft (February 2005). GICT, World Bank, Washington, DC.

World Bank Dispute Settlement in Telecommunications: Current Practices and Future Directions; A Joint Study Undertaken with the International Telecommunication Union., World Bank, Washington, DC. 2005.

WSIS (World Summit on the Information Society). 2003. "Declaration of Principles." Document WSIS-03/GENEVA/DOC/0004. WSIS, ITU, Geneva. <http://www.itu.int/wsis/docs/geneva/official/dop.html>. Accessed July 2005.

————. 2003. "Plan of Action." Document WSIS-03/GENEVA/DOC/0005. WSIS, ITU, Geneva. <http://www.itu.int/wsis/docs/geneva/official/poa.html>. Accessed July 2005.

WTO (World Trade Organization). 1996. "Reference Paper." WTO Negotiating Group on Basic Telecommunications, WTO, Geneva. <http://www.wto.org/english/tratop_e/serv_e/telecom_e/tel23_e.htm>. Accessed July 2005.

Zawaydeh, Serene. 2003. "Tunisia Internet & Datacomm Landscape Report." Arab Advisors Group, Strategic Research Service, Amman, Jordan.

Zawaydeh, Serene. 2004. "Algeria Internet & Datacomm Landscape Report." Arab Advisors Group, Strategic Research Service, Amman, Jordan.

Chapter 3

Achikbache, B., M. Belkindas, G. Eele and E. Swanson. 2004. "Strengthening Statistical Systems." In *PRSP Source Book.* Washington, DC: World Bank. (An overview of the publication can be accessed at http://web.worldbank.org/WBSITE/EXTERNAL/TOPICS/EXTPOVERTY/EXTPRS/0,,contentMDK:20177230~page PK:148956~piPK:216618~theSitePK:384201,00.html. Accessed 12 July 2005.

Adamali, A., B. Lanvin and R. Schware. 2005. *'E-Strategies Monitoring and Evaluation Toolkit /Monitoring and Evaluation Toolkit for E-strategies Results.* Washington, DC: GICT Department, World Bank.

APC (Association for Progressive Communications). 2003. "ICT Policy: A Beginner's Handbook." San Francisco, California: APC.

bridges.org. 2001. "Comparison of E-Readiness Assessment Models." bridges.org, Cape Town, South Africa and Washington, DC. <http://www.bridges.org/ereadiness>. Accessed 12 July 2005.

————. 2002 (updated February 2005). "E-readiness Assessment: Who is Doing What and Where." bridges.org, Cape Town, South Africa and Washington, DC. <http://www.bridges.org/ereadiness>. Accessed 12 July 2005.

CBC (Commonwealth Business Council). 2003. *E-government: Modernizing Commonwealth Governments.* London: CBC.

Choucri, N., Maugis, V., Madnick, S. and Siegel, M.. 2003. "E-readiness for What?" MIT Working Paper. MIT, Cambridge, Massachussetts.

De Wulf, Luc and Jose B. Sokol, eds. 2004. "Customs Modernization Handbook.", World Bank Trade and Development Series , World Bank, Washington, DC

Digital Opportunity Task Force. 2001. "Digital Opportunities for All: Meeting the Challenge; Report of the Digital Opportunity Task Force including a Proposal for a Genoa Plan of Action." DOT Task Force, G8 Information Centre, <http://www.g7.utoronto.ca/summit/2001genoa/dotforce1.html>. Accessed 12 July 2005.

E-Europe 2005. Thematic Portal of European Union Website. 2001. "E-government Indicators for Benchmarking E-Europe." European Union, Brussells. <http://europa.eu.int/information_society/eeurope/2002/action_plan/pdf/egovindicators.pdf>. Accessed 12 July 2005.

————. 2002. "E-Europe 2005: An Information Society for All." European Union, Brussells. <http://europa.eu.int/information_society/eeurope/2005/all_about/action_plan/index_en.htm>. Accessed 12 July 2005.

E-Europe, Cap Gemini and Ernst & Young. 2003. "Web-based Survey on Electronic Public Services: Report of the Fourth Measurement, October 2003." European Union, Brussels. <http://europa.eu.int/information_society/eeurope/2005/all_about/benchmarking/index_en.htm>. Accessed 12 July 2005.

EU (European Union) Information Society Website. 2000. "Public Strategies for the Information Societies in the Member States of the European Union." In "European Survey of the Information Society (ESIS) Report." EU, Brussels.

Grace, J., C. Kenny and C. Qiang. "Information and Communication Technologies and Broad-Based Development: A Partial Review of the Evidence." World Bank Working Paper, no. 12. GICT Department, World Bank, Washington, DC.

Hanna, N. 2003. "Why National Strategies are Needed for ICT-Enabled Development." ISG Staff Working Papers. ISG Department, World Bank, Washington, DC.

infoDev and CDT (Center for Democracy and Technology). 2003. The e-Government Handbook for Developing Countries. Washington, DC: infoDev, GICT Department, World Bank. Available at http://www.infodev.org/files/841_file_eGovernment_Handbook.pdf or http://www.cdt.org/egov/handbook/2002-11-14egovhandbook.pdf.

G-8 Kananaskis Summit. 2002. "The Italian Initiative on e-Government for Development." G-8 Summit, Kananaskis, Canada. <http://www.innovazione.gov.it/eng/egov4dev/iniziativa/contesto.shtml>. Accessed 12 July 2005.

Kenny, C., and C. Qiang. 2003. "ICT and Broad-Based Development." In ICT and Development: Enabling the Information Society. Wash-

ington, DC: GICT Department, World Bank. <http://info.worldbank.org/ict/WSIS/docs/comp_ICTBroad.pdf>. Accessed 12 July 2005.

Lanvin, B., and C. Qiang. 2003. "Poverty 'e-Readication:' Using ICT to the Meet MDG; Direct and Indirect Roles of e-Maturity." The Global Information Technology Report 2003-2004. New York and Oxford: Oxford University Press.

McNamara, K. 2004. Information and Communication Technologies, Poverty and Development—Learning from Experience. Washington, DC: infoDev, GICT Department, World Bank. <http://www.infodev.org/files/833_file_Learning_From_Experience.pdf>. Accessed 12 July 2005.

National Audit Office of the United Kingodm. 2002. "Government on the Web II." National Audit Office, London, United Kingdom. <http://www.nao.org.uk/pn/01-02/0102764.htm>. Accessed 12 July 2005.

NORAD (Norwegian Agency for Development Cooperation). 1999. The Logical Framework Approach. NORAD, Oslo, Norway. <http://www.baltichealth.org/customers/baltic/lfa/LFA%20handbook.htm>. Accessed 12 July 2005.

Nordic-Dutch Trade Union Centers. 2003. "Handbook of Participatory Project Planning." FNV, The Netherlands. <www.fnv.nl/download.do/id/6226/>. Accessed 12 July 2005.

OECD (Organisation for Economic Cooperation and Development). 2003. The e-Government Imperative. OECD, Paris. <http://www1.oecd.org/publications/e-book/4203071E.PDF>. Accessed 12 July 2005.

———. 2004. "Role of Infrastructure in Economic Growth and Poverty Reduction—Lessons

Learned from PRSPs of 33 Countries." DCD/DAC/POVNET(2004)16. OECD, Development Co-operation Directorate, DAC, Paris. <http://www.oecd.org/dataoecd/57/60/33919674.pdf>. Accessed July 2005.

Prennushi, G., G. Rubio and K. Subbarao. 2004. "Monitoring and Evaluation." In *PRSP Source Book*. Washington, DC: World Bank.

Qiang, C., and A. Pitt, with S. Ayers. 2003. "Contribution of Information and Communication Technologies to Growth." In *ICT and Development: Enabling the Information Society*. Washington, DC: GICT Department. <http://info.worldbank.org/ict/WSIS/docs/comp_ICTGrowth.pdf>. Accessed 12 July 2005.

Schware, R. 2003. "Information and Communications Technology (ICT) Agencies: Functions, Structures, and Best Operational Practices." *Info—The Journal of Policy, Regulation and Strategy for Telecommunications* 5, no. 3:3–7. Emerald Group Publishing Ltd., London, United Kingdom.

Schware, R., and A. Deane. 2003. "Deploying e-Government Programs: The Strategic Importance of 'I' before 'E.'" *Info—The Journal of Policy, Regulation and Strategy for Telecommunications* 5, no. 4:10–19. Emerald Group Publishing Ltd., London, United Kingdom. (A copy of the article can be accessed from http://www1.worldbank.org/publicsector/egov/ReinventingGovWorkshop/Deployingegovt.pdf. Accessed 12 July 2005).

Tan, Eng Pheng. 2004. "The Singapore e-Government Experience." Paper presented at "Foro Internacional: Hacia una Sociedad Digital" conference in Panama City, Panama, April 6, 2004.

UNCTAD. 2004. *E-commerce and Development Report*. Geneva: UNCTAD. <http://www.unctad.org/en/docs/ecdr2003_en.pdf>. Accessed 12 July 2005.

UNPAN (United Nations Online Network in Public Administration and Finance). "Benchmarking e-Government: A Global Perspective; Assessing the Progress of the UN Member States." UNPAN, New York, NY.

World Bank. (2001) "The LogFrame Handbook – A Logical Framework Approach to Project Cycle Management". <http://imagebank.worldbank.org/servlet/WDSContentServer/IW3P/IB/2005/06/07/000160016_20050607122225/Rendered/PDF/31240b0LFhandbook.pdf>. Accessed 12 July 2005.

World Bank. 2002. *ICT Sector Strategy Paper*. GICT Department, World Bank, Washington, DC. <http://info.worldbank.org/ict/ICT_ssp.html>. Accessed 12 July 2005.

WSIS (World Summit on the Information Society." 2003. "Action Plan." WSIS, International Telecommunications Union, Geneva, Switzerland. <www.itu.int/wsis/docs/geneva/official/poa.html>. Accessed 12 July 2005.

Chapter 4

Annunzio, S. 2001. *E-Leadership: Proven Techniques for Creating an Environment of Speed and Flexibility in the Digital Economy*. New York: The Free Press.

Avolio, B., S. Kahaiand G. Dodge. 2000. "E-Leadership: Implica-tions for Theory, Research, and Practice." *Leadership Quarterly* 11, no. 4:615–68.

Bjelland, O., J. Carr and K.R. Gordon. 2005. "The E-Leadership Debate." Xyntéo Ltd., London, www.xynteo.com.

Deloitte Touche Tohmatsu. 2000 "E-Leadership? Beyond the Hype: Perceptions vs. Reality about e-Leadership." Deloitte Research, DDT, New York.

Hanna, J., A. I. Carrasco and C. Watt. 2004. "Building Leadership for e-Business Development." *En Breve*, no. 56. Washington, DC: Latin America and Caribbean Division, World Bank.

Hargrove, R. 2000. *E-Leader: Reinventing Leadership in a Connected Economy*. Cambridge, Massachusetts: Perseus Publishing.

Hoenig, C. 2000. "Total Leadership: Lose the 'E.'" *CIO Magazine* (September 1). <http://www.cio.com/archive/090100_lead_content.html>. Accessed June 2005.

Lanvin, B. 2003. "Leaders and Facilitators—The New Roles of Governments." In *Global Information Technology Report 2002–2003*. Geneva: World Economic Forum, *info*Dev and INSEAD, 2003.

Mills, D.Q. 2001. *E-Leadership: Guiding Your Business to Success in the New Economy*. Paramus, New Jersey: Prentice Hall Press.

Kotter, J.P. 1996. *Leading Change*. Cambridge, Massachusetts: Harvard Business School Press.

Raffoni, M. 2001. "Rethinking E-Leadership." in "E--Leadership, Take Two." *Harvard Management Update* 6, no. 6 (June).

Chapter 5

Adamali, A., B. Lanvin and R. Schware. 2005. *Monitoring and Evaluation Tookit for E-strategies Results*. Washington, DC: GICT Department, World Bank. <http://wbln0018.worldbank.org/ict/resources.nsf/ a693f575e01ba5f385256b500062af05/ b3590b631857789885256f970057de12/$FILE/ estrategiesToolkit_Jan2005.pdf>. Accessed July 28, 2005.

AGIMO. 2004. "Agency Overview". Parkes: Australian Government Information Management Office. <http://www.agimo.gov.au/publications/ 2004/10/annrep03-04/part_2_- _agency_overview>. Accessed July 28, 2005.

_____. 2002. "Efficient Application of Technology: Organizing for e-Government". Parkes: Australian Government Information Management Office. <http://www.agimo.gov.au/ publications/ 2002/11/bsbg/application_of_technology>. Accessed July 28, 2005.

ATICA. 2002. "Guide to choosing and using free software licences for government and public sector entities". <http://www.adae.gouv.fr/up- load/documents/free_software_guide.pdf>. Accessed July 28, 2005.

Allega, Philip J. 2005. "'Do It Yourself' Is Not Sufficient for British Government and Enterprise Architecture Projects" (June 8). Gartner Research, Stamford, Connecticut.

Baum, Christopher H., and Andrea Di Maio. 2000. "Gartner's Four Phases of E-Government Model." Gartner Research, Stamford, Connecticut.

Bennoit, Kenneth. "Appendix 2J: Experience of Electronic Voting Overseas". Dublin: The Policy Institute, Trinity College. <http://www.cev.ie/htm/ report/first_report/pdf/Appendix%202J.pdf>. Accessed July 28, 2005.

Capgemini. 2005. *Online Availability of Public Services: How is Europe Progressing? Web-based Survey on Electronic Public Services, Report of the Fifth Measurement, October 2004*. Brussels: Directorate General for

Information and Media, European Commission. <http://europa.eu.int/information_society/soccul/egov/egov_benchmarking_2005.pdf>. Accessed July 28, 2005.

Caseley, Jonathan. 2004. "Public Sector Reform and Corruption: CARD Façade in Andhra Pradesh" (Vol.39, Issue 11, pages 1151-1156). *Economic and Political Weekly.*

Castells, Manuel. 2001. *The Internet Galaxy: Reflections on the Internet, Business, and Society.* New York: Oxford University Press.

Clark, Matthew. 2004. "Irish people want m-government: survey" (December 10). *electricnews.net.* <http://new.enn.ie/news.html?code=9569739>. Accessed July 30, 2005.

Component Organization and Registration Environment. <http://www.core.gov>. Accessed July 31, 2005.

Compranet. <http://www.compranet.gob.mx/>. Accessed July 28, 2005.

Computer Business Review Online. 2005. "Venezuelan government opts for open source approach" (January 5). <http://www.cbronline.com/article_news.asp?guid=B4AD0DAB-0611-4F6C-8C9F-8846A38A6525>. Accessed July 28, 2005.

Dorgan, Stephen J. and John J.Dowdy, "When IT lifts productivity". *The McKinsey Quarterly,* 2004 number 4.

E-Government Act of 2002, 107th Congress, USA (January 23, 2002).

E-Government Unit. 2004. *Open Source Software Use with UK Government.* Ver. 2. London: U.K. Cabinet Office. <http://www.govtalk.gov.uk/documents/oss_policy_version2.pdf>. Accessed July 28, 2005.

Edulinux. <http://www.edulinux.cl/english/index_p2.php?id_contenido=730&id_seccion=1473&id_portal=1>. Accessed July 28, 2005.

Electricnews.net. 2005. "Ireland Faces •50m E-voting Write-off" (February 4). *The Register.* <http://www.theregister.co.uk/2005/02/04/ireland_evoting_bill>. Accessed July 28, 2005.

European Commission. 2002. "eEurope 2005: An information society for all" (May 28). COM(2002) 263 final, Brussels. <http://europa.eu.int/information_society/eeurope/2002/news_library/documents/eeurope2005/eeurope2005_en.pdf>. Accessed July 28, 2005.

_____. 2004. "European Interoperability Framework for Pan-European e-Government Services, ver.1". Luxembourg: EC. <http://europa.eu.int/idabc/servlets/Doc?id=19528>. Accessed August 1, 2005.

_____. Information Society Thematic Portal. <http://europa.eu.int/information_society/soccul/egov/index_en.htm>. Accessed July 28, 2005.

_____. 2003. "The Role of E-Government for Europe's Future." SEC (2003) 1038 (September 26). EC, Brussels. <http://europa.eu.int/information_society/eeurope/2005/doc/all_about/egov_communication_en.pdf>. Accessed July 28, 2005.

European Union. 2004. "Directive 2004/18/EC of the European Parliament and of the Council on the Coordination of Procedures for the award of Public Works Contracts, Public Supply Contracts and Public Service Contracts" (March 31). Strasbourg.

_____. "Free and Open Source Software Directory of Key Terms". Europe's Information

Society Thematic Portal, Brussels. <http://europa.eu.int/information_society/ activities/opensource/doc/pdf/key_terms.pdf>. Accessed July 28, 2005.

General Manager (BD) BSNL Hyderabad. 2004. Letter to Director Communications IT&C Department, Government of Andhra Pradesh (April 16). (Lr. No.TA/10-40/2004/TP.

Gill, Robin. "Cooperation between the Public and Private Sectors to Improve Service Delivery: The Hong Kong Experience". <http://www.info.gov.hk/digital21/e-gov/eng/press/doc/20031118.pdf>. Accessed July 28, 2005.

Government of Andhra Pradesh. 2005. "Contract for development, implementation, operation and maintenance of AP Broadband Network between AP Aksh Broadband Limited and Aksh Broadband Limited and Andhra Pradesh Technology Services Limited on behalf of Information Technology and Communications Department" (April 21).

_____. 2002. GOMs.39, Information Technology and Communications Department (September 12). <http://www.apvatonline.com/ctportalnew/gosnotifications/GO3912092002.htm>. Accessed July 28, 2005.

Greene, Thomas C. 2005. "FBI Blew $170m on Doomed IT Upgrade" (January 14). *The Register*. <http://www.theregister.co.uk/2005/01/14/fbi_flushes_trilogy_money/print.html>. Accessed July 28, 2005.

Gresham, Maria T. and Jeremy Andrulis. 2002. "Using hybrid funding strategies to support the State of Arizona". New York: IBM Institute for Business Value. <http://www-1.ibm.com/services/us/imc/pdf/g510-1678-01-wheres-the-money-hybrid-funding.pdf>. Accessed July 28, 2005.

Holmes, Douglas. 2005. Email to author attaching a paper on "eGov in Latin America" (March 3).

Haines, Lester. 2005. "MPs Condemn e-Uni Disaster – Again" (March 4). *The Register*. <http://www.theregister.co.uk/2005/03/04/e_uni_committee_report/print.html>. Accessed July 28, 2005.

Heeks, Richard. 2003. "Success and Failure Rates of eGovernment in Developing/Transitional Countries: Overview". Manchester: IDPM, University of Manchester, UK. <http://www.egov4dev.org/sfoverview.htm>. Accessed July 28, 2005.

IDC. 2004. "IT Spending on eGovernment Continues to Grow in Western Europe, Says IDC" (October 12), Press release. <http://www.idc.com/getdoc.jsp?containerId=pr2004_10_05_171108>. Accessed July 28, 2005.

Input/Output. 2004. "Federal Government Requests $59.8 billion for FY2005 IT Spending" (February). Reston. <http://www.newsletterscience.com/ejkrause/pdf/00000034.pdf>. Accessed July 28, 2005.

International Council for Information Technology in Government Administration. 2004. "The Office of the e-Envoy Transitions to the e-Government Unit". ICA Information No. 82: General Issues. Surrey: ICA. <http://www.ica-it.org/docs/issue82/ICA_Issue_82_2004_05.pdf>. Accessed July 28, 2005.

Kost, John, and Andrea Di Maio. 2003. "Creating a Business Case for a Government IT Project" (January 6). Gartner Research, Stamford, Connecticut.

Kost, John, Richard G.Harris and John P.Roberts. 2005. "New Appointment in Victoria, Australia,

Is Seen as a Vote of Confidence for CIOs" (May 5). Gartner Research, Stamford, Connecticut.

Lallana, Emmanuel C. 2004. "eGovernment for Development: mGovernment Applications and Purposes Page". <http://www.egov4dev.org/mgovapplic.htm>. Accessed July 30, 2005.

Larrain, Claudio Orego. "Chile's E-procurement System: Transparency, Efficiency and PPP". <http://www.transparency.org/integrity_pact/dnld/orrego_e-procurement.pdf>. Accessed July 28, 2005.

Lobo, Albert, and Suresh Balakrishnan. 2002. *Report Card on Service of Bhoomi Kiosks: An Assessment of Benefits to Users of the Computerized Land Records System in Karnataka.* Draft. Bangalore: Public Affairs Centre. <http://unpan1.un.org/intradoc/groups/public/documents/APCITY/UNPAN015135.pdf>. Accessed July 28, 2005.

Maio, Andrea Di. 2003. "How to Measure the Public Value of IT" (July 8). Gartner Research, Stamford, Connecticut.

————. 2004. "It's Time for a New Way to Measure Progress of E-Government" (October 14). Gartner Research, Stamford, Connecticut.

————. 2005. "Local Governments in France Move to Open-Source Applications" (July 8). Gartner Research, Stamford, Connecticut.

Maio, Andrea Di, and John Kost. 2004. "Hype Cycle Shows E-Government Overcoming Disillusionment" (March 17). Gartner Research, Stamford, Connecticut.

Millard, Jeremy, and Jonas Iversen Svava. 2004. "Reorganization of Government Back Offices for Better Electronic Public Services: European Good Practices (Back-office Reorganization)." Final Report to the European Commission. Danish Technological Institute, Taastrup, Denmark.

National Assembly of Canada. 2004. *An Act respecting the Agence des parternariats public-privé du Québec.* Bill 61 (chapter 32), Thirty-seventh Legislature. Québec: Québec Official Publisher. <http://www2.publicationsduquebec.gouv.qc.ca/dynamicSearch/telecharge.php?type=5&file=2004C32A.PDF>. Accessed July 28, 2005.

Open Source Observatory, Interchange of Data between Administrations. 2003. "Case Study: Extremadura LinEx" (November). <http://europa.eu.int/idabc/servlets/Doc?id=1641>. Accessed July 28, 2005.

Public Procurement Service, Government of the Republic of Korea. <http://www.pps.go.kr/neweng/>. Accessed August 1, 2005.

Public Sector Technology & Management. 2005. "Migrating Citizens to e-government Channels in Hong Kong" (February 3). PSTM.net, Singapore. <http://www.pstm.net/article/index.php?articleid=511>. Accessed July 28, 2005.

Queensland Government. "About the Shared Service Initiative". <http://www.qld.gov.au/sharedservices/about_ssi/index.html>. Accessed July 31, 2005.

Select Committee on Work and Pensions. 2004. "Assessment of CSA's IT and telephony System". The United Kingdom Parliament. <http://www.publications.parliament.uk/pa/cm200304/cmselect/cmworpen/311/31109.htm>. Accessed August 1, 2005.

Sheriff, Lucy. 2005. "E-gov to Cost Europe •4bn+" (February 4). *The Register.* <http://www.theregister.co.uk/2005/02/04/idc_euro_gov_spend/print.html>. Accessed July 28, 2005.

Simpson, Robin and Eleana Liew. 2005. "Globe Telecom's G-Cash a Mobile Commerce Success

Story" (March 1). Gartner Research, Stamford, Connecticut.

Sisodia, R.P. 2005. Email to author (May 2).

Swedish Tax Agency. 2004. "Taxes in Sweden 2004: An English Summary of Tax Statistical Yearbook of Sweden". <http://www.skatteverket.se/broschyrer/104/10405.pdf>. Accessed July 30, 2005.

The e-GIF Accreditation Authority. <http://www.egifaccreditation.org/introduction.html> Accessed July 29, 2005.

The Economist. 2005. "Behind the Digital Divide." *Technology Quarterly* (12 March).

The Government of Malta. "m-Government". <http://www.gov.mt/egovernment.asp?p=106&l=1>. Accessed July 30, 2005.

The Government of the Hong Kong Special Administrative Region. "m-Government". <http://sc.info.gov.hk/gb/www.info.gov.hk/digital21/e-gov/eng/init/mgov.htm>. Accessed July 30, 2005.

The McKinsey Quarterly Chart Focus Newsletter. 2005. "Does IT improve performance?" (June 2005). <http://www.mckinseyquarterly.com/newsletters/chartfocus/2005_06.htm>. Accessed July 31, 2005.

United Nations. 2004. *Global E-Government Readiness Report 2004: Towards Access for Opportunity*. New York: United Nations.

World Bank. 2004. "Korea's Move to E-Procurement." *PREM Notes*, no. 90 (July). Washington, DC: Poverty Reduction and Economic Management Network, World Bank.

World Bank. 2004 *World Development Report 2005: Investment Climate Surveys*. New York: World Bank and Oxford University Press.

Wulf, Luc De and Jose B.Sokol. 2004. *Customs Modernization Initiatives: Case Studies*. Washington:

World Bank and Oxford University Press. <http://www.worldbank.org/transport/learning/learning%20week/trade_facil_2005/Case%20Studies/World%20Bank%20(2004f)%20Customs%20Modernization%20Initiatives%20Case%20Studies.pdf>. Accessed August 1, 2005.

Chapter 6

Apollo Group, Inc. 2003 and 2004. *Annual Reports*. Phoenix, Arizona: Apollo Group, Inc. <http://www.apollogrp.edu/Investor/AnnualReports.aspx>. Accessed January and July 2005.

Arts, J.A., W.H. Gijselaers and M.R.S. Segers. 2002. "Cognitive Effects of an Authentic Computer-supported Problem-Based Learning Environment." *Instructional Science* 30:465–95.

American Society for Training and Development and National Governors Association. 2000. *A Vision of E-Learning for America's Workforce*. Alexandria, Virginia: ASTD. <http://www.astd.org/NR/rdonlyres/8C76F61D-15FD-4C57-8554-D7E940A59009/0/pp_jh_ver.pdf>. Accessed January 2005.

Austria Ministry for Education, Science and Culture. 2004. "Information on Tuition Fees at Universities" (January). Ministry for Education, Science and Culture, Vienna, Austria. <http://www.bmbwk.gv.at/fremdsprachig/ en/univ/English_-_Universities_I7478.xml#H2>. Accessed May 2003 and July 2005.

Bates, A.W. 2005. *Technology, E-Learning and Distance Education.* London: Routledge.

Cao, X. 2004. "Workplace Learning and E-Learning Adoption: Experience of the Private Sector in the United States." World Bank Institute, Washington, DC. Unpublished.

Charles Schwab Corporation. 2004. Company Research Report on Apollo Group (September 15). Charles Schwab Corporation, San Francisco, CA.

China Ministry of Education. 2003. *China Education Yearbook 2002.* Ministry of Education of China, Beijing. <http://www.moe.edu.cn/english/basic_b.htm>. Accessed January and July 2005.

CERNET (China Education & Research Network). 2001. "CERNET Evolution" (August 15). Beijing, China. <http://www.edu.cn/20010815/188550.shtml>. Accessed July 2005.

———. Various dates. Statistical information in English. Beijing, China. <http://www.edu.cn/HomePage/english/statistics/education/index.shtml>. Accessed January and July 2005.

Epic Group Plc. 2003. "Epic Survey 2003: The Future of E-Learning." White paper. Epic Group Plc., Brighton, United Kingdom. <http://www.epic.co.uk/content/resources/white_papers/survey2003.htm>. Accessed January 2005.

Foley, M. 2005. Unpublished paper. World Bank Institute, Washington, DC.

Galagan, P.A. 2002. "Delta Force." *Training & Development.* July 2002.

Goh, A., and C. Lim. 2004. "Teachers and Students as Investigators: The Collaborative Project in Technology-based Learning Environments." *Educational Technology*, USA. November–December 2004.

Green, Madeleine, Peter Eckel and Barblan Andris. 2002. *The Brave New and Smaller World of Higher Education: A Transatlantic View.* Washington, DC: Center for Institutional and International Educational Initiatives, American Council on Education.

Hall, B. 2000. *Benchmark Study of Best Practices.* e-Learning, a Forbes special advertising section. <http://www.forbes.com/specialsections/elearning/e-05.htm#b>. Accessed January 2005.

Horton, W. 2000. *Designing Web-based Training: How to Teach Anyone Anything Anywhere Anytime.* Hoboken, New Jersey: John Wiley & Sons, Inc.

ITU (International Telecommunications Union). 2005. ITU database. ITU, Geneva.

Labi, A. 2004. "British Tuition Increase Passes Final Hurdle." *The Chronicle of Higher Education* 50, no. 45. July 16.

Larocque, Norman, and Michael Latham. 2003. "The Promise of e-Learning in Africa: The Potential for Public-Private Partnerships." IBM E-Government Series. Arlington, Virginia: IBM.

Larsen, Kurt, and Stephan Vincent-Lancrin. 2005. "The Impact of ICT on Tertiary Education: Advances and Promises." OCED, Paris.

Laureate Education, Inc. 2003 and 2004. *Annual Report.* Baltimore, Maryland: Laureate Education, Inc. <http://phx.corporate-ir.net/phoenix.zhtml?c=91846&p=irol-reportsannual>. Accessed January and July 2005.

———. N.d. Website. <http://www.laureate-inc.com/univOnline.php>. Laureate Education, Inc., Baltimore, Maryland. Accessed January and July 2005.

MERLOT (Multimedia Educational Resource for Learning and Teaching Online). N.d. Website. <www.merlot.org/Home>. Accessed July 2005.

Moe, Michael T. 2000. "The Book of Knowledge: Investing in the Growing Education and Training Industry." Merrill Lynch & Co., Inc., New York.

NationMaster. 2003–2005. "Encyclopedia: Demographics of India." NationMaster, Sydney, Australia. <http://www.nationmaster.com/encyclopedia/Demographics-of-India>. Accessed July 2005.

OBHE (Observatory on Borderless Higher Education). 2002 and 2004. "Online Learning in Commonwealth Universities" (surveys). OBHE, London, UK. http://www.obhe. ac.uk. Accessed May 2005.

OECD. 2003. *Education at a Glance.* Paris: OCED.

———. 2004. "OECD Economic Survey of the United Kingdom: Graduate Contributions For Higher Education." In *OECD Economic Survey of the United Kingdom.* Paris: OECD. <http://www.oecd.org/dataoecd/50/25/24834806.pdf>. Accessed July 2005.

Perkinson, Ron. 2001. "IFC Appraisal" (Cambodian education project). IFC, Washington, DC.

———. 2003. "Summary of Education Investment Workshop." International Finance Corporation, Washington, DC.

Prensky, M. 2001. *Digital Game-based Learning.* New York: McGraw Hill.

Ruth, Stephan, and Min Shi. 2001. "Distance Learning in Developing Countries: Is Anyone Measuring Cost Benefits?" George Mason University, Virginia, USA.

Saint, William. 2000. *Tertiary Distance Education and Technology in Sub-Saharan Africa.* Document 20992. Education & Technology Technical Notes Series 5, no. 1. Washington, DC: World Bank.

Shea-Shultz, H., and J. Fogarty. 2003. "Online Learning Today: 7 Strategies That Work." *Learning and Training Innovations* (January).

Sloan Consortium. 2004. *Entering the Mainstream: The Quality and Extent of Online Education in the United States, 2003 and 2004.* Sloan Center, Olin and Babson Colleges, Franklin W. Olin College of Engineering, Needham, Massachusetts. <http://www.sloan-c.org/resources/survey.asp>. Accessed July 2005.

Starner, T. 2003. "Increasing e-Learning Adoption." *IQ Magazine* (September/October).

Statistics Canada. 2002. "University Tuition Fees." *The Daily* (August 21). <http://www.statcan.ca/Daily/English/020821/d020821b.htm>. Accessed July 2005.

Thomson NETg USA. N.d. "Honeywell." Thompson NETg, Scottsdale, Arizona. <http://www.netg.com/content.asp?link=212>. Accessed January 2005.

Twigg, Carol A. 2003. "Improving Learning and Reducing Costs: New Models For Online Learning." The Observatory on Borderless Higher Education, London, UK.

Universities and Colleges Admission Service (ucas.com). N.d. Website. UCAS, Cheltenham, UK. <http://www.ucas.ac.uk/ instit/index.html>. Accessed July 2005.

Voth, Danna. 2003. "The Army Boots up for e-Learning." *Learning & Training Innovations.* Advanstar Communications, Lansing, Michigan. <http://www.sfu.ca/ ~dchen/Cmns453/html/reading1.htm>. Accessed July 2005.

Chapter 7

bridges.org. 2002 (updated February 2005). "E-readiness Assessment: Who is Doing What and Where." bridges.org, Cape Town, South Africa and Washington, DC. <http://www.bridges.org/ereadiness>. Accessed July 2005.

Dutta, S., B. Lanvin and F. Paua, eds. 2003. *The Global Information Technology Report, 2002–2003*. New York and Oxford: Oxford University Press. Excerpts from the work can be found on the website of the World Economic Forum, Geneva,

———. 2005. *Global Technology Information Report, 2004–2005*. New York: Palgrave MacMillan. Excerpts from the work can be found on the website of the World Economic Forum, Geneva,

Glaessner, T., T. Kellerman and V. McNevin. 2004. *Electronic Safety and Soundness: Securing Finance in a New Age*. World Bank Working Paper, no. 26. Washington, DC: The World Bank.

Guislain, Pierre, Mavis A. Ampah, Laurent Besançon, Cécile Niang and Alexandre Sérot. *Connecting Sub-Saharan Africa: A World Bank Group Strategy for ICT Sector Development*. World Bank Working Paper, no. 51. Washington, DC: World Bank. <http://wbln0018.worldbank.org/ict/resources.nsf/a693f575e01ba5f385256b500062af05/ddec6b6a3479f3b785257018005e447a/$FILE/ConnectingSub-SaharanAfrica.pdf>. Accessed June 2005.

Hanna, Nagy K. 2003. *Why National Strategies are Needed for ICT-enabled Development*. ISG Staff Working Papers, no. 3 (June). Washington, DC: Information Solutions Group Informatics Advisory Services, World Bank.

<http://www.apdip.net/ documents/policy/misc/policy_strategy1.pdf>. Accessed July 2005.

High-level Forum on Harmonization. N.d. Co-operative website. <http://www1.worldbank.org/harmonization/romehlf>. Accessed August 2005.

ITU. 2002. *World Telecommunications Development Report: Re-inventing Telecoms*. Geneva: ITU. <http://www.itu.int/ITU-D/ict/publications/wtdr_02/index.html>. Accessed June 2005.

———. 2003. *World Telecommunications Development Report: Access Indicators for the Information Society*. Geneva: ITU. <http://www.itu.int/ITU-D/ict/publications/wtdr_03/material/Chap4_WTDR2003_E.pdf>. Accessed July 2005.

Kessides, Ioannis N. 2004. *Reforming Infrastructure: Privatization, Regulation, and Competition*. World Bank Policy Research Report, no. 28985. Washington, DC: World Bank and Oxford University Press. <http://econ.worldbank.org/prr/reforming_infrastructure>. Accessed July 2005.

Lanvin, B., and C. Qiang. 2003. "Poverty 'e-Readication:' Using ICT to the Meet MDG; Direct and Indirect Roles of e-Maturity." *The Global Information Technology Report 2003-2004*. New York and Oxford: Oxford University Press.

McNamara, K. 2004. *Information and Communication Technologies, Poverty and Development—Learning from Experience*. Washington, DC: *info*Dev, GICT Department, World Bank. <http://www.infodev.org/files/833_file_Learning_From_Experience.pdf>. Accessed June 2005?

OECD (Organisation for Economic Cooperation and Development). DAC (Development Assistance Committee). 2003. *Donor ICT Strategies Matrix*. Paris: OECD. <http://www1.oecd.org/dac/ictcd>. Accessed July 2005.

———. 2003. "Donor Information and Communication Technology (ICT) Strategies: Summary Matrix." OECD, Paris. <http://www.oecd.org/dataoecd/53/55/2499900.pdf>. Accessed June 2005.

———. 2003. *Harmonising Donor Practices for Effective Aid Delivery*. DAC Guidelines and Reference Series. Paris: OECD. <http://www.oecd.org/dataoecd/ 0/48/20896122.pdf>. Accessed June 2005.

———. 2003. "Survey of Donor ICT for Development Activities and the Lessons Learnt." OECD, Paris. Available on the Eldis Gateway to Development Information, Sussex, UK, <http://www.eldis.org/static/DOC13762.htm>. Accessed June 2005.

———. 2005. *Financing ICTs for Development: Efforts of DAC Members; Review of Recent Trends of ODA and its Contribution*. Report to the U.N. Task Force on Finance Mechanisms for ICT for Development. Paris: OECD. <http://www.oecd.org/ dataoecd/41/45/34410597.pdf>. Accessed June 2005.

Sadowsky, G., J.X. Dempsey, A. Greenberg, B.J. Mack and A. Schwartz. 2003. *Information Technology Security Handbook*. Washington, DC: *info*Dev, World Bank and Global Internet Policy Initiative. <http://www.infodev.org/files/834_ file_IT_Security.pdf>. Accessed June 2005.

UNCTAD (United Nations Conference on Trade and Development). N.d. "Partnership for Measuring International Development." Website of the UNCTAD E-commerce Branch. UNCTAD, Geneva. <http://measuring ict.unctad.org/QuickPlace/ measuring ict/Main.nsf/h_Toc/ 281E7067B40AD764C1256EE80048DACC/ ?OpenDocument>. Accessed June 2005.

———. 2004. *E-Commerce and Development Report 2004*. New York and Geneva: UNCTAD.

U.N. ICT Task Force. N.d. "Informal Summary of the Open Consultations on the Global Alliance, 13 April 2005, Dublin." Website of the U.N. ICT Task Force. New York. <http://unicttaskforce.org/perl/documents.pl?id=1523>. Accessed July 2005.

USAID (U.S. Agency for International Development). Bureau for Economic Growth, Agriculture and Trade (EGAT). 2004. *Information and Communication Technology for Development: USAID's Worldwide Program*. Washington, DC: EGAT, USAID. <http://www.dec.org/partners/ict/USAID_ICT_Report_May2004.pdf>. Accessed June 2005.

Weimann, Gabriel. 2004. "Cyberterrorism: How Real is the Threat?" Special Report 119. U.S. Institute of Peace, Washington, DC. <www.usip.org/reports>. Accessed August 2005.

Wireless Internet Institute. N.d. "Digital Cities Convention." Website of the Wireless Internet Institute. Boston, Massachusetts. <http://www.w2idigitalcitiesconvention. com>. Accessed July 2005.

World Bank. 2002. Knowledge Assessment Methodology. World Bank, Washington, DC. <http://info.worldbank.org/etools/kam2005>. Accessed July 2005.

———. 2003. "ICT and MDGs: A World Bank Group Perspective." Washington, DC: GICT Department, World Bank. <http://info.worldbank.org/ict/WSIS/docs/mdg_Complete.pdf>. Accessed July 2005.

————. 2005. *Doing Business in 2005: Removing Obstacles to Growth.* Washington, DC: World Bank and Oxford University Press.

————. GICT. 2005. "Financing Information and Communication Infrastructure Needs in the Developing World: Public and Private Roles." Draft (February 2005). GICT, World Bank, Washington, DC.

————. Forthcoming. *World Information and Communication for Development Report 2006: Trends and Policies for the Information Society.* Washington, DC: World Bank.

————. N.d. Private Participation in Infrastructure (PPI) Database. Website of the World Bank. Washington, DC. <http://ppi.worldbank.org>. Accessed July 2005.

WSIS (World Summit on the Information Society). 2003. "Action Plan." WSIS, International Telecommunications Union, Geneva, Switzerland. <www.itu.int/wsis/docs/geneva/official/poa.html>. Accessed March 2005.

————. 2004. "The Report of the Task Force on Financial Mechanisms for ICT for Development: A Review of Trends and an Analysis of Gaps and Promising Practices." WSIS, ITU, Geneva. <http://www.itu.int/wsis/documents/doc_multi.asp?lang=en&id=1372|1376|1425|1377>. Accessed June 2005.